The Light Body

A Transformational Cooking Guide To Health-Supportive Eating

by

Marita Rose Collins

Illustrations by

Gina Rowan

Honeoye, New York

The Traveling Gourmet
P. O. Box 702
Honeoye, N.Y. 14471-0702

Cover design by Marita Rose Collins and Favorite Recipes Press
Illustrations by Gina Rowan

Library of Congress Number: 96-61615.
ISBN 0-9654751-0-7

Marita Rose Collins
The Light Body / Marita Rose Collins.

Manufactured in the United States by:
Favorite Recipes Press

This book is dedicated to the memory of my mother, Valeria Silsbe,
and her mother, Mary Kuhn,
whose culinary talents and love of good food
continue to inspire me.

Acknowledgements

Writing this book has been both a challenge and a joy. The time spent in recipe development and in the test kitchen have been happy, creative hours. As I look back to when the idea for the book was first conceived, I am deeply grateful to so many people that shared my vision -- my husband, family and friends, far and wide. Their encouragement, support and confidence in me are what made this book possible.

Special thanks to my friend **Bonnie Klein** for being on hand from the beginning of this project, for her expert counsel and computer wizardry, her willing and patient participation; to my husband and best friend **Rick Collins** for his patience and willingness to give-up weekends and evenings to tirelessly enter and edit data, for his enthusiasm, encouragement and constant support throughout the two and a half years spent writing this book; many thanks to my friend **Gina Rowan** not only for the incredible artwork that I love but for inspiring my artistic abilities too; to my friend **Janet Lueck** for her unwavering support, sage advice, and creative writing talents; to **Ray Czapkowski** for sharing his extensive knowledge and guidance in getting this project off the ground; to my friends **Jo-Ann Alibrandi** and **Steven Jarose** for sharing their delicious recipes; to my students who kept after me to turn my recipes into a cookbook; and to **Bill Branch** and all the staff at **Favorite Recipes Press** for their professionalism, enthusiasm and support, and for their sensitivity to my artistic endeavors and to me.

Why The Light Body?

My love of cooking probably began when I was a small child in my maternal grandmother's kitchen. Mary Kuhn, a German American, loved baking and preparing special dishes for her family. At her aproned side, I began what would be a lifelong enjoyment and study of food preparation. Yet, my real mentor and most significant influence was my mother, Valeria Silsbe, a nurse who also combined a love of cooking with an emphasis on choosing foods that were nutritionally superior and which supported wellness. This was not too unusual a beginning and probably accounts for why cooking, with an eye towards nutrition, came naturally to me.

For the past 25 years, I have studied the way in which food interacts with both the emotional and physical bodies. Along the way, I made appropriate dietary changes to fit a busy life-style which included frequent entertaining of guests. I eagerly rose to the challenge of creating dishes that were not only nutritious and satisfying, but aesthetically pleasing. The adaptations I made were never just dietary. In my twenties and thirties, I was plagued with recurring bronchial and intestinal infections, accompanied by frequent episodes of eczema, specifically *dermatitis herpetiformis*, a type associated with intestinal and immune disorders. (Recent evidence appears to support the theory that this type of dermatitis may be triggered by the consumption of dairy products and/or gluten). During this same time, my young daughter was facing similar health-challenges. It was then I began to take a closer look at the relationship between diet and wellness, and was astounded to learn that hundreds of nutritional studies, conducted over the last decade, have provided irrefutable evidence against the assumption that our bodies require a traditional diet of meat, eggs and dairy to be healthy. In fact, it is these very habits of excess that are largely responsible for many of the modern diseases such as cancer, osteoporosis and coronary artery disease that afflict us.

My whole relationship to food began to change and take on new meaning. I gradually eliminated all meat, starting with beef and pork. At the same time, I began introducing more fresh vegetables, fruits and whole grains into my diet while eliminating processed foods, refined flours and sugars. I also made a conscientious choice to reduce my total fat intake. At this point, my glucose levels stabilized and my immune system and adrenals became stronger. My dermatitis began to clear and I noticed that I became sick less often. Two years later, I gave-up poultry, followed by fish and dairy. The results were dramatic and, for the first time in years, I had a glow to my skin and energy to spare. A new-found morning clarity replaced the fogginess I had come to take for granted. My lungs were clear and I felt stronger. During this time, I was thrilled to learn that my reputation, as a whole-foods gourmet cook, had grown as my healthy life-style continued to evolve. There was nothing to "give up". It seemed that I had created a style of cooking where one could have it all!

This life-style change had a profound effect on me, and was the catalyst in my decision to formally study nutrition with the Clayton College of Natural Health. In 1991, I began nutrition and wellness consulting, guiding people toward making appropriate life-style and dietary changes for optimal health. One year later, I established *The Traveling Gourmet School of Cooking* dedicated to providing people with instruction in how to create health-supportive, inspiring meals without compromise. Classes emphasized the importance of a varied diet of fruits, vegetables, grains and legumes in supporting wellness. Creative dishes were prepared, using fresh, seasonal, organically-grown ingredients high in flavor and low in fat with no animal products.

Over the years, I recognized a need for a comprehensive cookbook that would meet the necessary criteria for attaining optimal health. In response to this need, *The Light Body* was born. Written for people with hectic lives, sophisticated tastes and a strong inclination toward healthy eating, *The Light Body* is a collection of imaginative recipes for everyday meals and special occasions. Many of the recipes are quick and easy to prepare while others are a bit more challenging. Dishes range from down-home comfort food and regional-America favorites to international haute cuisine all reflecting the latest findings concerning the importance of diet in the preservation and enhancement of well-being. Realizing that eating healthfully can be challenging for today's busy life-styles, I have included a number of helpful tips for preparing healthy meals, keeping preparation time to a minimum. One timesaving tip is to cook extra amounts when preparing rice, grains, pasta or dried beans. Simply double or even triple the amount needed for one meal and refrigerate or freeze extras. This gives a head-start on creating many quick, flavorful dishes utilizing the newest whole superfoods, including amaranth, quinoa, spelt and kamut as well as many traditional foods.

Based on our current, scientific understanding of clinical nutrition, the healthiest diet is predominantly vegetarian, which is high in complex carbohydrates and low in saturated fat and protein. Vegetarian diets have been linked to decreased risk of many health conditions including coronary artery disease, cancer, diabetes, and obesity. The ideal diet is about 70 percent complex carbohydrates, 20 percent protein and 10 percent fat. However, not all vegetarian dishes are created equal on the health front. Some vegetarian dishes, especially prepared foods, can overcompensate for the lack of meat with an abundance of high-fat ingredients such as cheese and oils.

My philosophy on eating is not about denial, but rather an awareness of how fresh, whole foods can benefit us both in regaining, and maintaining, health and wellness. I believe that what we put into our bodies has a direct effect on our health, our moods and the quality of our lives. The Standard American Diet (SAD) eaten by the majority of Americans today is filled with chemicals and preservatives, grown in nutrient-depleted soil and stored on shelves for long periods of time resulting in mass nutritional loss. All this adds up to a dead-food diet. By combining fresh, wholesome foods and low-fat cooking methods, we can transform both our mental and physical bodies into happier, lighter beings.

Marita Rose Collins
June 1997

Contents

Preparation and Technique

How To Make Sun-Dried Tomatoes 3
How To Roast Peppers 3
How To Make A Buttermilk Substitute 3
How To Make Coconut Milk 4
How To Make Prune Purée 4
How To Keep Bananas 4
How To Cook Without Eggs 5
How To Prepare Mangoes 5
How To Cook Beans 6
How To Cook Grains 7
How To Make Stock 8
How To Make Multi Grain Baking Mix 9
How To Toast Nuts and Seeds 10

Appetizers

Baked Tortilla Chips 13
Black Bean Hummus 13
Chile Dilly Carrot Paté 14
"Cheezy" Zucchini Squares 15
Artichoke Paté 16
Zesty Daikon Dip 16
Hummus Canapes with Sun-Dried Tomatoes 17
Hole Guacamolé 18
Onion Dill Dip with Capers 18
Braised Mushroom Caps
with Tarragon Tomato Tapenade 19
Dolmades (Stuffed Grape Leaves) 20
Swedish Nut Balls In Mushroom Sauce 21
Spinach Balls 22
Caponata 23

Beverages

Blueberry Heaven Smoothie 27
Peachy Keen Frappé 27
Nectar of the Gods 28
Purple Passion Lemonade 28
"Champagne" Spritzer 29
Cranberry Mulled Cider 29
Iced Relaxation Tea 30
Pooh Bear Smoothie 30
Coral Reef 31
Holiday Nog 31

Breads, Muffins and Rolls

Amaranth Focaccia
with Herbs de Provence 35
Chapatis 36
Banana Date Bread 37
Hawaiian Ti Bread 38
Cranberry Pumpkin Bread 39
Honey Wheat Rolls 40
E-Z Tarragon Rolls 41
South of the Border Skillet Cornbread 42
Seven Grain Bread 43
Savory Sunflower Bread 44
Ginger Scented Banana Muffins 45
Harvest Moon Muffins 46
Blueberry Muffins with Lemon Glaze 47
Pineapple Date Bran Muffins 48
PB & J Muffins (Peanut Butter and Jelly) 49

Breakfast and Brunch

Plum Kuchen 53
Golden Corn Waffles 54
Banana Nut Waffles
with Apricot Orange Syrup 55
French Toast Mimosa 56
Blueberry Griddle Cakes
with Cinnamon Blueberry Syrup 57
Hacienda Breakfast Burritos 58
Cauliflower Leek Quiche with Rice Crust 59
Fruits of the Sun Fiesta with Ambrosia Sauce 60
Rise 'n Shine Granola 61

Dressings, Sauces, Etc.

Cinnamon Apple Butter ... 65
Mint Chutney ... 65
Herbal Seasoning ... 66
Curry Powder ... 66
Garam Masala ... 67
Gomasio ... 67
Harissa (Hot Pepper Sauce) ... 68
Italian Seasoning ... 68
Cilantro Lime Vinaigrette ... 69
Citrus Poppy Seed Dressing ... 69
Heart Beet Dressing ... 70
Herbal Vinaigrette ... 70
Creamy Cucumber Dill Dressing ... 71
Thousand Island Dressing ... 71
Island Dressing ... 72
Mango Fandango Dressing ... 72
Zorba the Greek Dressing ... 73
Dijon Eggless "Mayo" ... 74
Asian Marinade ... 74
Zesty Ketchup ... 75
Border Salsa ... 76
Salsa Verde ... 77
Basil Spinach Pesto ... 78
Tarragon Tomato Tapenade ... 78
Southwest Chile Pesto ... 79
Howling Coyote Hot Sauce ... 80
Mellow Yellow Sauce ... 81
Sweet 'n Sour Sauce ... 81
Gingery Plum Sauce ... 82
Sunny Citrus Sauce ... 82
Alfrézo Sauce ... 83
Tomato "Cream" Sauce ... 83
Holiday Gravy ... 84
Toasted Cumin Black Bean Sauce ... 85
Horsey Sauce ... 85
Herbed Pomadoro Sauce with Roasted Garlic ... 86
Sedona Sauce with Roasted Sweet Peppers ... 87
Figgy Cranapple Chutney ... 88

Desserts

Apple Spice Cake with Cinnamon Glaze ... 91
Apricot Glazed Carrot Cake ... 92
Celebration Cake ... 93
Chocolate Surprise Cake ... 94
Hawaiian Gingerbread ... 95
Pumpkin Maple "Cheese" Cake ... 96
Almond Sun Cookies ... 98
Cranberry Nut Gems ... 99
Honey Drop Cookies ... 100
Chewy Molasses Energy Cookies ... 101
Coconut Apricot Balls ... 102
Orange Apricot Bars with Cardamom ... 103
Pie Crusts ... 104
Canadice Grape Pie ... 105
Banana Coconut "Cream" Pie ... 106
Plum Empanadas ... 107
Strawberry Glazed Tart ... 108
Kona Banana Bake ... 109
Blueberry Peach Crisp ... 110
Peach Melba Croustade ... 111
Tropical Dream Tapioca with Papaya and Macadamias ... 112
Orange Quinoa Pudding with Almonds ... 113
Lemon Saffron Granita with Blueberry Coulis ... 114
Coconut Mango Sorbet ... 115
Razzle Berry Mousse ... 116

Entrées

Mandarin Orange Stir Fry with Apricots and Snow Peas ... 119
Kealakekua Stir Fry ... 120
Mediterranean Cabbage Rolls ... 121
Lemon Tempeh Picatta with Capers ... 122
Black Bean Enchiladas Grande ... 123
Asparagus Risotto with Mushrooms and Fennel ... 124
Moroccan Tagine with Couscous ... 125
Black Bean Primavera with Saffron Orzo ... 126
Chayote Kamut Medley with Toasted Cashews ... 127
Hickory Grilled Portabellas ... 128
Artichoke Stuffed Portabellas ... 129
Zesty Glazed Neat Loaf ... 130
Lemon Pineapple Kabobs Maui ... 131
Pecan Lime "Chick" Fingers ... 132
Pueblo Tortilla Casserole ... 133
Ratatouille Ragout with Fresh Herbs ... 134
Potatoes El Greco ... 135
Roasted Veggie Medley with Garlic Polenta ... 136
Stuffed Peppers Ranchero ... 138

Scorned Woman Chili
with Cornmeal Dumplings 139
Thanksgiving Hubbard
with Apricot Sourdough Stuffing 140
Cajun Creole 142
Shepherdess Pie 143
Curry In A Hurry 144
Stuffed Tomatoes
Provencale 145
Three Sisters Stew 146

Pasta

Far East Noodle Salad
with Gingery Plum Sauce 149
Pesto Pasta Salad with Toasted Pine Nuts 150
Orzo Salad with Pineapple Salsa 151
Puttanesca Insalate 152
Gnocchi and Garbanzos
with Herbed Pomadoro Sauce 152
Tomato Zucchini Bolognése 153
Amazing Grains
with Pasta, Greens and Mushrooms 154
Caponata Stuffed Shells 155
Penne Four Pepper Pasta 156
Pasta Monterey 157
Confetti Roll-Ups with Alfrézo Sauce 158
Wild Mushroom Stroganoff 159

Salads

German Potato Salad (A Warm Salad) 163
Berry Green Salad
with Raspberry Walnut Vinaigrette 164
Broccoli Salad with Pineapple Dressing 165
Pinwheel Salad 165
Sweet 'n Sour Salad 166
Squaw Salad (Black Beans and Corn) 167
Quinoa Tabouleh 168
Hasta la Pasta 169
Lemon Couscous Salad 170
Dilly Barley Salad 171
Orange Wheatberry Salad
with Apricots, Asparagus and Almonds 172

Pockets, Sandwiches and Wraps

Mock Chicken Wraps 175
Tofuna Waffle Club 176
Garden of Eat'n Burgers 177
Anasazi Bean Burgers 178
Baba Ganouj Pockets 179
Garden Patch Bagels
with Creamy Cucumber Dill Dressing 180
Reuben James 181
Sloppy Josettes 182
Mesquite Summer Grill
with Basil Spinach Pesto 183

Sides

Cucumber Mint Raita 187
Saffron Scented Rice with Peas 187
Quinoa and Wild Rice Avocados 188
Thai Rice Bake with Lemon Grass and Basil 189
Cranberry Wheatberry Pilaf 190
Acropolis Pilaf 191
Cornmeal Dumplings 191
Mom's Baked Beans 192
Beets Normandy 193
Brussels Almondine 193
Lemon Dill Green Beans 194
Sautéed Greens with Apple and Currants 194
Couscous Filled Orange Blossom Cups 195
Summer Squash Medley
with Limas and Millet 196
Honey Glazed Acorn Rings 196
E-Z Beanz and Greenz 197
Pineapple Glazed Carrots 198
Baked Acorn Boats with Apple Pear Purée 199
Oven Roasted Potatoes
with Onion and Rosemary 200
Maple Roasted Yams 200
Bavarian Späetzle (Miniature Dumplings) 201
Spicy Udon Noodles 202
Ginger Sesame Broccoli 202

Soups

Chestnut Apple Bisque 205
Asparagus Velouté 206
Black Bean Soup Taos 207

Bombay Carrot Bisque 208
Chinatown Soup 209
Barley Bean Pistou 210
Frosty Raspberry Lime (A Chilled Soup) 211
Garden Gazpacho 212
Indonesian Red Lentil Soup 213
Olde World Minestrone 214
Potato Leek Pottage 215
Savory Garlic Broth 216
Red Pepper Velouté
with Tarragon Tomato Tapenade 217
Jamaican Salsa Soup (A Chilled Soup) 218
Summertime Cucumber Dill
(A Chilled Soup) 219
Chile Corn Chowder Cripple Creek 220
Butternut Bisque 221

Glossary

Index

Preparation and Technique

"Man has an infinite capacity to rationalize his rapacity, especially when it comes to something he wants to eat."

Cleveland Amory

How To Make Sun-Dried Tomatoes

- Preheat oven to 175° F. Be sure to check temperature with an oven thermometer before attempting drying as even a new oven can be off as much as 100° F.

- Wash tomatoes, core and slice. Spread slices in single layer over lightly oiled, nonreactive baking sheet(s).

- Place baking sheet(s) in oven overnight and into the next day, 14 to 18 hours. When tomatoes are done, they should look wrinkled, dark red and show no signs of moisture.
  Note: check tomatoes frequently after 12 hours.

- When tomatoes are completely cool, store in airtight container (mason jars work well), add 2 or 3 cloves garlic or fresh basil sprigs, if desired. Pour extra-virgin olive oil over tomatoes to cover. Will keep refrigerated several months.
  Note: the seasoned oil can be used to flavor sauces and salad dressings.

The ideal time to make these is at summers end when tomatoes are abundant. Slow baking concentrates their flavor.

How To Roast Peppers

- Roast peppers (chiles and bell) directly over gas flame or 4 inches below very hot broiler, until blackened on all sides, about 5 minutes for open flame, about 10 minutes for broiler.

- Transfer peppers to brown paper bag, close and let "sweat" 5 minutes.

- Peel peppers, pull out stem and seed pods, rinse briefly to remove bits of skin and seeds. Prepare as directed.

How To Make A Buttermilk Substitute

- Whisk 1 tablespoon lemon juice or apple cider vinegar into 1 cup soy milk. Let stand 5 to 10 minutes.

How To Make Coconut Milk

1 cup dried coconut, unsweetened*
1½ cups hot water

- In blender, combine coconut and hot water, let stand 5 minutes, process until smooth.
- Strain milk through mesh sieve or cheese cloth, discard solids. Store in airtight container with tight-fitting lid. Will keep refrigerated up to 4 days, can be frozen indefinitely.

Yield: about 1½ cups

* Available in natural food stores.

How To Make Prune Purée

An excellent fat replacer that also adds sweetness. Substitute prune purée for the fat called for in your favorite recipes. Use a 1:1 ratio.

Prunes are high in calcium, magnesium, iron, potassium, vitamins and fiber.

1½ cups dried prunes, pitted
1 cup apple juice or water

- In blender, combine prunes and water, process until smooth. Store purée in airtight container with tight-fitting lid. Will keep refrigerated up to 3 weeks.

Yield: about 2¼ cups

Variation: make apricot purée by substituting dried apricots for the prunes, add 1 teaspoon orange zest and ⅛ teaspoon freshly ground nutmeg.

How To Keep Bananas

Keep frozen bananas on hand for making frosty smoothies, Banana-Date Bread *[p. 37]* *or any recipe calling for puréed bananas.*

Peel overripe bananas that have darkened, cut in half. Freeze in airtight container with tight-fitting lid. Will keep several months.

How To Cook Without Eggs

Eggs are not the healthy food everyone believes them to be. Consider this: eggs are about 70 percent fat. One egg contains a whopping 250 milligrams of cholesterol! Eggs are frequently contaminated with salmonella bacteria and are high in protein which we, as Americans, already consume too much of. The main function of eggs in a recipe is to provide moistness, tenderness, lightness, and stability. In baked goods, eggs make things rise.

Here are some ideas for replacing the egg in your favorite recipes:

- In baked goods: applesauce, prune or pumpkin purée have a neutral taste and can replace some or all of the fat in a recipe. A good rule of thumb, use 1/4 to 1/3 cup of fat substitute for each egg you replace.

- To hold things together: try substituting moistened bread crumbs, rolled oats, mashed potatoes, tahini or nut butters.

- To bind or leaven in savory dishes (i.e. casseroles): try substituting powdered egg replacer, arrowroot powder, potato starch or tapioca.

- Ground flax seed gets foamy and frothy when whipped with water in a blender, and can be folded into baked goods like egg whites. The amount used will vary depending on the recipe.

- If the recipe calls for just 1 egg, you can skip replacing it with no noticeable effect. If the recipe calls for 2 or more eggs, then you have to consider what would be appropriate to use in place of the egg. With a little bit of experimenting, you can come up with a tasty finished product and not even miss the egg.

How To Prepare Mangoes

A mango contains a long, thin central stone. Cut through the mango on either side of the stone in the center, slicing mango into three pieces. Remove the peel from the section that contains the stone. Trim the fruit from around the stone. Make diagonal crosshatches on each of the two remaining mango pieces, slicing down to (but not through) the peel. Place your hand under each mango section and push upward to invert the fruit. The cubes of fruit will rise and separate, remove them by slicing with a knife along the base of the fruit.

How To Cook Beans

Beans really are the perfect food—low in fat with almost no sodium, loaded with vitamins, minerals and complex carbohydrates. They taste great and are very versatile.

When you cook beans for a meal—cook extra. Refrigerate or freeze meal-size portions in airtight containers or resealable freezer bags. Leftover beans will give a head start on the weeks' meals.

Bean (1 cup dry measure)	Water	Cooking Time	Yield
Aduki*	3½ cups	1 hour, 15 minutes	2½ cups
Anasazi	4 cups	1 hour, 15 minutes	2½ cups
Black, Turtle	4 cups	1 hour, 15 minutes	2½ cups
Black-Eyed Peas	3½ cups	1 hour	2½ cups
Garbanzos (chickpeas)	4 cups	3 hours	2½ cups
Great Northerns	4 cups	2 hours	2½ cups
Kidney (red or white)	4 cups	1 hour, 30 minutes	2½ cups
Lentils* (red and green)	3 cups	30 minutes	2¼ cups
Limas	2½ cups	1 hour, 30 minutes	1¼ cups
Mung	2½ cups	1 hour, 30 minutes	2¼ cups
Navy	3 cups	2 hours, 30 minutes	2½ cups
Pinto	3 cups	2 hours, 15 minutes	2½ cups
Soybeans	4 cups	3 hours	2½ cups
Split Peas*	3 cups	45 minutes	2¼ cups

Helpful tips:

- Before soaking overnight, sort and rinse beans to remove dirt, dust and any tiny stones. Cover beans with 4 cups water for each cup of beans, swirl water, discarding any beans that float (beans that float are hollow and won't cook properly).

- Beans, also known as legumes, contain complex sugars. The human digestive system can't break down these sugars, so they end up in the large intestine where bacteria ferment them, producing gas. Here are some things you can do to reduce flatulence (gas):
  - Drain soaking water, adding fresh water for cooking. For more flavor, cook beans in vegetable stock and add a sprig or two of fresh rosemary or thyme.
  - Consume smaller quantities until your digestive system adapts.
  - Add a 3 inch piece of kombu (see Glossary) or a couple sprigs of dried epazote (a Mexican herb) at the beginning of cooking time.
  - Sprout beans, prior to cooking, to promote better assimilation.

- Cook beans until tender. Add ¼ teaspoon sea salt, low-sodium tamari, or miso (optional) at end of cooking, if added at beginning, it will toughen beans and lengthen cooking time.

- Store uncooked beans, in an airtight container, in a cool, dry place. Will keep indefinitely. After a year, beans will begin to lose flavor and require longer to cook.

---
* Presoaking not required where noted.

How To Cook Grains

Grain (1 cup dry measure)	Water	Cooking Time	Yield
Amaranth	2 cups	30 minutes	2½ cups
Barley, whole	3 cups	50 minutes	4 cups
Barley, pearled	2½ cups	35 minutes	3 cups
Buckwheat, (kasha)*	3 cups	30 minutes	3½ cups
Bulgur, whole wheat*	2 cups	15 minutes	3 cups
Cornmeal, coarse*	4 cups	25 minutes	3 cups
Couscous, whole wheat*	2½ cups	10 minutes	3 cups
Kamut	3 cups	1 hour	3 cups
Millet*	3 cups	30 minutes	3½ cups
Oats, rolled*	2½ cups	30 minutes	3½ cups
Quinoa	2 cups	15 minutes	3½ cups
Rice, Brown (short grain)	2 cups	1 hour	3 cups
Rice, Brown (medium grain)	1½ cups	50 minutes	2½ cups
Rice, Brown (long grain)	1½ cups	50 minutes	2½ cups
Rice, Brown Basmati	1½ cups	30 minutes	2½ cups
Rice, Wild	3 cups	50 minutes	4 cups
Whole Wheat Berries	3 cups	2 hours	2⅔ cups

Whole grains contain the majority of basic nutrients essential for life in humans and animals—water, carbohydrates, fats, protein, vitamins, minerals and fiber.

When you cook grains for a meal—cook extra. Refrigerate or freeze meal-size portions in airtight containers or resealable freezer bags. Leftover grains will give a head start on the weeks' meals.

Helpful Tips:

- Cooking times are approximate and can vary several minutes either way. Age of the grain can affect cooking time. Older grains that have become more dry may require a bit more liquid and take longer to cook.
- After measuring, rinse bulk grains in cool water before cooking to remove dust and debris from harvesting. With rice, rinsing removes some of the starch resulting in a lighter, fluffier grain. With quinoa, rinsing removes the natural saponin coating.
- Toast grains before cooking to enhance their nutty flavor and impart a lighter, fluffier texture. Toast grain in heavy-bottomed skillet, over medium heat, stirring constantly until fragrant, 5 to 8 minutes.
- Presoak grains with hard coats (such as whole barley, wheat and rye) for several hours or overnight to reduce cooking time.
- Store whole grains in airtight container in cool, dry place (or refrigerate). Will keep indefinitely. Whole grains that are cracked or ground into flour begin to lose freshness and should be kept in the refrigerator or freezer to retain freshness and avoid rancidity.

---
* Do not rinse before cooking.

How To Make Stock

Vegetable-based stocks have a clear advantage over meat stock—they are extremely easy to make, healthier and require no skimming of fat.

Will keep refrigerated up to 4 days. Freezes well.

Basic Vegetable Stock

4 quarts water
2 large unpeeled onions, quartered
3 large unpeeled carrots, cut into thick slices
1 head unpeeled garlic, cut tips off cloves
2 ribs celery (including leaves), cut into chunks
2 large Roma tomatoes, quartered
2 leeks (including tops), cut into chunks
8 cups vegetable trimmings
1/2 cup assorted fresh herbs
bouquet garni (see Glossary)
1 teaspoon black peppercorns
1/4 cup liquid aminos

- Scrub vegetables. Combine all ingredients in stockpot, bring to boil, reduce heat. Cover, simmer 45 minutes, add water, as necessary, to keep vegetables from drying out. Strain stock, discard vegetables.

Yield: 7 cups

Savory Garlic Broth

see Soups (p. 216)

Mushroom Stock

This stock is simple to make with rich, complex flavor. The mushrooms lend a meat-like, rich earthy taste.

Will keep refrigerated up to 4 days. Freezes well.

1 cup crimini, shitake or porcini mushrooms
2 cups white button mushrooms, sliced
8 cups boiling water
3 teaspoons sesame oil
1 large unpeeled onion, quartered
2 ribs celery (including leaves), cut into chunks
1 teaspoon black peppercorns
bouquet garni (see Glossary)

- In large bowl, combine dried mushrooms and boiling water, let soak 15 minutes to reconstitute. Drain, reserve soaking liquid for stock.

- In stockpot, heat oil, sauté onion and celery until soft and golden, 4 to 6 minutes. Add reserved soaking liquid, peppercorns and bouquet garni to pot with onion and celery, simmer 45 minutes. Strain stock and discard vegetables.

Yield: about 7 to 8 cups

Helpful Tips

Freezing stock: to insure having stock on hand, after cooking, strain stock and pour into ice cube trays. When frozen, pop stock cubes into large, resealable freezer bag. (This way only the amount called for in a recipe can be defrosted). Will keep several months in freezer.

Rule of thumb: 7 or 8 cubes = 1 cup defrosted stock.

Helpful Tip: out of stock and no time to make any? Substitute natural Vogue Instant Vege Base, it's organic and low in sodium.

How To Make Multi Grain Baking Mix

1 cup rolled oats
1 cup white or yellow stone ground cornmeal
2½ cups unbleached flour with germ
2½ cups whole wheat bread flour
½ cup amaranth flour
½ cup powdered soy milk*
3 teaspoons baking soda
2 tablespoons aluminum-free baking powder
1 teaspoon sea salt, fine grind

- Grind oats and cornmeal to powder.
  Helpful Tip: a coffee grinder works well for this.
- In large bowl, combine all ingredients, whisking to blend. Store in an airtight container with tight-fitting lid in refrigerator or freezer.

Yield: 8 cups

This recipe is a healthier, less expensive version of all-purpose, commercially prepared baking mixes and contains no milk products or aluminum-based baking powder, using whole grain flours instead of white, bleached flour.

---
* Available in natural food stores and some supermarkets.

How To Toast Nuts and Seeds

All nuts and seeds can benefit from toasting which brings out their flavor while adding crunch.

- **Pan Method:** in small heavy-bottomed skillet, toast nuts or seeds, over medium heat, stirring constantly until fragrant and golden (check table for toasting time).

Nut	Time	Seed	Time
Almonds, blanched*	4 to 6 minutes	Sesame	1 to 2 minutes
Cashews	3 to 4 minutes	Sunflower	2 to 3 minutes
Macadamias	3 to 4 minutes	Other	1 to 2 minutes
Pecans	4 to 6 minutes		
Pine nuts	3 to 4 minutes		
Walnuts	4 to 6 minutes		

The oven method of toasting requires less attention but more time compared to the pan method. [Oven method not recommended for seeds, use pan method instead].

- **Oven Method:** preheat oven to 325° F.
  Note: if you prefer, a toaster oven can be used.
  Spread nuts over bottom of shallow, ungreased pan. Bake until fragrant, about 8 to 10 minutes. Shake pan once or twice during toasting.
  Note: age and size of nuts may affect toasting time.

---

* To blanch almonds: in small saucepan, bring enough water to cover almonds by 1 inch to rolling boil, cook 2 minutes. Drain, submerge in ice water 30 seconds. Drain, squeeze almonds out of skins.
Note: blanching the almonds allows them to toast up golden, making them easier to purée.

Appetizers

"The person who is afraid to alter his living habits, and especially his eating and drinking habits, because he is afraid that other persons may regard him as queer, eccentric, or fanatic forgets that the ownership of his body, the responsibility for its well-being, belongs to him, not them."

Dr. Paul Brunton

Baked Tortilla Chips

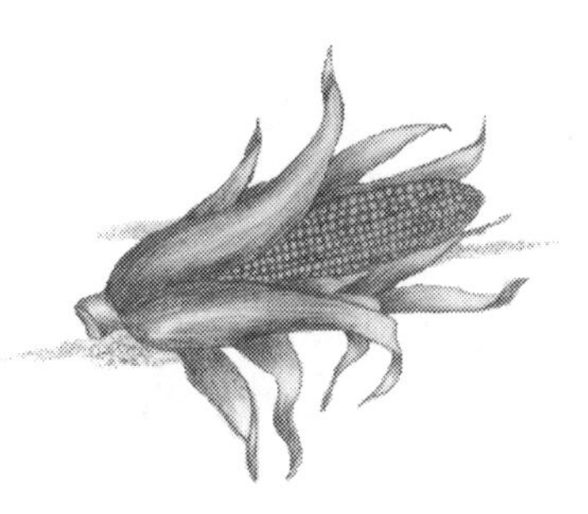

12 6-inch corn tortillas
sea salt, optional

- Preheat oven to 350° F.
- Cut tortillas into quarters. Spread pieces evenly over baking sheets, sprinkle with sea salt, if desired.
- Bake until crisp, 10 to 12 minutes.

Yield: 48 large chips

A low-fat, healthy alternative to fried tortilla chips. One whole tortilla contains just 0.6 grams of fat.

Serve with Border Salsa [p. 76], Salsa Verde [p. 77] or Black Bean Hummus [recipe below].

Black Bean Hummus

1 1/2 cups cooked black beans
1 cup cooked garbanzo beans
2 teaspoons garlic, minced
1/4 cup tahini
1 tablespoon freshly squeezed lemon juice
1 tablespoon balsamic vinegar
1 1/2 tablespoons liquid aminos
1/3 cup fresh parsley, minced
2 tablespoons fresh chives, chopped
1 tablespoon red hatcho miso
3 teaspoons ground cumin
1/4 to 1/2 teaspoon hot pepper sauce, to taste

- In food processor, combine all ingredients, process to desired consistency.

Yield: 3 cups

Serving suggestions: as an Appetizer, thin with a little water, for dipping tortilla chips; as a Salad, add a scoop to a bed of fresh greens; as a Pocket Sandwich, spread hummus in whole grain pita pocket, add sprouts, lettuce and tomatoe slices.

Middle East meets Mexico in this version of hummus with a twist.

Chile Dilly Carrot Paté

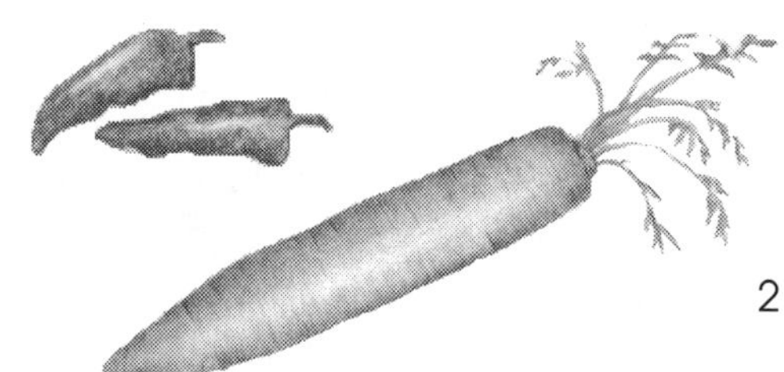

1 cup vegetable stock (p. 8)
2 large cloves garlic, minced
¼ cup sweet onion, diced
2 cups carrot, diced
2 tablespoons fresh dill weed or 2 teaspoons dried
~
2 tablespoons mellow white miso dissolved in 2 tablespoons water
¼ teaspoon Vege Sal®
2 tablespoons tahini
2 tablespoons mild green chile, seeded and diced
1 to 2 tablespoons prepared horseradish, to taste

Your eyes will shine when you indulge in this heavenly paté!

One cup of carrots contain over 20,000 iu of vitamin A.

Green chiles and horseradish wake up your palate with an unexpected burst of flavor.

Serve with whole grain crackers, sesame sticks or assorted crudités [raw veggies].

- In medium saucepan, bring ½ cup stock (reserve remainder) to simmer, sauté garlic, onion and carrot, 5 minutes.
- Whisk dill and remaining stock into carrot mixture. Cover, simmer until tender, 12 to 15 minutes. Transfer mixture to blender or food processor, process until smooth.
- In blender, combine carrot mixture, miso and all remaining ingredients. Pulse-chop mixture just until blended and small pieces of chile are visible.
- Transfer paté to small serving dish. Serve at room temperature.

Yield: 2 cups

"Cheezy" Zucchini Squares

Great party fare!

The nutritional yeast is the secret ingredient that lends a "cheesy" flavor to this easy make-ahead appetizer.

3 cups unpeeled zucchini, coarsely grated
1 cup Multi-Grain Baking Mix (p. 9)
1/4 cup onion, finely chopped
3 cloves garlic, minced
3 tablespoons nutritional yeast flakes
2 tablespoons fresh parsley, chopped
1/4 teaspoon Vege Sal®
1 teaspoon dried oregano
1 tablespoon egg replacer powder
1/4 cup water
2 teaspoons extra-virgin olive oil
1 teaspoon lecithin granules*

- Preheat oven to 350° F. Lightly oil bottom of 9 inch baking pan.
- In medium bowl, combine all ingredients, beating to blend. Spread mixture evenly in prepared pan.
  Helpful Tip: for easier spreading, moisten fingertips with water; pat batter evenly into corners of pan.
- Bake until lightly golden and toothpick inserted in center comes out clean, 40 to 45 minutes.
- Transfer pan to wire cooling rack. Let stand 20 minutes before cutting. Cut into 6 rows, 6 squares per row. Arrange squares on large serving tray. Serve room temperature with cocktail picks.

Yield: 36 squares

---

* Available in natural food stores.

Artichoke Paté

Enjoy this taste-tempting, heart-healthy version of a favorite without feeling guilty! The cheese and fat-laden mayo have been replaced with heart-healthy soy without sacrificing flavor.

High in folic acid [an important B vitamin] and potassium, artichokes tone up the liver and are thought to help keep arteries clean and smooth.

Serve with petite rye rounds or toasted wheat crackers.

14 ounces water-packed artichokes, drained
1 cup Dijon Eggless Mayo (p. 74)
1/3 cup parmesan-style cheese alternative, grated
1 tablespoon freshly squeezed lemon juice
1 to 2 tablespoons prepared horseradish, to taste
1 tablespoon fresh dill, minced or 1 teaspoon dried
2 cloves garlic, minced
1/8 teaspoon hot pepper sauce

- Preheat oven to 325° F.
- Chop artichokes into bite-size pieces.
- Combine all ingredients in medium nonreactive bowl, stirring to blend, transfer to 11 by 7 inch baking dish.
- Bake until mixture is bubbly and golden, 25 to 30 minutes (do not over bake).
- To reheat, microwave on medium-high until bubbly, 1 to 2 minutes.

Yield: 6 to 8 servings

Zesty Daikon Dip

Daikon is a long, white Japanese radish with a pungent-sweet flavor. An excellent blood cleanser, daikon assists in the digestion of fatty foods.

Serve with assorted crudites [raw veggies] or sesame crackers.

8 ounces reduced-fat firm tofu, drained
2/3 cup Dijon Eggless Mayo (p. 74)
1/3 cup daikon, peeled and coarsely grated
1/4 cup fresh Italian flat-leaf parsley, minced
1 1/2 teaspoons low-sodium tamari sauce
1 tablespoon freshly squeezed lemon juice
1 tablespoon fresh summer savory, minced or 1 teaspoon dried
2 teaspoons Gomasio (p. 67)
~
1 parsley sprig
1 tablespoon unhulled sesame seeds

- Drain tofu, squeeze gently to remove excess water. In blender, combine tofu with all remaining ingredients, except sesame seeds, process until smooth.
- Transfer mixture to small serving bowl. Sprinkle sesame seeds over top, garnish with sprig of parsley. Cover, chill 1 hour before serving.

Yield: about 2 cups

Hummus Canapes
with Sun-Dried Tomatoes

1 cup Black Bean Hummus (p. 13)
~
1 cup boiling water
1 cup sun-dried tomatoes
~
36 party-size slices rye or pumpernickel cocktail bread (about 1 loaf)
1¼ cups Dijon Eggless Mayo (p. 74)
1 cup pitted black olives, sliced

- Make hummus as directed, reserve one cup, refrigerate remainder. Note: can be made ahead, if desired.
- In heat-resistant measuring cup, pour boiling water over tomatoes. Let soak 15 minutes to reconstitute. Drain, discard any remaining liquid. Chop tomatoes into small pieces. Set aside.
- Arrange bread slices on large serving tray, cover with plastic wrap while working to prevent bread drying out.
- In small bowl, combine hummus and mayo, beating to blend, spread small amount over each slice, top with 2 or 3 olive slices and ½ teaspoon sun-dried tomatoes. Cover with plastic wrap. Refrigerate until ready to serve.

Yield: 36 canapés (6 servings)

Terrific make-ahead party fare for that special brunch.

These attractive open-faced mini-sandwiches are bursting with flavor and good nutrition.

Holé Guacamole

Guacamole bursting with sunny Southwest flavor. A tantalizing way to use overripe avocados. Garbanzos add a new dimension to this popular dip, high in protein, fiber and vitamin A.

Serve with Baked Tortilla Chips [p. 13].

2 very ripe Haas avocados, peeled, pitted, and quartered

~

1 cup cooked garbanzo beans
juice of 1 freshly squeezed lime
1 teaspoon hot pepper sauce
1/4 teaspoon sea salt
2 teaspoons ground cumin

~

1 cup Salsa Verde (p. 77)

- In blender, combine all ingredients, except salsa, process until smooth.
- Transfer guacamole to medium serving bowl, stir in salsa. Cover, chill 1 hour before serving.

Yield: 4 cups

Onion Dill Dip with Capers

A fabulous low-fat, low-calorie, dairy-free dip!

Serve with assorted crudités [raw veggies] or sesame sticks.

1 package natural onion dip mix*
10 ounces low-fat extra-firm silken tofu
2 teaspoons umeboshi vinegar
2 tablespoons soy milk
2 tablespoons Dijon Eggless Mayo (p. 74)
2 tablespoons fresh dill, minced or 2 teaspoons dried
2 tablespoons capers, drained and chopped

- In food processor or blender, combine all ingredients, process until smooth.
- Transfer to small serving bowl, stir in capers. Chill 1 to 2 hours before serving.

Yield: 1 2/3 cups

---

* The Spice Hunter® makes an excellent one.

Braised Mushroom Caps

with Tarragon Tomato Tapenade

2 cups Tarragon Tomato Tapenade (p. 78)
36 jumbo mushroom caps
~
1 tablespoon extra-virgin olive oil
3 tablespoons mirin
2 tablespoons liquid aminos
~
½ cup pine nuts, toasted (p.10)

- Wipe mushroom caps with damp paper towel (or mushroom brush) to remove dirt. Grasp stem where it attaches to cap, using a twisting motion, turn wrist clockwise until stem detaches. Reserve stems for mushroom stock (p. 8).

- In large wide-bottomed pan, bring oil, mirin and liquid aminos to simmer. Place caps, gill side up, in pan, braise 4 to 5 minutes, moving mushrooms around pan with spatula to prevent sticking. Turn, braise gill side, 3 to 4 minutes.
  Note: depending on size of pan, it may be necessary to braise mushrooms in 2 or 3 batches.

- Arrange mushrooms, gill side up, in lightly oiled jelly roll pan. Spoon tapenade into caps, mounding over top.

- Position pan 4 to 6 inches from broiler, broil 3 to 4 minutes. Press pine nuts lightly into tapenade for garnish. Serve warm.

Yields: 6 servings

A favorite hors d' oeuvre for "wowing" guests.

The sunny, concentrated flavor of sun-dried tomatoes complements the earthy flavor of mushrooms.

Preparation time can be minimal, if you have Tapenade in the freezer. Simply thaw and voila - instant appetizer!

Dolmades (Stuffed Grape Leaves)

2 cups cooked brown rice
1/2 cup onion, finely chopped
2 cloves garlic, minced
2 tablespoons fresh mint, minced or 2 teaspoons dried
2 tablespoons fresh dill weed, minced or 2 teaspoons dried
1 tablespoon fresh oregano, minced or 1 teaspoon dried
1/4 teaspoon freshly ground pepper
juice of 2 freshly squeezed lemons
2 teaspoons extra-virgin olive oil
1/3 cup dried currants
~
16 ounces grape leaves (about 24 to 30), drained
3/4 cup mushroom or vegetable stock (p. 8)

Guests tend to love these savory little rollups so you may want to make a double batch to be sure there's enough to go around!

If desired, can be made ahead. Remove from refrigerator 30 minutes before serving.

- In medium nonreactive bowl, combine all ingredients, except grape leaves and stock.
- Preheat oven to 350° F. Lightly oil 11 by 7 inch baking dish.
- Drain brine from grape leaves, carefully spread leaves out over work area. Spoon 1 1/2 tablespoons filling into center of each leaf. Fold leaf, sides to center, roll up beginning at stem end. Arrange dolmades, seam side down, in prepared baking dish. Repeat procedure with remaining leaves and filling, pour stock over top. Cover.
- Bake 20 to 25 minutes. Serve warm, or room temperature, with cocktail picks.

Yield: 24 to 30 dolmades

Swedish Nut Balls
In Mushroom Sauce

1½ cups cooked brown rice
2 cups walnuts, ground
⅔ cup cheddar-style cheese alternative, grated
¾ cup Multi-Grain Baking Mix (p. 9)
¾ cup onion, diced
2 teaspoons garlic, minced
1 teaspoon herbal seasoning (p. 66)
1 tablespoon egg replacer powder
½ teaspoon ground cardamom
⅓ cup water
~
12 ounces white button mushrooms, diced
¼ cup whole wheat pastry flour
3 cups mushroom stock (p. 8)
~
2 tablespoons brown miso
1 tablespoon vegetarian Worcestershire sauce

- Preheat oven to 400° F. Lightly oil two lip-edged baking sheets.
- In large bowl, combine all ingredients. Shape mixture into 1½ inch balls, arrange on prepared baking sheets.
  Helpful Tip: periodically moisten fingers with water to prevent mixture sticking to hands.
- Bake 20 minutes. Turn nut balls halfway through baking time, transfer to large serving dish.*
- Meanwhile, in large wide-bottomed skillet, heat 3 tablespoons stock (reserve remainder). Sauté mushrooms until they release their juices, 3 to 5 minutes.
- Stir flour into mushrooms, cook until bubbly, add reserved stock, stirring to blend. Bring mixture to simmer, stirring frequently until thickened. Remove pan from heat.
- Stir miso and Worcestershire into sauce, pour sauce over nut balls. Serve warm with cocktail picks.

Yield: 10 to 12 servings

Containing half the fat of traditional meat balls, these tempting treats are an instant hit.

Walnuts contain mono unsaturated fats [the heart-healthy kind] high in protein, magnesium, copper, vitamin E and Omega-3 oils.

Variation: as an entrée, ladle over eggless noodles and accompany with a salad of fresh greens.

---
* A chafing dish or crockpot (low setting) will keep nut balls warm several hours.

Spinach Balls

Remember those spinach balls you loved so much, laden with tons of dairy, cholesterol and fat? Well, guess what... now you can indulge, without the guilt!

This healthy rendition of a favorite contains no dairy or eggs with only a 1/4 of the fat of traditional spinach balls.

Spinach is rich in vitamin A, potassium, magnesium and calcium.

10 ounces fresh spinach (about 12 cups)
~
1 cup whole grain bread crumbs
1/2 cup cheddar-style cheese alternative, grated
1 medium onion, finely chopped
1/2 cup raw cashews, ground
1/4 cup raw sunflower seeds, ground
2 tablespoons nutritional yeast flakes
1/4 teaspoon freshly ground pepper
1 1/2 teaspoons dried oregano
1 tablespoon liquid aminos
1 tablespoon freshly squeezed lemon juice

- Rinse spinach thoroughly to dislodge any sand particles, repeat, if necessary. Remove and discard stems. Chop leaves into bite-size pieces.
- In large wide-bottomed skillet, add small amount of water, bring to boil, add spinach. Cover, cook until wilted, 4 to 6 minutes. Drain spinach thoroughly, transfer to colander or mesh sieve, press with back of metal spoon to remove excess water.
  Note: if using frozen spinach, thaw and cook according to package directions. Drain same as with fresh spinach.
- In medium nonreactive bowl, combine spinach and all remaining ingredients, stirring to blend.
- Preheat oven to 325° F. Lightly oil baking sheet.
- Shape mixture into 1 1/2 inch balls, arrange on prepared baking sheet.
- Bake 20 to 25 minutes. Transfer spinach balls to serving dish. Serve warm with cocktail picks.

Yield: 18 to 20 balls

Caponata

1 large eggplant (about 2 pounds)
~
1/3 cup Savory Garlic Broth (p. 8)
3 cloves garlic, minced
2/3 cup onion, diced
2/3 cup celery, diced
~
1 pound Roma tomatoes, cored and diced
1/4 cup fresh basil, snipped
1/4 cup fresh oregano, snipped
1/4 teaspoon freshly ground pepper
2 teaspoons low-sodium tamari sauce
2 teaspoons brown rice syrup
1/2 cup pitted black olives, coarsely chopped
3 tablespoons capers, drained and chopped
1/3 cup dried currants
2 1/2 tablespoons balsamic vinegar
1 teaspoon extra-virgin olive oil

- Preheat broiler. Lightly oil broiler pan.
- Cut eggplant in half, lengthwise (do not peel), lay halves, cut side down, on broiler pan. Broil until skins are charred and puffed, 12 to 14 minutes. Transfer eggplant to wire rack until cool enough to handle.
- In medium heavy-bottomed skillet, bring broth to boil. Reduce heat, sauté garlic 2 minutes, add onion and celery, sauté until soft, 4 to 5 minutes.
- Using large metal spoon, scoop pulp from skins, chop into small pieces.
- Transfer sautéed veggies to medium serving bowl, add eggplant and all remaining ingredients, stirring to blend. Cover, chill 1 hour to allow flavors to meld. Serve at room temperature.

Yield: about 5 cups

This Italian classic can be served as an appetizer with toasted whole grain pita triangles or as a savory filling for Caponata Stuffed Shells [p. 155].

Beverages

"When Health is absent,
Wisdom cannot reveal itself,
Art cannot become manifest,
Strength cannot be exerted,
Wealth is useless and
Reason is powerless."

Herophiles, 300 B.C.

Blueberry Heaven Smoothie

1 1/2 cups fresh or frozen blueberries
1/2 cup raw almonds, blanched (p.10) and ground
1 1/2 cups vanilla flavor rice milk, chilled
2 teaspoons plain or fruit flavor lecithin granules*
1/4 teaspoon ground cinnamon
1 1/2 tablespoons dark amber maple syrup
1 teaspoon lemon zest

- In blender, combine all ingredients, process until smooth.

Yield: 2 servings

* Available in natural food stores.

If you're a blueberry fan, you're gonna love this heavenly, nourishing drink with just a hint of lemon. Almonds are a good protein source; blueberries are high in vitamins A and C, iodine and manganese.

Peachy Keen Frappé

2 1/2 cups fresh or frozen peaches, peeled and sliced
1 1/2 cups frozen non-dairy vanilla dessert*
1 cup raspberry juice (no added sweeteners)
2 tablespoons all-fruit peach jam
1/4 teaspoon pure almond extract
2 teaspoons freshly squeezed lime juice
8 ice cubes
~
4 unpeeled peach slices

- In blender, combine all ingredients, process in 2 batches until smooth.
- Serve in tall, chilled glasses. Garnish rim with peach slice.

Yield: 4 servings

* Frozen Rice Dream® by Imagine Foods is excellent.

Whip up this cool refreshing drink when those dog-days of summer arrive and ripe, juicy peaches are plentiful!

Peaches are good sources of vitamins A and C, potassium and phosphorus.

Nectar of the Gods

The taste alone is worth the preparation time for this ambrosial drink. Choose mangoes that are ripe but not mushy. If mangoes aren't ripe when purchased, seal in brown paper bag until soft and fragrant, 2 to 3 days.

Mango is a voluptuous, perfumy fruit native to Asia, fairly high in vitamin C, zinc, magnesium and potassium.

3 large ripe mangoes
juice of 1 freshly squeezed lime
1 cup unsweetened pineapple juice, chilled
1 cup freshly squeezed orange juice, chilled
2 cups water, chilled
½ to 1 teaspoon liquid fruit sweetener, to taste

- Prepare mangoes as directed (p. 5).
- In blender, combine all ingredients, process in 2 batches until smooth.

Yield: 4 servings

Purple Passion Lemonade

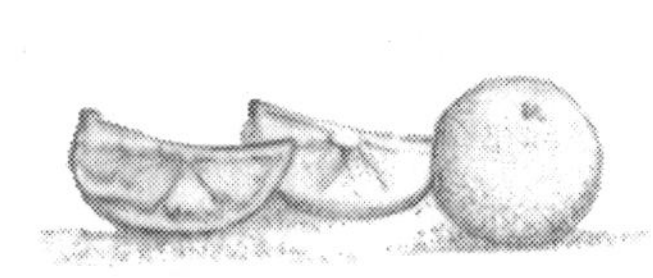

A new twist on lemonade, naturally sweetened with grape juice [contains no refined sugar].

Lemons are a wonderful detoxifier and cleanser for the liver, high in potassium and vitamin C.

1 cup freshly squeezed lemon juice (4 to 5 large lemons)
3 cups frozen unsweetened purple grape juice concentrate, undiluted
3 cups water, chilled
2 tablespoons liquid fruit sweetener
~
4 lemon slices, for garnish

- In blender, combine all ingredients, except lemon slices, process until blended.
- Chill 1 to 2 hours, pour lemonade over ice. Garnish rim with lemon slice.

Yield: 4 (14 ounce) glasses

"Champagne" Spritzer

12 ounces frozen unsweetened white grape juice concentrate, undiluted
32 ounces low-sodium seltzer water, chilled

- Combine grape juice and seltzer water, whisk until blended.
- Pour into fluted champagne or wine glasses. Serve immediately.

Yield: 8 servings

A nice touch to Sunday brunch.

Tastes like the real thing!

Cranberry Mulled Cider

64 ounces fresh-pressed natural apple cider
32 ounces unsweetened cranberry juice*
16 whole cinnamon sticks
10 whole cloves
1 teaspoon whole allspice

- Make bouquet garni (see Glossary) with 4 cinnamon sticks (reserve remainder), cloves and allspice.
- In stockpot, bring cider and cranberry juice to slow boil. Gently drop bouquet garni into mixture. Reduce heat, simmer 15 minutes. Remove pan from heat, discard bouquet garni.
- Ladle cider into mugs. Serve piping hot with cinnamon stick, for stirring.

Yield: 16 (10 ounce) servings

When there's a chill in the air, cook up a batch of this tangy, warming, beverage. Great for serving a crowd!

Keep refills warm in crock pot on low setting.

Helpful Tip: save considerably by buying cinnamon sticks in bulk section of your favorite natural food store.

* After The Fall®, Apple and Eve® and Knudsen® are all excellent.

Iced Relaxation Tea

Equally delicious hot.

Good for easing tension and as a digestive aid. Ginger soothes the digestive system; chamomile and lemon balm have a mild, sedative-effect on the nervous system.

8 cups water
~
1/2 cup fresh ginger root, peeled and chopped
1/2 ounce dried chamomile*
1/2 ounce dried lemon balm*
~
1 large lemon, cut into wedges, for garnish

- In 3 quart saucepan, bring water to rolling boil. Add ginger root, chamomile and lemon balm, lower heat, simmer 12 to 15 minutes. Remove pan from heat, let steep 15 minutes. Strain mixture, through mesh sieve or cheesecloth, into serving pitcher.
- Chill 2 to 3 hours. Serve tea over ice in tall chilled glasses. Garnish rim with lemon wedge.

Yield: 6 to 8 servings

---
* Available in herbal and natural food stores.

Pooh Bear Smoothie

Winnie would be quite fond of this yummy smoothie in his tummy—so will your kids!

Bananas, almost complete carbohydrate, are Americas' favorite fruit, high in magnesium, potassium, iron and vitamin B6.

2 large bananas, frozen
2 cups vanilla flavor rice or soy milk, chilled
1/4 cup unsweetened coconut, finely shredded
2 tablespoons honey
1/2 teaspoon ground cinnamon
1 tablespoon plain or fruit flavor lecithin granules*

- In blender, combine ingredients, process until smooth.

Yield: 2 servings

---
* Available in natural food stores.

Coral Reef

3 cups ripe papaya, peeled, seeded* and cubed
2 cups fresh strawberries (1 pint)
1 to $1\frac{1}{2}$ tablespoons liquid fruit sweetener, to taste
12 ice cubes
~
4 large fresh strawberries, for garnish

- In blender, combine all ingredients, process on low until ice begins to break up, increase speed and liquefy.
- Serve Coral Reef in tall chilled glasses. Spear two strawberries with cocktail pick, float in glass.

Yield: 2 generous servings

* Reserve and freeze seeds for making Island Dressing (p. 72).

The beautiful color of this refreshing drink reminds me of the coral in the Florida Keys.

Papayas' sunset colors range from golden yellow to burnt orange. The seeds of the papaya have a mild peppery taste.

Holiday Nog

10 ounces low-fat firm silken tofu,* chilled
5 cups vanilla flavor rice milk, chilled
$\frac{1}{2}$ cup dark amber maple syrup, chilled
2 teaspoons pure vanilla extract
$\frac{1}{8}$ teaspoon ground tumeric
$1\frac{1}{2}$ tablespoons egg replacer powder
1 tablespoon plain or fruit-flavor lecithin granules
~
1 teaspoon freshly ground nutmeg

- In blender, combine all ingredients, except nutmeg, process in 2 or 3 batches until smooth.
- Serve cold in chilled roly-poly glasses or mugs, dust tops with nutmeg.

Yield: 6 (10 ounce) servings

* Mori-Nu® makes one with only 1 percent fat.

Since eliminating eggs and dairy from my diet, the one thing I sorely missed at holiday-time was eggnog. I had resigned myself to the fact that I probably wouldn't ever have eggnog again, when I decided to experiment. After numerous attempts, this low-fat, dairy-free version was born. It has managed to pass the "taste-test" at family gatherings—being eagerly quaffed down! [Just keep them guessing what's in it.]

Breads, Muffins and Rolls

"I have no doubt that it is part of the destiny of the human race in its gradual development to leave off the eating of animals, as surely as the savage tribes have left off eating each other when they came into contact with the more civilized."

Thoreau

Amaranth Focaccia
with Herbs de Provence

4 teaspoons active baking yeast
1 teaspoon unsulphured molasses
2 cups warm water (105° to 115° F)
~
3/4 teaspoon coarse sea salt
2 cups whole wheat bread flour
1 1/2 cups unbleached bread flour with germ
1 1/2 cups amaranth flour
~
1/4 cup whole grain stone ground yellow corn meal
~
2 tablespoons extra-virgin olive oil
1 1/2 teaspoons herbs de Provence
2 tablespoons fresh sage leaves, coarsely chopped
2 tablespoons garlic, minced

- In large heat-resistant measuring cup, combine yeast, molasses and water, let stand until bubbly and fragrant, about 10 minutes.
- In separate bowl, whisk salt and flours together. Set aside.
- In large nonreactive bowl, beat yeast and flour mixture, with heavy duty mixer, until dough pulls away from sides of bowl, about 3 to 4 minutes.
- Turn dough out onto lightly floured work surface. Knead dough forming a springy ball, add flour, 1 tablespoon at a time, as needed, to prevent sticking. Dough should remain moist and pliable.
- Lightly oil large bowl. Transfer dough to bowl, cover with damp dish towel or plastic wrap, let rise in warm place, free from drafts, until double in size, about 1 to 1 1/2 hours.
- Sprinkle flour over work surface. Using heel of hand, gently press and flatten dough. Lift and gently pull dough, stretching it to fit a jelly roll pan. Lay plastic wrap lightly over dough, let rise again until double in size, about 30 to 45 minutes.
- While dough is rising, in small bowl combine olive oil, herbs de Provence, and sage, let stand 30 minutes to allow herbs to infuse oil.
- Heat oven to 450° F. Sprinkle cornmeal over lightly oiled jelly roll pan.
  Note: omit oil if using non-stick pan.
  Using your knuckles, poke dimples in surface of dough. Drizzle oil over dough allowing it to flow into dimples, sprinkle herbs and garlic over top. Reduce temperature to 400° F. Bake focaccia until top is golden and bottom sounds hollow when tapped, 20 to 25 minutes, cut into wedges. Serve warm.

Yield: 6 to 8 servings

Focaccia, a traditional Italian flatbread, is a cousin to pizza dough, topped with olive oil, herbs and garlic.

This rustic bread dates back thousands of years to when flatbreads were cooked on open hearths. The dimpling of the dough gives focaccia its characteristic look of hills and valleys.

In Italy, people traditionally make focaccia with refined flour. This version uses a combination of whole wheat, unbleached bread flour with germ and amaranth to give the dough a heartier flavor and higher nutritional value.

Amaranth, revered by the Aztecs for its excellent balance of amino acids, high protein and calcium content, lends a nutty, somewhat-sweet flavor to the bread.

Serve with Olde World Minestrone soup [p. 214] and a salad of leafy greens with Herbal Vinaigrette [p. 70] for a satisfying dinner.

Chapatis

Fat and cholesterol-free!

Chapatis are unleavened flatbreads traditionally served in India, usually torn into pieces for scooping vegetables, dals and spicy curries. Great as a wrapper for beans, rice and vegetables.

½ teaspoon sea salt
½ cup whole wheat pastry flour
1 cup whole wheat bread flour
½ cup chick pea flour*
1 cup water

- In medium nonmetallic bowl, whisk together salt and flours. Add water to flour mixture, stirring to make a soft, kneadable dough. Turn dough out onto lightly floured work surface, cover with dish towel, let dough rest 5 minutes. Wash, dry and lightly oil bowl.

- Knead dough, 8 to 10 minutes. Sprinkle additional flour over work surface to prevent dough from sticking, if necessary. When dough is smooth and springy, form into ball. Place dough ball in bowl, cover with damp dish towel or plastic wrap, set aside until slightly risen, about 1 hour.

- Divide dough into 12 equal pieces. Roll each piece into a 7 inch circle. Sprinkle small amount of flour over work surface to prevent dough sticking, if necessary. Stack chapatis between sheets of waxed paper, cover with damp dish towel or plastic wrap to prevent dough drying out.

- Heat griddle or cast-iron skillet, on high, until water dripped on surface sizzles. Cook chapatis, one at a time, until edges begin to curl and bottom is lightly browned, about 1 minute. Turn, cook until small brown spots appear (not quite 1 minute). Periodically press spatula against chapati to allow air pockets to rise between layers of dough. If chapati doesn't puff-up, hold over gas flame briefly, with tongs.
  Note: if cooking on an electric stove, place wire rack over burner coil, lay chapati on rack and heat 5 or 6 seconds. This should be done quickly so chapati remains soft, flexible and doesn't dry out. (Not to worry, even if they don't puff, they'll still taste good).

- Wrap chapatis in dry dish towel to keep warm, cover with inverted bowl or plate. Will keep refrigerated several days or stack between layers of waxed paper in resealable freezer bags and freeze.
  To reheat chapatis, place in covered dish, 10 to 12 minutes in a 300° F oven.

Yield: 12 chapatis

---

* Available in Indian markets and natural food stores.

Banana Date Bread

½ cup pitted dates, coarsely chopped
1½ teaspoons baking soda
⅔ cup boiling water
~
3 large very ripe bananas
2 teaspoons expeller-pressed canola oil
¼ cup dark amber maple syrup
1 teaspoon pure vanilla extract
~
1½ cups whole wheat pastry flour
½ cup amaranth flour
1 tablespoon egg replacer powder
½ cup date sugar
1 teaspoon aluminum-free baking powder
~
½ cup chopped walnuts, toasted (p.10)

How sweet it is!

Dates and bananas team up with date sugar and maple syrup to naturally sweeten this moist rendition of an old favorite. Full of potassium, protein, vitamins and fiber.

- Preheat oven to 350° F. Lightly oil one standard 9 inch, or two mini, loaf pan(s).
  Note: omit oil if using non-stick pan(s).
- In small nonreactive bowl, add dates, baking soda and boiling water, stirring to blend. Let stand 10 minutes (mixture will be frothy).
- In blender, combine banana and next 3 ingredients, process until smooth and no lumps remain.
- In large bowl, whisk together dry ingredients.
- Combine date mixture with wet and dry ingredients, stirring just until blended, fold in nuts.
- Pour mixture evenly into prepared pan(s); using rubber spatula, push batter into corners.
- Bake until toothpick inserted in center comes out clean, 50 to 60 minutes (mini-loaves, 40 to 50 minutes), transfer to wire rack. Cool 20 minutes before removing bread.

Yield: 1 standard or 2 mini-loaves

Hawaiian Ti Bread

(pronounced tea)

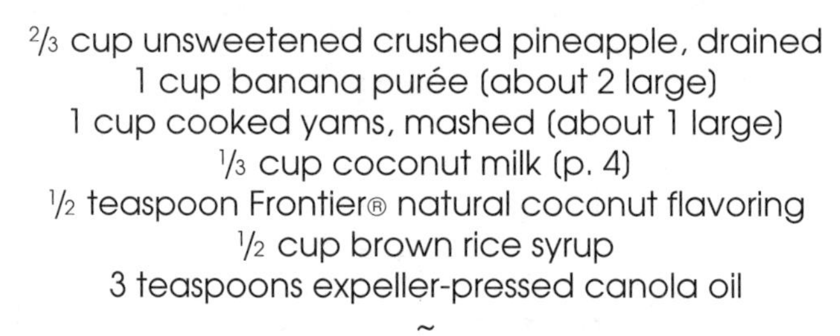

2/3 cup unsweetened crushed pineapple, drained
1 cup banana purée (about 2 large)
1 cup cooked yams, mashed (about 1 large)
1/3 cup coconut milk (p. 4)
1/2 teaspoon Frontier® natural coconut flavoring
1/2 cup brown rice syrup
3 teaspoons expeller-pressed canola oil

~

1 cup whole wheat pastry flour
3/4 cup unbleached flour with germ
2 teaspoons aluminum-free baking powder
1 teaspoon baking soda
1 tablespoon egg replacer powder
1/2 teaspoon ground cardamom
1/2 teaspoon freshly grated nutmeg

~

1/4 cup macadamia nuts,* ground

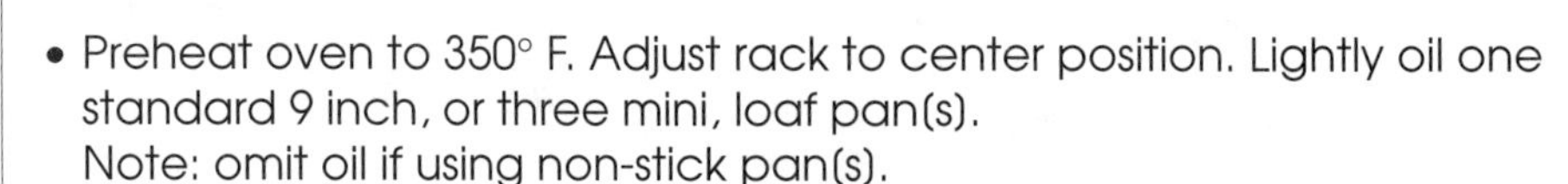

The exotic tastes of Hawaii meld to create this moist, sensationally-flavored dessert bread packed with vitamins and minerals.

Pineapple, commonly grown in Hawaii, is mildly acidic, high in magnesium and rich in bromelain, a digestive enzyme. [Bromelain appears to have an anti-inflammatory action in the body].

Bananas are an excellent source of potassium and contain many vitamins and minerals including iron, selenium and magnesium.

Yams are rich in vitamins A and C, potassium and iron.

- Preheat oven to 350° F. Adjust rack to center position. Lightly oil one standard 9 inch, or three mini, loaf pan(s).
  Note: omit oil if using non-stick pan(s).
- In medium nonreactive bowl, combine wet ingredients.
- In large bowl, whisk together dry ingredients. Combine wet and dry ingredients, stirring just until blended (do not over mix).
- Pour mixture evenly into prepared pan(s); using rubber spatula, push batter into corners, sprinkle macadamias over top.
- Bake until toothpick inserted in center comes out clean;, 50 to 60 minutes (mini-loaves, 40 to 50 minutes), transfer to wire rack. Cool 20 minutes before removing bread.

Yield: 1 large or 3 mini-loaves

---

* If macadamias aren't available, substitute pecans.

Cranberry Pumpkin Bread

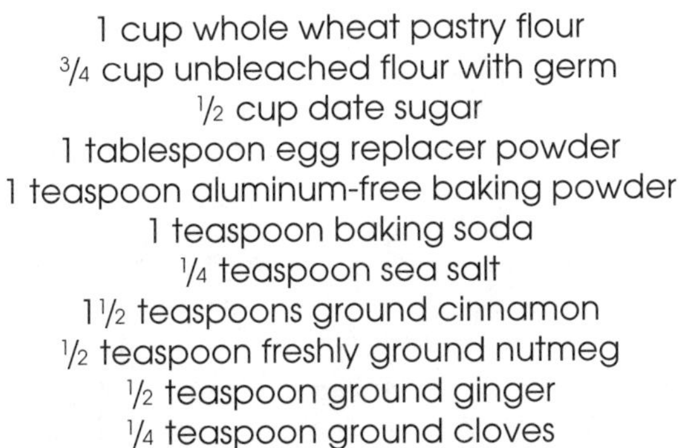

1 cup fresh or frozen cranberries, rinsed and picked over
1/3 cup date sugar

~

2/3 cup banana purée
1 cup pumpkin purée
1 tablespoon expeller-pressed canola oil
3 drops pure orange oil* or
1 1/2 teaspoons freshly grated orange zest
1/4 cup freshly squeezed orange juice

~

1 cup whole wheat pastry flour
3/4 cup unbleached flour with germ
1/2 cup date sugar
1 tablespoon egg replacer powder
1 teaspoon aluminum-free baking powder
1 teaspoon baking soda
1/4 teaspoon sea salt
1 1/2 teaspoons ground cinnamon
1/2 teaspoon freshly ground nutmeg
1/2 teaspoon ground ginger
1/4 teaspoon ground cloves

~

1/2 cup pecans, coarsely chopped, optional

- Preheat oven to 350° F. Lightly oil one standard 9 inch, or two mini, loaf pan(s).
  Note: omit oil if using non-stick pan(s).

- In mini chopper or food processor, pulse-chop cranberries 8 to 10 times (do not over process). Transfer cranberries to small bowl, add date sugar, tossing to coat. Set aside.

- In small nonreactive bowl, combine wet ingredients.

- In large bowl, whisk together dry ingredients. Combine wet and dry ingredients, stirring just until blended (do not over mix), fold in cranberries and nuts.

- Pour mixture evenly into prepared pan(s); using rubber spatula, push batter into corners.

- Bake until toothpick inserted in center comes out clean, 50 to 60 minutes (mini-loaves, 40 to 50 minutes), transfer to wire rack. Cool 20 minutes before removing bread.

Yield: 1 standard or 2 mini-loaves

This fragrant "quick" bread [see Glossary] is wonderful for the holidays. Low-fat, delicious, crusty and moist.

For holiday giving, mini-loaves of this scrumptious bread make welcome gifts. Wrap in colored plastic wrap and top with a bow.

---

* Available at kitchen specialty stores.

Honey Wheat Rolls

This master recipe can be used for making delicious burger buns with just a few, easy modifications.

After the first rise, divide dough into 8 equal portions. Cover, let rest 10 minutes. Lightly oil baking sheet and sprinkle with cornmeal. Shape each portion of dough into a ball. Gently flatten ball into bun shape, using thumb and fingers. Arrange buns on prepared baking sheet, 2 inches apart, press dough down firmly. Cover with damp dish towel, let rise in warm place free from drafts, about 30 minutes.

Bake in a 350 °F oven until lightly browned, 15 to 20 minutes.

Yield: 8 burger buns

1/2 cup boiling water
1/2 cup seven-grain cereal
~
2 cups whole wheat bread flour
1 1/2 cups unbleached bread flour with germ
~
1 package active baking yeast
1/2 teaspoon sea salt
3/4 cup warm water (105° to 115° F)
2 tablespoons honey
1 tablespoon expeller-pressed canola oil

- In heat-resistant measuring cup, combine boiling water and cereal, stirring to blend. Let stand 10 minutes, drain any remaining water.
- In small bowl, whisk flours together. Set aside.
- In large bowl, combine **1 cup** of flour mixture with yeast, salt, water, honey, oil and soaked cereal, beat 30 seconds on low, with heavy-duty mixer,* scraping sides of bowl, continue beating 3 minutes on high. Gradually add remaining flour until moderately stiff dough is formed.
- Turn dough out onto lightly floured work surface, knead until smooth and elastic, about 6 to 8 minutes. Add flour, a little at a time, to prevent dough sticking, if necessary.
- Transfer dough to large, lightly oiled nonmetallic bowl, turning to coat. Cover, let rise in warm place, free from drafts, until double in size, about 1 hour.
- Punch dough down and divide into 16 equal portions, cover with damp dish towel or plastic wrap. Let rest 10 minutes. Shape each portion into a 3 inch oval and lay on lightly oiled baking sheet, 2 inches apart, recover rolls. Let rise in warm place, free from drafts, until double in size and dough springs back slowly when pressed with finger, about 30 minutes.
- Halfway through rise time, preheat oven to 350° F. Bake rolls until lightly browned, 15 to 18 minutes.

Yield: 16 rolls

---

* If heavy-duty mixer isn't available, beat by hand, 5 to 6 minutes.

E-Z Tarragon Rolls

3/4 cup whole wheat bread flour
3/4 cup unbleached bread flour with germ
1/2 cup barley flour
1/2 cup rye flour
~
2 packages rapid-rise yeast
2 teaspoons egg replacer powder
1 teaspoon celery seeds, crushed
1/2 teaspoon sea salt
1 tablespoon fresh Italian flat-leaf parsley, minced
2 tablespoons fresh tarragon, chopped
~
1 1/4 cups warm water (105° to 115° F)
1 tablespoon barley malt syrup
1 tablespoon extra-virgin olive oil

- In small bowl, whisk flours together. Set aside.
- In large bowl, combine **half** of flour mixture with yeast and next 5 ingredients.
- In separate bowl, combine water, barley malt and oil. Add to flour/yeast mixture, beat 30 seconds on low, with heavy-duty mixer,* scraping sides of bowl, continue beating 3 minutes on high. Gradually add remaining flour until moderately stiff dough is formed.
- Transfer dough to large, lightly oiled nonmetallic bowl, turning to coat. Cover with damp dish towel or plastic wrap, let rise in warm place, free from drafts, until double in size, about 30 minutes.
- Spoon dough into one standard 12 cup, or jumbo 6 cup, lightly oiled muffin pan. Fill each cup just over half full.
- Preheat oven to 350° F. Recover rolls, let rise in warm place, free from drafts, until double in size, about 15 minutes.
- Bake rolls until lightly browned, 15 to 18 minutes (jumbo, 23 to 28 minutes).

Yield: 12 standard or 6 jumbo rolls

You'll love the aroma of tarragon wafting through your kitchen as these quick, whole grain rolls bake.

Barley malt gives them a light golden color and acts as a sweetener to activate the yeast.

A heavy-duty mixer does the kneading and rapid-rise yeast cuts rise time in half.

---
* If heavy-duty mixer isn't available, beat by hand 5 to 6 minutes.

South of the Border Skillet Cornbread

When cornbread was first made in Mexico, it was baked in a cast-iron skillet over hot coals. This moist, dairy-free version uses whole grain stone ground cornmeal for the fullest flavor. The addition of onion, chile and bell peppers, cumin and cayenne take it to another dimension.

Soaking the cornmeal in the "clabbered" soy milk gives the bread a tender crumb. Red bell and green chile peppers add flecks of color and boldness. Baking the cornbread in a sizzling cast-iron skillet gives it a crisp, chewy crust with a light cake-like crumb.

Pair this flavorful cornbread with Black Bean Primavera [p. 126] or Scorned Woman Chili [p. 139] for a terrific meal.

1 cup whole grain stone ground yellow cornmeal
3/4 cup soy milk
3/4 cup yogurt, dairy-free
1 tablespoon freshly squeezed lemon juice
2 tablespoons honey
1 tablespoon liquid aminos

~

2 teaspoons extra-virgin olive oil
1/3 cup shallots, finely chopped
1/3 cup red bell pepper, diced
1 mild green chile pepper, diced

~

2 tablespoons oat bran
1 cup unbleached bread flour with germ
1/4 teaspoon Vege Sal®
pinch of cayenne pepper
1 teaspoon ground cumin
1/4 teaspoon dried thyme
3 teaspoons aluminum-free baking powder
1 teaspoon baking soda
1 tablespoon egg replacer powder

- In medium nonreactive bowl, combine cornmeal and next 5 ingredients, whisking to blend. Let stand 10 minutes.
- In 9 inch cast-iron skillet,* heat oil, sauté onion, bell and chile peppers until soft, 4 to 5 minutes.
- Preheat oven to 375° F.
- In large bowl, whisk together dry ingredients. Set aside.
- Combine sautéed veggies with wet and dry ingredients, stirring just until moistened. Spoon batter into skillet.
- Bake until toothpick inserted in center comes out clean, 20 to 25 minutes.

Yield: 6 to 8 servings

---

* If cast-iron skillet isn't available, use 9 inch baking pan. Bake an additional 8 to 10 minutes, until toothpick inserted in center comes out clean.

Seven Grain Bread

1 1/2 cups soy milk
1 1/2 tablespoons freshly squeezed lemon juice
~
1 cup boiling water
1/2 cup seven-grain cereal*
1/4 cup unsulphured molasses
1 tablespoon expeller-pressed canola oil
~
1 1/4 cups whole wheat bread flour
1 cup unbleached bread flour with germ
2 teaspoons aluminum-free baking powder
1 teaspoon baking soda
2 teaspoons egg replacer powder
1/2 teaspoon sea salt

A satisfying accompaniment to winter meals, this hearty "quick" bread has distinctive character.

Seven-grain cereal is coarse and earthy, rich in fiber and nutrients. Most blends contain barley, corn, cracked rye, flax, millet, rice and triticale.

- In small nonreactive bowl, combine soy milk and lemon juice, stirring to blend. Let stand 10 minutes.
- In separate bowl, pour boiling water over cereal, stirring to blend. Let stand 10 minutes, drain any remaining water. Stir molasses and oil into cereal. Set aside.
- Preheat oven to 350° F. Lightly oil one standard 9 inch loaf pan. Note: omit oil if using non-stick pan.
- In large bowl, whisk together dry ingredients. Combine soy milk and cereal with dry ingredients, stirring just until blended.
- Pour mixture into prepared pan; using rubber spatula, push batter into corners.
- Bake until toothpick inserted in center comes out clean, 55 to 60 minutes, transfer to wire rack. Cool 10 minutes before removing from pan. Cool completely before storing.

Yield: 1 large loaf

---
* Sold in natural food stores and some supermarkets.

Savory Sunflower Bread

You probably didn't know making yeasted bread could be so quick, foolproof and incredibly delicious.

The extra rapid-rise yeast called for cuts rise time considerably, producing fragrant bread in half the time.

This recipe makes three generous loaves. You can freeze some for later—if they don't disappear first!

1 tablespoon expeller-pressed canola oil
5 cups warm water (105° - 115° F)
1 tablespoon unsulphured molasses
~
6 cups whole wheat bread flour
2½ cups unbleached bread flour with germ
1 tablespoon flax seed, ground
2 tablespoons rapid-rise yeast
1½ teaspoons sea salt
1 teaspoon garlic, minced
1 tablespoon herbal seasoning (p. 66)
1 tablespoon fresh thyme, minced or 1 teaspoon dried
1 tablespoon fresh savory or 1 teaspoon dried
~
⅔ cup raw sunflower seeds, toasted (p.10)
½ cup rolled oats

- Lightly oil three standard 9 inch loaf pans. Set aside.
  Note: omit oil if using non-stick pans.
- Divide water equally between two mixing bowls, add molasses to one bowl, whisking to blend. Set aside.
- In separate bowl, whisk bread flour and next 8 ingredients together.
- Gradually pour molasses water into dry ingredients, beat 30 seconds on low, with heavy-duty mixer,* scraping sides of bowl, continue beating 3 minutes on high. Gradually add remaining water, stirring until dough is wet but not sticky.
  Note: you may not need entire amount of water.
- Turn dough out onto lightly floured work surface, knead until smooth and elastic, about 6 to 8 minutes. Add flour, a little at a time, to prevent dough sticking, if necessary. Divide dough evenly into thirds, press firmly into prepared pans to release any air bubbles.
- Preheat oven to 375° F.
- Cover loaves with damp dish towels or plastic wrap, let rise in warm place, free from drafts, until double in size and dough springs back slowly when pressed with finger, about 15 minutes.
- Scatter sunflower seeds and oats over tops, pressing lightly into dough.
- Bake until tops are golden and bottom sounds hollow when tapped, 40 to 50 minutes, transfer to wire racks. Cool 10 minutes before removing from pans. Cool completely before storing.

Yield: 3 loaves

Ginger Scented Banana Muffins

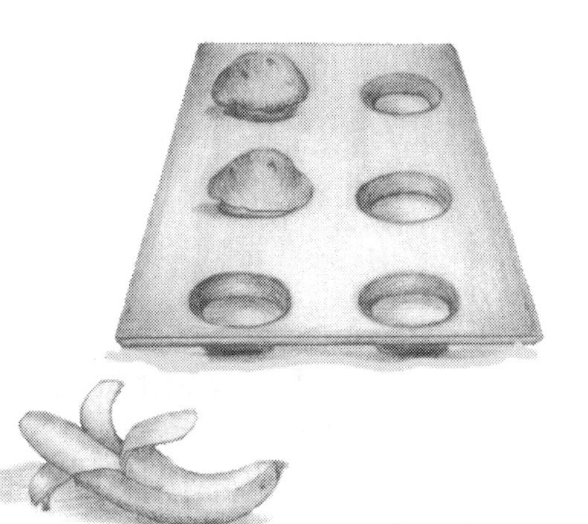

1 teaspoon flax seed, ground
1/2 cup amasake (see Glossary)
3/4 cup banana purée (about 2 medium)
1/4 cup freshly squeezed orange juice
1/4 cup brown rice syrup
1 tablespoon expeller-pressed canola oil
~
1 cup whole wheat pastry flour
1 cup amaranth flour
2 teaspoons aluminum-free baking powder
1 tablespoon egg replacer powder
1/4 teaspoon sea salt
1/2 teaspoon ground ginger
1 tablespoon crystallized ginger, minced
1 teaspoon ground cinnamon

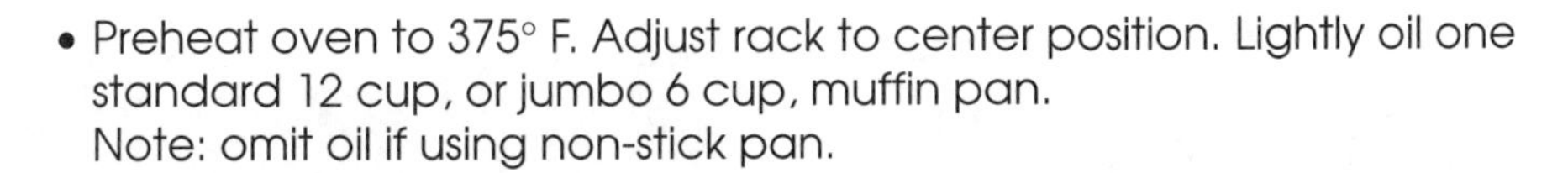

- Preheat oven to 375° F. Adjust rack to center position. Lightly oil one standard 12 cup, or jumbo 6 cup, muffin pan.
  Note: omit oil if using non-stick pan.
- In medium nonreactive bowl, with electric mixer, beat flax seed and soy milk, on high, until frothy, about 1 to 2 minutes, add banana purée and next 3 ingredients to mixture, beat on low 30 seconds to blend. Set aside.
- In large bowl, whisk dry ingredients together. Combine wet and dry ingredients, stirring just until blended (do not over mix).
- Spoon batter into prepared pan, filling each cup 3/4 full.
- Bake until toothpick inserted in center comes out clean, 15 to 20 minutes (jumbo, 25 to 30 minutes).
- Transfer pan to wire rack. Cool 10 minutes before removing muffins from pan.

Yield: 12 standard or 6 jumbo muffins

Serve these elegant muffins for breakfast or brunch.

Flax seeds are rich in Omega-3 fatty acids which have vitally important properties for strengthening immunity and cleaning the heart and arteries.

Bananas replace the fat and add moistness, ginger adds sweet, distinctive flavor and irresistible aroma.

Amaranth, prized by the Aztecs and Mayans for its high protein, iron and calcium content, gives the muffins their light texture.

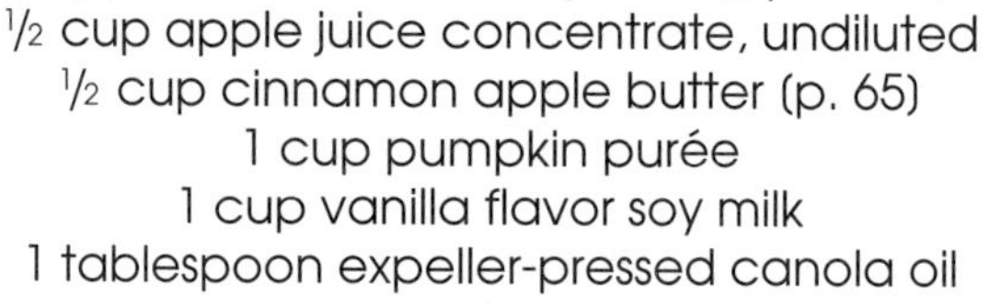

Harvest Moon Muffins

1 cup tart cooking apples (such as Granny Smith), peeled, cored and grated
1/2 cup apple juice concentrate, undiluted
1/2 cup cinnamon apple butter (p. 65)
1 cup pumpkin purée
1 cup vanilla flavor soy milk
1 tablespoon expeller-pressed canola oil

~

1 cup whole wheat pastry flour
1/2 cup soy flour
1/2 cup oat bran
2 teaspoons aluminum-free baking powder
1 teaspoon baking soda
3 teaspoons egg replacer powder
1/4 teaspoon sea salt
1/4 teaspoon ground cloves
1/2 teaspoon ginger
1 teaspoon ground cinnamon
1/4 teaspoon freshly grated nutmeg

The Autumn Equinox heralds the harvesting of juicy, red apples and sweet orange pumpkins... a perfect time for making these terrific-tasting muffins, loaded with vitamins and fiber!

- Preheat oven to 375° F. Adjust rack to center position. Lightly oil one standard 12 cup, or jumbo 6 cup, muffin pan.
  Note: omit oil if using non-stick pan.
- In small bowl, combine wet ingredients. Set aside.
- In large bowl, whisk dry ingredients together. Combine wet and dry ingredients, stirring just until blended (do not over mix).
- Spoon batter into prepared pan, filling each cup 3/4 full.
- Bake until toothpick inserted in center comes out clean, 15 to 20 minutes (jumbo, 25 to 30 minutes).
- Transfer pan to wire rack. Cool 10 minutes before removing muffins from pan.

Yield: 12 standard or 6 jumbo muffins

Blueberry Muffins
with Lemon Glaze

1/2 cup dark amber maple syrup
1/2 cup prune purée (p. 4)
6 ounces lemon flavor yogurt, dairy-free
1 teaspoon pure vanilla extract
3 drops pure lemon oil or 3/4 teaspoon pure lemon extract
3 tablespoons freshly squeezed lemon juice
1/2 cup vanilla flavor rice milk
1 tablespoon expeller-pressed canola oil

~

1 cup amaranth flour
1/2 cup rice flour
1/2 cup oat bran
3 teaspoons aluminum-free baking powder
1 teaspoon baking soda
1 tablespoon egg replacer powder
1/4 teaspoon sea salt
1/2 teaspoon freshly ground nutmeg
1 cup fresh or frozen blueberries

~

1/2 cup freshly squeezed lemon juice
3 tablespoons dark amber maple syrup
2 teaspoons kudzu
1/8 teaspoon ground tumeric
2 teaspoons lemon zest

- Preheat oven to 375° F. Adjust rack to center position. Lightly oil one jumbo 6 cup muffin pan.
  Note: omit oil if using non-stick pan.
- In small nonreactive bowl, combine wet ingredients. Set aside.
- In large bowl, whisk dry ingredients together. Combine wet and dry ingredients, except blueberries, stirring just until blended (do not over mix), fold in blueberries.
  Note: if using frozen blueberries, fold into batter without thawing or juice will turn muffins purple.
- Spoon batter into prepared pan, filling each cup 3/4 full.
- Bake until toothpick inserted in center comes out clean, 25 to 30 minutes.
- Transfer pan to wire rack. Cool 10 minutes before removing muffins from pan.
- Prepare glaze in small nonreactive saucepan by combining all ingredients, except lemon zest, stirring to blend. Bring mixture to boil, stirring constantly. Remove pan from heat, cool slightly. Drizzle glaze over muffins, sprinkle lemon zest over tops.

Yield: 6 jumbo muffins

For a treat you can't beat, whether morning or night, these blueberry-studded giants will surely delight!

Dairy and wheat-free, these muffins are ideal for food-sensitive individuals.

Pineapple Date Bran Muffins

These tangy bran muffins are uncommonly moist thanks to the added pineapple.

Have one with breakfast to keep you going all morning long. Ummm good.

1 1/2 cups pineapple juice, unsweetened
1/2 cup pitted Medjool dates, finely chopped
1 1/2 teaspoons baking soda
~
1/2 cup unsweetened crushed pineapple, drained
1 teaspoon pure vanilla extract
1 tablespoon expeller-pressed canola oil
~
3/4 cup date sugar
1 1/2 cups whole wheat pastry flour
1 1/2 cups wheat bran
2 teaspoons flax seed, ground
2 teaspoons aluminum-free baking powder
1 tablespoon egg replacer powder
1/4 teaspoon sea salt
~
1/2 cup chopped pecans, toasted (p.10)

- In 2-quart nonreactive sauce pan, bring pineapple juice to boil, remove pan from heat, add dates and baking soda, stirring to blend. Let stand 10 minutes (water will be frothy).

- Preheat oven to 375° F. Adjust rack to center position. Lightly oil one standard 12 cup, or jumbo 6 cup, muffin pan.
  Note: omit oil if using non-stick pan.

- In small nonreactive bowl, combine date mixture with crushed pineapple, vanilla and oil, beating to blend. Set aside.

- In large bowl, whisk dry ingredients together. Combine wet and dry ingredients, stirring just until blended (do not over mix), fold in nuts.

- Spoon batter into prepared pan, filling each cup 3/4 full.

- Bake until toothpick inserted in center comes out clean, 15 to 20 minutes (jumbo, 25 to 30 minutes).

- Transfer pan to wire rack. Cool 10 minutes before removing muffins from pan.

Yield: 12 standard or 6 jumbo muffins

PB & J Muffins

(Peanut Butter and Jelly)

2/3 cup crunchy natural reduced-fat peanut butter
1/2 cup cinnamon apple butter (p. 65)
1 cup vanilla flavor soy milk
1/4 cup water
1/2 cup liquid fruit sweetener
~
1 1/2 cups whole wheat pastry flour
1/2 cup unbleached flour with germ
1 tablespoon egg replacer powder
1/4 teaspoon sea salt
~
1/3 cup all-fruit jam (flavor of your choice)

- Preheat oven to 375° F. Adjust rack to center position. Lightly oil one standard 12 cup, or two jumbo 6 cup, muffin pans.
  Note: omit oil if using non-stick pans.
- In small bowl, combine peanut butter and next 4 ingredients, beating to blend. Set aside.
- In large bowl, whisk dry ingredients together. Combine wet and dry ingredients, stirring just until blended (do not over mix).
- Spoon batter into prepared pans, filling each cup 1/2 full, add 1 teaspoon jam to each muffin cup. Spoon remaining batter over jam, filling each cup 2/3 full.*
- Bake until toothpick inserted in center comes out clean, 15 to 20 minutes (jumbo, 25 to 30 minutes).
- Transfer pans to wire racks. Cool 10 minutes before removing muffins from pans.

Yield: 16 standard or 8 jumbo muffins

Keep plenty of these tempting muffins on hand for after-school snacks. Kids love 'em. The trick is getting the grown-ups to share them!

---

* Fill empty cups 2/3 full with water to ensure even baking.

Breakfast and Brunch

"The natural force within each of us is the greatest healer of disease."

Hippocrates

Plum Kuchen

1 tablespoon kudzu dissolved in
3 tablespoons freshly squeezed lemon juice
1/3 cup apple juice concentrate, undiluted
2 teaspoons ground cinnamon
3 cups ripe pitted prune-plums, halved

~

6 ounces vanilla flavor yogurt, dairy-free*
1/2 cup prune purée (p. 4)
2 teaspoons pure vanilla extract
1/4 cup apple juice concentrate, undiluted
3 teaspoons expeller-pressed canola oil

~

1 cup unbleached flour with germ
1 cup amaranth flour
3 teaspoons aluminum-free baking powder
1 teaspoon baking soda
1 tablespoon egg replacer powder

~

1/2 cup walnuts or pecans, coarsely chopped, optional
1 teaspoon ground cinnamon

- In medium nonreactive saucepan, dissolve kudzu in lemon juice, add apple juice concentrate, cinnamon and plums to pan. Bring mixture to boil, reduce heat. Simmer, stirring frequently until thickened, 2 to 3 minutes. Set aside.
- Preheat oven to 350° F. Lightly oil and flour 13 by 9 inch glass baking dish. Note: If using metal pan, increase temperature to 375° F.
- In small bowl, combine yogurt and next 4 ingredients, stirring just until blended.
- In large bowl, whisk dry ingredients together. Combine wet and dry ingredients, beating until blended. Set aside.
- Pour half of batter into bottom of prepared dish. Scatter nuts evenly over batter. Pour remaining batter over nuts, spoon plum mixture over top.
- Bake until toothpick inserted in center comes out clean, 40 to 45 minutes, transfer to wire rack, sprinkle cinnamon over top. Let stand 15 minutes before cutting. Serve warm or room temperature.

Yield: 8 to 10 servings

"Kuchen" is German for cake!

This sensational breakfast cake was my Grandma Kuhn's recipe. I've made it heart-healthy, eliminating the eggs and refined sugar and reducing the fat. The plum topping is its crowning glory.

Sure to become a favorite at your house.

---

* White Wave® makes an excellent one.

Golden Corn Waffles

Waffles aren't just for breakfast anymore–you can enjoy them morning, noon and night in a myriad of ways.

My ideal of the perfect waffle is a crisp, lightly-browned exterior and a fluffy interior. These delectable waffles, with the goodness of corn, reflect my ideal.

Serve them for breakfast with a little warm maple syrup drizzled over top. For lunch, they become the "bread" for Tofuna Waffle Club [p. 176]. For Tex-Mex dinner fare, add ½ cup diced red bell pepper to waffle batter; ladle Toasted Cumin Black Bean Sauce [p. 85] over waffle, top with shredded lettuce, diced tomatoes and a small amount of grated Jack-style cheese alternative.

¾ cup unbleached flour with germ
¼ cup amaranth flour
1 cup whole grain stone ground yellow cornmeal
2 teaspoons aluminum-free baking powder
1 tablespoon egg replacer powder
¼ teaspoon sea salt
~
½ cup frozen corn kernels
1 cup soy milk
1 tablespoon unrefined corn oil
8 ounces low-fat firm silken tofu*
3 tablespoons brown rice syrup
~
extra corn oil for waffle grids

- In medium bowl, whisk dry ingredients together. Set aside.
- In blender, combine corn kernels and next 4 ingredients, process until smooth.
- Combine wet and dry ingredients, stir batter just until moistened and lumps disappear (do not over mix).
  Note: if batter is too thick, add extra soymilk, a little at a time, stirring to blend.
- Preheat oven to 200 F. Cooked waffles can be kept warm on a cake rack until ready to serve (will keep exterior crisp).
- Brush waffle grids with oil. Preheat on medium setting. Ladle ¾ cup batter (or amount recommended by manufacturer) evenly over hot cooking surface. Close lid, bake until crisp and golden, 2 to 3 minutes. Re-oil grids every 2 or 3 waffles, if necessary.

Yield: 6 waffles

---
* Mori-Nu® makes one with only 1 percent fat.

Banana Nut Waffles
with Apricot Orange Syrup

1 cup whole wheat pastry flour
1/2 cup amaranth flour
1/4 cup oat flour
1 tablespoon aluminum-free baking powder
2 teaspoons baking soda
1 tablespoon egg replacer powder
1/4 teaspoon sea salt
~
1 cup vanilla flavor rice milk
1/2 cup amasake
2/3 cup banana purée
2 teaspoons pure vanilla extract
1 tablespoon expeller-pressed canola oil
~
3 large ripe bananas, sliced
1/2 cup pecans, coarsely chopped and toasted (p.10)

- In medium bowl, whisk dry ingredients together. Set aside.

- In blender, combine rice milk and next 4 ingredients, process just until smooth. Combine wet and dry ingredients, gently mixing with a rubber spatula. Toward end of mixing, use a folding motion to blend ingredients (do not over mix).

- Preheat oven to 200° F. Cooked waffles can be kept warm on a cake rack until ready to serve (will keep exterior crisp).

- Brush waffle grids with vegetable oil. Preheat on medium setting. Ladle 3/4 cup batter (or amount recommended by manufacturer) evenly over hot cooking surface. Close lid, bake until crisp and golden, 2 to 3 minutes. Re-oil grids every 2 or 3 waffles, if necessary.

- Garnish with sliced banana and pecans, drizzle Apricot Orange Syrup over top (recipe below). Serve immediately.

Yield: 6 waffles

Sunday mornings are eagerly awaited at our house...that's when my husband makes breakfast. These melt-in-your-mouth waffles are his specialty.

Make extra to freeze for a quick, nourishing weekday breakfast. Will keep 1 month in freezer. To reheat: place waffles directly on oven rack in preheated 350°F. oven for 8 to 10 minutes. [It is not necessary to defrost waffles before reheating.]

Apricot Orange Syrup

1 cup all-fruit apricot jam
2 teaspoons kudzu dissolved in
1/2 cup freshly squeezed orange juice
2 drops pure orange oil or 1/4 teaspoon pure orange extract

- In small nonreactive saucepan, whisk all ingredients together.

- Bring mixture to boil, reduce heat, simmer, stirring occasionally, until thickened, 2 to 3 minutes.

Yield: about 1 1/2 cups

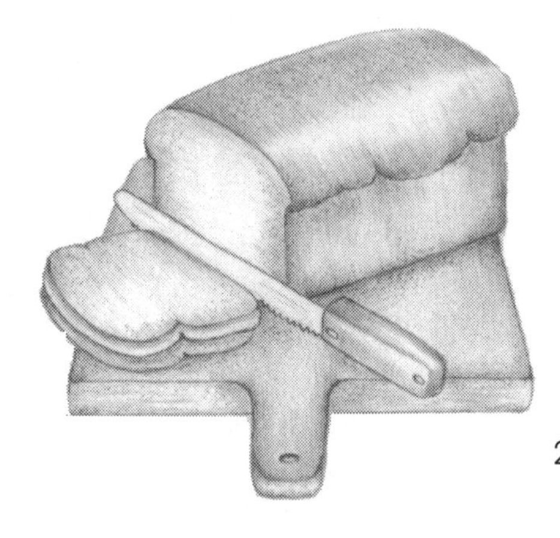

French Toast Mimosa

8 slices whole grain bread (such as oat, spelt or wheat)
~
1 cup pineapple juice, unsweetened
2 large ripe bananas
1 teaspoon ground cinnamon
2 teaspoons pure vanilla extract
1/4 teaspoon Frontier® coconut flavoring*
2 drops pure orange oil* or 1/2 teaspoon pure orange extract
~
2 large ripe bananas, sliced
8 large fresh strawberries, halved
Sunny Citrus Sauce (p. 82)

You'll love this easy egg and dairy-free version of traditional french toast with a taste of the tropics.

A delicious addition to Sunday brunch.

Bananas are an excellent source of potassium, with a good amount of iron, selenium and magnesium.

Strawberries are high in vitamin C, with a fair amount of iron and potassium.

- Leave bread out overnight to "stale".
- Prepare Sunny Citrus Sauce as directed.
  Note: can be prepared the night before, if desired.
- In blender, combine pineapple juice and next 5 ingredients, process until smooth. Pour fruit batter into shallow nonreactive pan.
- Preheat oven to 250° F. Meanwhile, preheat pancake griddle or cast-iron skillet until hot, lightly oil cooking surface.
- Dip bread into fruit batter, turning several times to saturate, cook until golden, 2 to 3 minutes (lift corner of bread with spatula to check color). Turn, cook 1 to 2 minutes, transfer to baking dish. Cover, keep warm while cooking remaining bread.
- Arrange french toast on plate (2 slices per serving), garnish with sliced banana and strawberries. Ladle sauce over top. Serve warm.

Yield: 4 servings

---
* Available in natural food stores and some supermarkets.

Blueberry Griddle Cakes
with Cinnamon Blueberry Syrup

2 cups vanilla flavor soy milk
1/2 cup amasake
1 1/2 tablespoons freshly squeezed lemon juice
1/4 cup barley malt syrup
1 tablespoon expeller-pressed canola oil
~
2 cups buckwheat flour
1/2 cup oat bran
2 tablespoons aluminum-free baking powder
1 1/2 tablespoons egg replacer powder
1/4 teaspoon sea salt
~
1 cup fresh or frozen blueberries

- In small bowl, combine soy milk, amasake and lemon juice, whisking to blend. Let stand 10 minutes, stir barley malt and oil into mixture.
- In large bowl, whisk dry ingredients together.
- Combine wet and dry ingredients, mix just until blended and lumps disappear. If batter appears thick, add more soy milk, a little at a time, fold blueberries into batter.
  Note: if using frozen blueberries, do not thaw or juice will turn griddle cakes purple.
- Preheat griddle or cast-iron skillet until hot, lightly oil cooking surface. Pour batter over hot griddle in pools, about 4 inches in diameter, leaving at least 1 inch between cakes, cook until puffy and full of bubbles. Turn, cook until golden, about 1 to 2 minutes.
- Drizzle Cinnamon Blueberry Syrup over cakes (recipe below).
  Serve immediately.

Yield: about 1 dozen

Cinnamon Blueberry Syrup

1 cup all-fruit blueberry jam
2 teaspoons kudzu dissolved in
1/3 cup freshly squeezed lemon juice
3 tablespoons water
1/2 to 1 teaspoon ground cinnamon to taste

- In small nonreactive saucepan, whisk all ingredients together.
- Bring mixture to boil. Reduce heat, simmer, stirring occasionally until thickened, 2 to 3 minutes.

Yield: about 1 1/2 cups

These light-textured, whole grain griddle cakes will get your day off to a healthy start and the mouth-watering Cinnamon-Blueberry Syrup will make you forget all about the butter.

Blueberries are fairly high in calcium, magnesium, iron and other minerals as well as vitamins A and C.

Hacienda Breakfast Burritos

8 10-inch whole wheat flour tortillas

~

1 cup vegetable stock (p. 8)
1 tablespoon low-sodium tamari sauce
1/2 cup white onion, coarsely chopped
1 large mild green chile pepper, seeded and minced
2/3 cup red bell pepper, diced
1 teaspoon ground tumeric
2 teaspoons ground cumin
1/4 to 1/2 teaspoon hot pepper sauce, to taste
16 ounces reduced-fat firm tofu,* well drained and crumbled

~

3 tablespoons fresh cilantro, chopped
1/2 cup Jack-style cheese alternative, grated
1 ripe (but firm) Haas avocado, peeled, pitted and diced
3/4 cup Roma tomatoes, seeded and diced

~

1 cup Salsa Verde (p. 77) or Howling Coyote Hot Sauce (p. 80)

A tried and true favorite from the Great American Southwest. These irresistible burritos are made with tofu filling standing in for the scrambled eggs.

Great for brunch. Serve with Oven Roasted Potatoes [p. 200].

- Preheat oven to 275° F.
- Layer tortillas between slightly damp paper towel in large, rectangular baking dish. Cover, keep tortillas warm in oven while preparing filling.
- In large heavy-bottomed skillet, bring stock and tamari to boil. Reduce heat, sauté onion and pepper until soft, 3 to 4 minutes. Add seasonings and tofu to onion mixture. Cook, stirring occasionally, 2 to 3 minutes. Remove pan from heat, set aside.
- Transfer warm tortillas to work area. Increase oven temperature to 375° F. Lightly oil baking dish.
- Spoon 1/3 cup filling into center of tortilla. Roll up burrito-style and arrange, seam side down, in prepared dish. Repeat procedure with remaining tortillas. Scatter cheese and cilantro over top, cover dish.
- Bake until tofu is puffy and cheese has melted, about 15 to 20 minutes.
- Remove pan from oven. Uncover, scatter avocado and tomatoes over burritos. Serve immediately and pass the salsa.

Yield: 4 servings (2 rollups per serving)

---

* White Wave® makes an excellent one.

Cauliflower Leek Quiche
with Rice Crust

2 cups cooked brown rice
1/2 cup cheddar-style cheese alternative, grated
2 teaspoons egg replacer powder
2 tablespoons unbleached flour with germ
2 1/2 tablespoons water
1/4 teaspoon sea salt
~
3 cups cauliflower flowerettes
2 large leeks, diagonally sliced (include some green)
2 teaspoons extra-virgin olive oil
~
1 cup rice milk
2 tablespoons mellow white miso
2 tablespoons freshly squeezed lemon juice
1 teaspoon lemon zest
3 teaspoons Dijon-style mustard
1/4 teaspoon freshly ground pepper
1/4 teaspoon ground marjoram
3 tablespoons unbleached flour with germ
3 teaspoons powdered egg replacer
~
2 teaspoons fresh tarragon, snipped or 1/2 teaspoon dried
1/3 cup cheddar-style cheese alternative, grated
1 medium green or red bell pepper, sliced thin and blanched

- Preheat oven to 375° F. Lightly oil 10 inch fluted quiche pan or deep-sided pie plate.
- Prepare crust by combining rice and next 5 ingredients. Press mixture evenly into prepared pan, bake until cheese melts, about 6 to 8 minutes, transfer to wire rack.
- Prepare cauliflower and leeks as directed. Steam cauliflower until crisp-tender, 6 to 8 minutes. In small heavy-bottomed skillet, heat oil, over medium heat, sauté leeks until soft, 3 to 4 minutes.
- In food processor or blender, combine rice milk and next 8 ingredients, process until smooth.
- Spoon cauliflower into crust, pour filling over cauliflower, sprinkle tarragon and cheese over top.
- Bake 20 to 25 minutes. Remove quiche from oven. Shape blanched pepper strips into circles and arrange around perimeter of quiche. Return quiche to oven, bake until set and knife inserted in center comes out clean, about 10 to 15 minutes.
- Transfer to wire rack, cool 5 minutes before cutting. Serve warm.

Yield: 4 to 6 servings

A wholesome rice crust complements this eggless, dairy-free quiche. The tangy filling tantalizes the taste buds with bursts of lemon and anise undertones.

Cauliflower, a member of the cruciferous family, is rich in potassium, folic acid, vitamin C and fairly high in protein. Crucifers have been found to contain cancer-preventative properties.

For lunch or a light dinner, serve with a side of Oven Roasted Potatoes [p. 200] and a medley of crisp greens.

Fruits of the Sun Fiesta
with Ambrosia Sauce

Perfect for Sunday brunch, this heavenly summertime treat is refreshing as a tropical breeze.

Silken tofu gives the sauce a creamy richness.

2 cups ripe mango
2 cups ripe banana, sliced
2 cups ripe pineapple, peeled and cut into chunks
2 cups ripe papaya, peeled and cut into chunks
2 cups ripe (but firm) kiwi, peeled and sliced
~
1 to 2 tablespoons liquid fruit sweetener, to taste
1½ tablespoons kudzu dissolved in
⅔ cup reserved pineapple juice
3 tablespoons freshly squeezed orange juice
3 tablespoons freshly squeezed lemon juice
~
8 ounces low-fat* firm silken tofu
~
⅔ cup coconut, unsweetened
16 fresh mint leaves

- Prepare mango as directed (p. 5).
- Prepare banana, pineapple (reserve juice), papaya and kiwi as directed, transfer to large serving bowl. Cover, refrigerate.
  Note: if pineapple doesn't yield ⅔ cup juice, simply add water to make up the difference.
- Prepare sauce in small nonreactive saucepan by combining fruit sweetener and next 4 ingredients, stirring to blend. Cook, over medium heat, stirring constantly, until thickened and clear, 2 to 3 minutes. Remove pan from heat, let cool 10 minutes.
- In blender, combine sauce with tofu, process until smooth, pour over fruit, tossing gently to coat. Chill 1 to 2 hours.
- Just before serving, fold in coconut. Serve in stemmed glasses or honeydew melons, halved and seeded. Garnish with mint leaves.

Yield: 6 to 8 servings

* Mori-Nu® make one with only 1 percent fat.

Rise'n Shine Granola

2 cups blanched almonds, toasted (p.10)
~
4 cups rolled oats, toasted
2 cups spelt flakes,* toasted
½ cup oat bran
~
⅔ cup dark amber maple syrup
¾ cup apple juice concentrate, undiluted
2 tablespoons expeller-pressed canola oil
2 teaspoons pure vanilla extract
1 teaspoon ground cinnamon
~
1 cup golden raisins
1½ cups dried unsulphured apricots, diced
1½ cups Medjool dates, pitted and diced

- Preheat oven to 325° F. Adjust rack to center position.
- In medium saucepan, combine maple syrup, apple juice concentrate and oil, heat until warm. Remove pan from heat. Whisk vanilla and cinnamon into mixture.
- In large mixing bowl, toss almonds, rolled oats, spelt flakes and oat bran together. Pour maple syrup mixture over top, tossing to coat.
- Spread mixture evenly over a 17 by 11 inch jelly-roll pan. Note: due to the volume of ingredients, it may be necessary to bake granola in two batches (do not overcrowd).
- Bake granola, stirring and re-spreading evenly in pan every 5 minutes until golden, about 15 to 20 minutes. Remove pan from oven, transfer granola immediately to large bowl to stop further cooking, let cool.
- Add raisins, apricots and dates to granola, spread over parchment paper or foil to cool. When completely cooled, break up large chunks with spatula, store in airtight container.

Yield: 12 cups

---

* Available in natural food stores and some supermarkets. If toasted spelt flakes aren't available, substitute rolled oats (not instant).

Commercially prepared granola tends to be high in fat, sugar and price. Try making this heart-healthy maple and fruit-juice sweetened version at home—big on taste with nutrition that's hard to beat.

Spelt, a member of the wheat family, has a slightly-sweet taste, high in gluten, protein, B vitamins, potassium and iron, it is an excellent alternative for people with celiac sprue [a gluten intolerance] and other wheat allergies.

Dressings, Sauces, Etc.

"No one knows the state of health of a person better than the person himself or herself. It is important to think about one's health and to act in such a way as to improve it."

Linus Pauling
Distinguished Scientist and Medical Researcher

Cinnamon Apple Butter

14 cups tart apples (such as Granny Smith or 20 ounce), peeled, cored and sliced
4 cups natural apple cider
~
1½ cups apple juice concentrate, undiluted
2 teaspoons ground cinnamon
¼ teaspoon ground cloves

- Combine apples and cider in crockpot. Cover, cook on low setting until soft and tender, about 10 hours, drain any remaining liquid.
- In blender or food processor, purée apples, in 2 or 3 batches, until smooth. Return mixture to crockpot.
- Whisk apple juice concentrate, cinnamon and cloves into apple mixture. Cover, cook until thickened, 1 to 2 hours, let cool.
- Store apple butter in container with tight-fitting lid. Will keep refrigerated up to 3 weeks.

To preserve: ladle apple butter into sterilized jars with tight-fitting lids. Process in boiling water bath, 10 minutes. When completely cool, test for seal. Will keep up to 9 months.

Yield: about 8 cups

Cooking apple butter in a crockpot ensures that the slow cooking process will produce a smooth, tasty butter. This naturally-sweetened butter is delicious in muffins, cookies and baked beans, great on hot cereal too.

Makes a welcome treat. Especially nice for gift giving.

Mint Chutney

2 cups fresh mint, firmly packed
3 tablespoons freshly squeezed orange juice
¼ cup water
1 tablespoon brown rice syrup
¼ teaspoon sea salt
¼ teaspoon hot pepper sauce

- In blender or food processor, combine all ingredients, process until smooth.
- Transfer mixture to small serving bowl. Cover, chill 1 hour before serving. Store leftovers in container with tight-fitting lid. Will keep refrigerated 2 to 3 days.

Yield: about 1 cup

A good digestive aide. This cooling condiment cleanses the palate and refreshes the taste buds. Serve with spicy dishes and curries to take the edge off.

Serving size = 2 tablespoons.

Herbal Seasoning

This delicious multi-purpose seasoning is salt-free, deriving its natural saltiness from kelp, a sea plant, rich in minerals.

1/3 cup dried dill weed
1 1/4 tablespoons kelp powder
1 1/4 tablespoons nutritional yeast flakes
1 tablespoon dried oregano
1/2 teaspoon dried marjoram leaves
1/2 teaspoon granulated garlic
1/2 teaspoon spirulina powder (see Glossary)
1/4 teaspoon cayenne pepper

- In spice mill, coffee grinder, or mortar bowl, grind all ingredients to fine powder.
- Store in container with tight-fitting lid. Will retain its flavor up to 6 months. Label jar with date prepared.

Yield: 1/2 + cup

Curry Powder

There are infinite varieties of curry mixtures each with their own special flavor... here's mine. Personalize it with your own additions or deletions.

The heat can be adjusted by the amount of cayenne pepper used.

2 tablespoons coriander seeds
1 1/2 tablespoons cumin seeds
2 teaspoons cardamom seeds
2 teaspoons mustard seeds
1/2 teaspoon fennel seeds
5 whole cloves
~
3 teaspoons ground tumeric
1/4 teaspoon freshly ground nutmeg
1/4 teaspoon ground cinnamon
1/8 to 1/2 teaspoon ground cayenne pepper, to taste
1/4 teaspoon ground white pepper

- Toast seeds as directed (p.10).
- In spice mill, coffee grinder or motar bowl, grind seeds and cloves to fine powder, combine with ground spices, whisking to blend.
- Store in container with tight-fitting lid. Will retain its flavor up to 3 months. Label jar with date prepared.

Yield: about 1/2 cup

Garam Masala

2 tablespoons cumin seeds
1 tablespoon fennel seeds
2 teaspoons cardamom seeds
2 teaspoons whole cloves
~
1 teaspoon ground mace
1 teaspoon freshly ground nutmeg
1 teaspoon ground ginger
1 teaspoon ground cinnamon

- Toast seeds as directed (p.10).
- In spice mill, coffee grinder, or mortar bowl, grind whole seeds and cloves to fine powder, combine with ground spices, whisking to blend.
- Store in container with tight-fitting lid. Will retain its flavor up to 6 months. Label jar with date prepared.

Yield: about 1/4 cup

Garam Masala translates to "hot spices" and is a staple in many Northern Indian and African dishes.

Toasting gives spices a deeper, nuttier flavor. Stove-top cooking lets you keep an eye on the spices while enjoying their fragrance.

Gomasio

1 cup raw unhulled sesame seeds*
2 teaspoons fine-ground sea salt
pinch cayenne pepper

- Toast sesame seeds as directed (p.10).
- In spice mill, coffee grinder or mortar bowl, grind sesame seeds to coarse consistency, combine with sea salt and cayenne, whisking to blend.
- Store in container with tight-fitting lid. Will keep refrigerated up to 3 weeks. Label jar with date prepared.

Yield: 1 cup

Gomasio, a staple in many Japanese households, is used as a seasoning in place of regular table salt.

* Available in natural food stores.

Harissa
(Hot Pepper Sauce)

This pungent, spicy North African condiment is commonly served with salads and other Moroccan dishes, such as Moroccan Tagine with Couscous [p. 125].

6 dried cayenne chile peppers (about 2 ounces)
~
2 teaspoons caraway seeds
1 teaspoon cumin seeds
1 teaspoon coriander seeds
2 large cloves garlic
~
1/8 teaspoon sea salt
1 1/2 tablespoons extra-virgin olive oil

- In heat-resistant measuring cup, cover dried chiles with boiling water, let soak 30 minutes to reconstitute. Drain, chop into small pieces. In mortar bowl with pestle, grind chiles, seeds and garlic to pulp consistency, stir in sea salt.
  Note: for thinner sauce, add freshly squeezed lemon juice, a little at a time, until desired consistency is achieved.

- Store in container with tight-fitting lid. Pour a thin layer of olive oil over harissa to prevent discoloration. Will keep refrigerated up to 4 months.

Yield: about 3/4 cup

Italian Seasoning

2 tablespoons dried basil
2 tablespoons dried marjoram
2 tablespoons dried oregano
2 tablespoons dried rosemary
2 tablespoons dried summer savory
2 tablespoons dried thyme
1 teaspoon crushed red pepper flakes
2 tablespoons ground coriander

- In spice mill, coffee grinder, or mortar bowl, combine all ingredients, except coriander, grind to fine consistency.

- Store in container with tight-fitting lid. Will retain its flavor up to 6 months. Label jar with date prepared.

Yield: 1 cup

Cilantro Lime Vinaigrette

2 large cloves garlic, blanched
2 teaspoons cumin seeds, toasted (p.10)
¼ cup freshly squeezed lime juice
1 tablespoon tomato paste
2 tablespoons water
2 tablespoons fresh cilantro, chopped
¼ cup rice vinegar
2 teaspoons walnut oil
⅛ teaspoon hot pepper sauce
¼ teaspoon sea salt
2 teaspoons honey
2 teaspoons lecithin granules*

- Peel garlic, blanch cloves in small, nonreactive saucepan, cover with water, bring to boil, simmer 1 to 2 minutes. Drain, repeat process two more times. Note: the more garlic is blanched, the milder it becomes taking away its bite.

- In blender, combine garlic, cumin seeds and all remaining ingredients, process just until blended. Chill 1 to 2 hours to allow flavors to meld. Store in container with tight-fitting lid. Will keep refrigerated up to 4 days. After standing, dressing may become thick, re-blend or add a little water.

Yield: about 1 cup

Zesty and colorful, bursting with complex flavors. This dressing is a hit with Mexican or Caribbean dishes.

Serve with fresh greens and strips of orange or yellow bell pepper. Terrific over Pinwheel Salad [p. 165] or as a marinade for veggie kabobs.

* Available in natural food stores.

Citrus Poppy Seed Dressing

⅔ cup freshly squeezed orange juice
3 tablespoons tahini
2 tablespoons rice vinegar
3 teaspoons honey mustard
1 tablespoon brown rice syrup
2 tablespoons poppy seeds

- In blender, combine all ingredients, except poppy seeds, process on high until creamy and smooth, about 1 minute, stir poppy seeds into dressing.

- Chill 2 hours before serving. Store in container with tight-fitting lid. Will keep refrigerated up to 2 weeks.

Yield: 1 cup

A tangy-sweet, oil-free dressing that goes great with fresh spinach greens. Garnish with tangerine segments and wedges of unpeeled red pear for a colorful presentation.

Tahini keeps the dressing from separating.

Heart Beet Dressing

This creamy soft-pink dressing is low in fat and cholesterol. Its sweet-tart flavor compliments bitter greens [such as endive, mustard, dandelion or escarole].

Beets are one of the most under-appreciated vegetables, high in folic acid, an important B vitamin.

1 1/2 tablespoons raw beet, peeled and diced
1 1/2 teaspoons brown rice syrup
1/3 cup Dijon Eggless Mayo (p. 74)
1/2 cup soy milk
2 teaspoons fresh dill, minced or 1 teaspoon dried

- In blender, combine all ingredients, process until smooth. Chill 1 hour before serving. Store in container with tight-fitting lid. Will keep refrigerated up to 2 weeks.

Yield: 1 1/4 cups

Herbal Vinaigrette

Let your imagination run wild!

*This low-fat versatile dressing has endless possibilities: drizzled over crisp salad greens, as a marinade for veggie kabobs or grilled porta-bellas, even dressing-up a chilled pasta salad.**

3 large cloves garlic, blanched
1 teaspoon herbal seasoning (p. 66)
1 tablespoon fresh basil, chopped
1 tablespoon fresh flat-leaf Italian parsley, chopped
1 tablespoon fresh tarragon, chopped
1 tablespoon extra-virgin olive oil
1/2 cup rice vinegar
3 tablespoons mellow white miso
1/4 cup mirin
2/3 cup vegetable stock (p. 8)
1 tablespoon liquid aminos
1 tablespoon shallots, diced
1 to 2 teaspoons brown rice syrup, to taste
1 tablespoon Dijon-style mustard

- Peel garlic, blanch cloves in small, nonreactive saucepan, cover with water, bring to boil, simmer 1 to 2 minutes. Drain, repeat process two more times. Note: the more garlic is blanched, the milder it becomes taking away its bite.

- In blender, combine garlic and all remaining ingredients, process just until blended. Chill 1 to 2 hours to allow flavors to meld. Store in container with tight-fitting lid. Will keep refrigerated up to 4 days.

Yield: 2 cups*

* Enough for 16 ounces of cooked pasta.

Creamy Cucumber Dill Dressing

3/4 cup cucumber, peeled, seeded and coarsely chopped
2 1/2 tablespoons carrot, coarsely chopped
5 ounces low-fat firm silken tofu, drained
1 tablespoon mellow white miso
3 tablespoons rice vinegar
2 tablespoons freshly squeezed lemon juice
1/3 cup soy milk
2 teaspoons lecithin granules
3 teaspoons honey mustard
1 tablespoon honey
1/4 teaspoon sea salt
2 cloves garlic, blanched
2 teaspoons sweet onion, minced
1 1/2 tablespoons fresh flat-leaf Italian parsley, snipped
3 tablespoons fresh dill, snipped

- Peel garlic, blanch cloves in small, nonreactive saucepan, cover with water, bring to boil, simmer 1 to 2 minutes. Drain, repeat process two more times. Note: the more garlic is blanched, the milder it becomes taking away its bite.

- In blender, combine all ingredients, process until blended and flecks of carrot are visible. Store in container with tight-fitting lid. Will keep refrigerated up to 1 week.

Yield: 1 1/2 cups

This sensational dressing has incredible taste-appeal and no oil! A real winner and probably my all-time favorite.

Drizzle dressing over a medley of mixed greens, on a garden burger, topping a baked potato or in a whole grain pita pocket with cucumber, tomato and shredded lettuce.

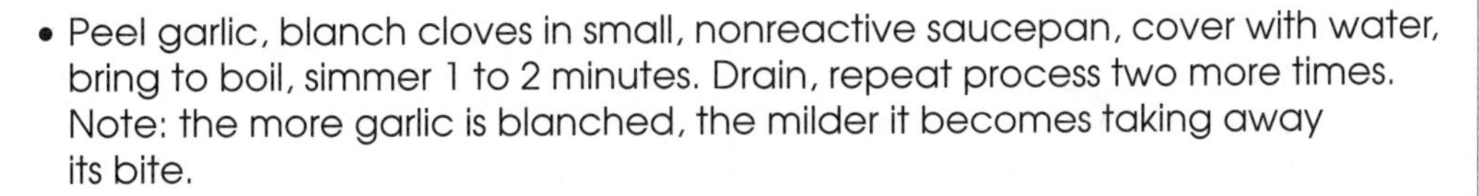

10 ounces low-fat firm silken tofu, drained
1/3 cup Zesty Ketchup (p. 75)
1/8 teaspoon hot pepper sauce
2 teaspoons brown rice syrup
3 tablespoons dill pickle, chopped
2 tablespoons dill pickle juice (from jar)
1 1/2 tablespoons red hatcho miso
3 teaspoons fresh chives, snipped
1 tablespoon fresh flat-leaf Italian parsley, snipped

- In blender, combine all ingredients, process until small pieces of pickle are visible. Store in container with tight-fitting lid. Will keep refrigerated up to 2 weeks. After standing, dressing may become thick, re-blend or add a little water.

Yield: 1 3/4 cups

Serve this tangy dressing with a salad of fresh spinach greens and red onion, thinly sliced.

Terrific on a Reuben James sandwich [p. 181].

Island Dressing

I first tasted this heavenly dressing at a renowned dining spot on the Big Island of Hawaii. After numerous attempts, this version was born.

Papaya seeds lend a mild peppery taste to the dressing; banana imitates the texture and viscosity of oil, creating an intensely flavorful dressing.

10 ounces low-fat firm silken tofu,* drained
1 large ripe banana
1/4 cup rice milk
2 teaspoons vegetarian Worcestershire sauce
1 tablespoon balsamic vinegar
2 tablespoons raspberry vinegar
1 tablespoon Dijon-style mustard
2 to 4 teaspoons dark amber maple syrup, to taste
2 teaspoons shallots, chopped
1 tablespoon fresh basil, chopped
2 teaspoons fresh lemon thyme, chopped
2 tablespoons papaya seeds

- In blender, combine all ingredients, process just until blended and flecks of papaya seed are visible.
- Chill 1 to 2 hours to allow flavors to meld. Store in container with tight-fitting lid. Will keep refrigerated up to 1 week. After standing, dressing may become thick, re-blend or add a little water.

Yield: 2 cups

* Mori-Nu Lite® is excellent with only 1 percent fat.

Mango Fandango Dressing

Serve this exotic dressing with complex flavors over a bed of crisp summer greens with chunks of ripe nectarine and fresh ripe figs.

Mango is a voluptuous perfumy fruit, native to Asia, extremely rich in vitamin A. One mango may contain as much as 10,000 iu's of vitamin A, also high in vitamin C, beta carotene, zinc, magnesium and potassium.

Lime juice brings out the mango's haunting flavor.

1 ripe mango
1 teaspoon honey mustard
3 tablespoons freshly squeezed lime juice
1 1/2 tablespoons walnut oil
1/8 teaspoon sea salt
2 teaspoons lecithin granules
2 teaspoons fresh cilantro, chopped

- Prepare mango as directed (p. 5).
- In blender, combine mango and all remaining ingredients, process until smooth and creamy. Store in container with tight-fitting lid. Will keep refrigerated up to 3 days. After standing, dressing may become thick, re-blend or add a little water.

Yield: about 1 1/2 cups

Zorba the Greek Dressing

¼ cup pine nuts, toasted (p.10)
4 large cloves garlic, blanched
3 scallions, chopped (white part only)
8 pitted Kalamata olives
1 tablespoon Dijon-style mustard
1 tablespoon red wine vinegar
2 tablespoons freshly squeezed lemon juice
1 teaspoon lemon zest
1 tablespoon extra-virgin olive oil
½ cup Roma tomatoes, cored, seeded and quartered
¼ teaspoon freshly ground pepper
¼ to ½ teaspoon sea salt, to taste
2 teaspoons lecithin granules*
⅓ cup Savory Garlic Broth or vegetable stock (p. 8)
1 tablespoon parmesan-style cheese alternative, grated
1 tablespoon fresh basil, chopped
1 tablespoon fresh oregano, chopped

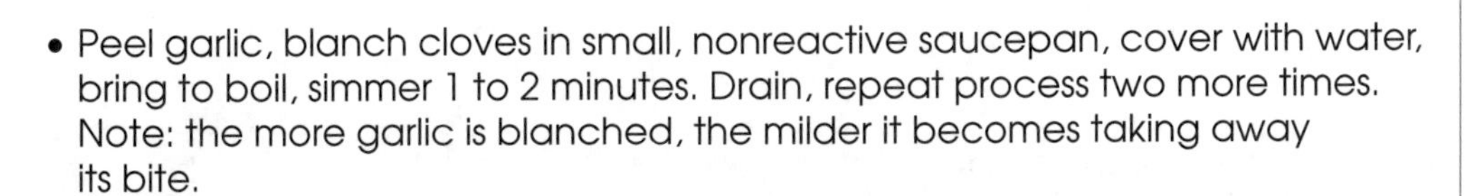

- Peel garlic, blanch cloves in small, nonreactive saucepan, cover with water, bring to boil, simmer 1 to 2 minutes. Drain, repeat process two more times. Note: the more garlic is blanched, the milder it becomes taking away its bite.

- In blender, combine pine nuts, garlic and all remaining ingredients, process until smooth and small flecks of basil and oregano are visible. Store in container with tight-fitting lid. Will keep refrigerated up to 4 days. After standing, dressing may become thick, re-blend or add a little water.

Yield: 1 cup

* Available in natural food stores.

Sparkling and sunny like the Mediterranean, this dressing has full-bodied flavor.

Goes well with a variety of cuisines. Delicious as a dressing for pasta salad [double the recipe for 16 ounces pasta].

Helpful Tip: assemble all ingredients before beginning—this will speed preparation time considerably.

Dijon Eggless "Mayo"

Lecithin, a fat emulsifier, is important to cell membranes, nerves and the brain. Used in this heart-healthy eggless recipe, lecithin granules help keep the mayo from separating.

10 ounces low-fat firm silken tofu,* drained
2 tablespoons expeller-pressed canola oil
2 tablespoons freshly squeezed lemon juice
1 tablespoon lecithin granules
2 tablespoons cashews, finely ground
2 teaspoons Dijon-style mustard
1 teaspoon brown rice syrup
1 teaspoon mirin
1/2 teaspoon herbal seasoning (p. 66)
1/4 teaspoon sea salt
1/8 teaspoon white pepper

- In blender or food processor, combine all ingredients, process until smooth. Note: if mayo seems thick, add water, a little at a time, until desired consistency is achieved.

- Transfer to container with tight-fitting lid. Chill 2 to 3 hours to allow flavors to meld. Will keep refrigerated up to 2 weeks.

Yield: 1 cup

---
* Mori-Nu Lite® is excellent with only 1 percent fat.

Asian Marinade

Complex flavors abound in this Eastern-inspired exotic marinade. Tangy-sour tamarind and pungent red curry are the predominant tastes.

Grill strips of marinated tempeh and serve with a side of Spicy Udon Noodles [p. 202] for a protein-packed ride on the Orient Express.

2 tablespoons tamarind paste (see Glossary)
2 tablespoons red curry paste*
6 cloves garlic, minced
2 tablespoons fresh ginger root, peeled and grated
3 tablespoons extra-virgin olive oil
4 tablespoons barley malt syrup
8 tablespoons low-sodium tamari sauce
6 tablespoons freshly squeezed orange juice

- Combine all ingredients in medium nonreactive bowl, whisking to blend.

Yield: about 1 1/2 cups

---
* Available in Asian markets, natural food stores and some supermarkets.

Zesty Ketchup

$1\frac{3}{4}$ pounds Roma tomatoes
1 cup onion, diced
3 cloves garlic, pressed
1 large red bell pepper, diced
$\frac{1}{2}$ to $\frac{3}{4}$ teaspoon sea salt, to taste
$\frac{1}{8}$ teaspoon cayenne pepper

~

1 large whole bay leaf
1 whole cinnamon stick
$1\frac{1}{2}$ teaspoons celery seeds, crushed
$\frac{1}{3}$ cup apple juice concentrate, undiluted

~

$\frac{1}{2}$ cup red wine vinegar
2 tablespoons fresh basil, minced
3 tablespoons tomato paste

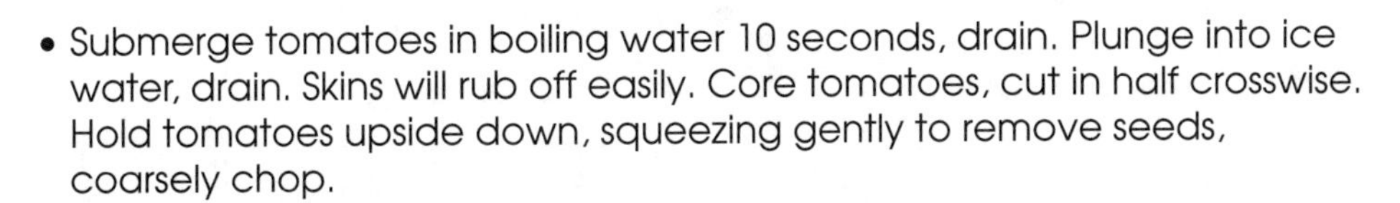

- Submerge tomatoes in boiling water 10 seconds, drain. Plunge into ice water, drain. Skins will rub off easily. Core tomatoes, cut in half crosswise. Hold tomatoes upside down, squeezing gently to remove seeds, coarsely chop.

- In large nonreactive saucepan, combine tomatoes and next 5 ingredients, bring to boil. Reduce heat, simmer until tomatoes are cooked into juice, about 30 minutes. Remove pan from heat, press mixture through mesh sieve or chinot, over bowl, to extract liquid, discard solids.

- Make bouquet garni (see Glossary) with bay leaf, cinnamon stick and celery seeds. Add bouquet garni and apple juice concentrate to tomato mixture, whisking to blend. Return mixture to boil, stirring occasionally. Reduce heat, simmer until mixture starts to thicken, about 30 to 45 minutes, (cooking time will depend on water content of tomatoes).

- Remove and discard bouquet garni. Whisk vinegar, basil and tomato paste into mixture, simmer 15 minutes. Remove pan from heat, let cool 10 minutes. Note: if ketchup seems thin, add more tomato paste, a little at a time, until desired consistency is achieved.

- Transfer mixture to food processor or blender, process until smooth. Store in container with tight-fitting lid. Will keep refrigerated up to 2 months.

Yield: 4 cups

Easy to prepare. Simmer a batch while you're working around the house on the week-end.

Once you've tried this tangy, fruit juice sweet-ened version, you'll never go back to commercially prepared ketchup again.

Tomatoes are rich in lycopene, a nutraceutical which protects against cell damage. Recent studies show that lycopene may decrease the risk of colon and bladder cancer.

Perk up dressings and sauces, also great on Oven-Roasted Potatoes [p. 200] or Garden of Eat'n Burgers [p. 177].

Border Salsa

Salsa has dethroned ketchup to become the king of condiments for the 90's.

This chunky salsa has big bold taste, loaded with live-energy enzymes. The subtle hint of aromatic cinnamon and cilantro contrast beautifully with the smoky undertones of the chipotles to create a unique taste with tantalizing fieriness.
Note: For milder salsa, cut the amount of chiles called for in half.

Serve with Baked Tortilla Chips [p. 13] or ladle over Black Bean Enchiladas Grande [p. 123].

4 large cloves garlic, finely chopped
2 cups beefsteak-style tomatoes, seeded and crushed
1 1/4 cups white onion, coarsely chopped
1 large mild green chile pepper, finely chopped
7 ounces chipotle chiles in adobo sauce (see Glossary)
1 large yellow bell pepper, coarsely chopped
1/4 cup fresh cilantro, chopped
1/4 teaspoon ground cinnamon
1 tablespoon ground cumin
1/2 teaspoon Vege Sal®
2 teaspoons dried oregano
1/4 to 1/2 hot pepper sauce, to taste
~
4 large Roma tomatoes, seeded and coarsely chopped

- In mortar bowl, mash garlic with pestle.
- In food processor or blender, combine garlic and all ingredients, except Roma tomatoes, pulse-chop 8 to 10 times. Mixture should be chunky (do not over process).
- Transfer salsa to serving bowl, stir in Romas. Store in container with tight-fitting lid. Chill 1 to 2 hours to allow flavors to meld. Will keep refrigerated up to 2 weeks.

Yield: about 5 cups

Salsa Verde

1½ pounds tomatillos, husked and coarsely chopped (about 4 cups)
1 tablespoon extra-virgin olive oil
3 large cloves garlic, finely chopped
1 cup white onion, diced
1 large mild green chile pepper, finely chopped

~

1 to 2 teaspoons brown rice syrup, to taste
½ teaspoon hot pepper sauce
1 teaspoon Frontier® Mexican seasoning*
1 teaspoon ground cumin
¼ teaspoon Vege Sal®

~

¼ cup freshly squeezed lime juice
¼ cup fresh cilantro, finely chopped

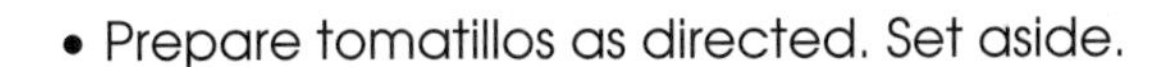

- Prepare tomatillos as directed. Set aside.
- In mortar bowl, mash garlic with pestle.
- In large wide-bottomed skillet, heat oil, sauté garlic, onion and green chile until soft, 3 to 4 minutes. Add all remaining ingredients, except lime juice and cilantro, to skillet, bring to boil over medium heat. Reduce heat, cover, simmer 20 minutes. Remove pan from heat.
- Transfer salsa to serving bowl. Cover, chill 1 to 2 hours to allow flavors to meld, add lime juice and cilantro **just before serving** to preserve the bright green color. Will keep refrigerated up to 2 weeks, though fresher is better. Note: to preserve, ladle salsa into sterilized ½ pint or pint jelly jars with tight-fitting lids. Process in boiling water bath, 10 minutes. When completely cool, test for seal. Store in cool dark place. Will keep up to 9 months.

Yield: 3½ to 4 cups

* Available in natural food stores and some supermarkets.

Salsa Verde [green salsa] a versatile condiment with pizzazz!

Tomatillos, used predominantly in Mexican cooking are similar to tomatoes, only smaller, with a tart lemon-herb flavor and papery husk. Be sure to choose ripe tomatillos [not shriveled] when making this pungent salsa.

Cilantro is a fairly strong-flavored herb reminiscent of lemon and sage. Widely used in Latin American dishes.

Basil Spinach Pesto

This low-fat version of Basil Genovese uses only a fraction of the fat [oil] typical of traditional pesto. Sunflower seeds replace higher-fat nuts while miso mellows basils' pungency. Make extra and freeze in pint containers or ice cube trays.

Toss a couple of pesto cubes into your favorite soup for added flavor; spread on crostini [grilled French baguette slices]; as a filling for Braised Mushroom Caps [p. 19] or topping your favorite pasta.

1/3 cup raw sunflower seeds, toasted (p.10)
12 cups fresh spinach, loosely packed (about 10 ounces)
1 1/2 cups fresh basil leaves, firmly packed
3 tablespoons extra-virgin olive oil
4 cloves garlic, blanched
1 tablespoon water
2 tablespoons mellow white miso

- Rinse spinach thoroughly to dislodge sand particles, repeat, if necessary. Remove and discard stems, cut into bite-size pieces. Cook spinach in large wide-bottomed skillet, over high heat, until wilted, 2 to 3 minutes. Drain, squeeze spinach to remove excess water. Blanch garlic (see Cilantro Lime Vinaigrette, step 1, p. 69).
- In food processor, combine spinach, garlic and all remaining ingredients, process until pesto is consistency of coarse paste. Store in container with tight-fitting lid. Cover pesto with thin layer of olive oil to prevent discoloration. Will keep refrigerated several weeks.

Yield: about 2 cup

Tarragon Tomato Tapenade

Sun-dried tomatoes, tarragon, toasted pine nuts and miso come together to give this tapenade its delicious, smoky-rich flavor.

As an appetizer, spread thinly on crostini [grilled baguette slices] or add a dollop to Red Pepper Veloute soup [p. 217].

3/4 cup sun-dried tomatoes (about 1 ounce)
1 cup boiling water
1/4 cup pine nuts, toasted (p.10)
1/2 cup fresh tarragon, firmly packed
3/4 cup fresh flat-leaf Italian parsley, chopped
2 tablespoons extra-virgin olive oil
1 tablespoon freshly squeezed lemon juice
2 teaspoons liquid aminos
1 1/2 tablespoons red hatcho miso
3 medium Roma tomatoes, seeded and quartered

- In small nonreactive bowl, pour boiling water over sun-dried tomatoes, let soak 15 minutes to reconstitute.
- In food processor, combine sun-dried tomatoes with soaking liquid, pine nuts and all remaining ingredients, except Roma tomatoes, process until smooth. Add Romas to mixture, process until consistency of coarse paste. Store in container with tight-fitting lid. Cover tapenade with thin layer of olive oil to prevent discoloration. Will keep refrigerated several weeks.

Yield: about 1 1/2 cups

Southwest Chile Pesto

3 tablespoons expeller-pressed canola oil
1 cup mild green chile peppers, diced
3 large cloves garlic, chopped
~
½ cup raw pepita seeds, toasted (p.10)
¼ cup freshly squeezed lime juice
1 cup fresh basil, firmly packed
½ cup fresh cilantro, firmly packed
2 teaspoons ground cumin
½ teaspoon ground coriander
1 to 2 teaspoons brown rice syrup, to taste
2 tablespoons mellow white miso

- In small heavy-bottomed skillet, heat oil, sauté chile pepper and garlic stirring frequently until soft, 3 to 5 minutes. Remove pan from heat. Note: if you prefer a milder pesto, remove seed ribs from chiles before chopping.
- In food processor, combine chile/garlic mixture and all remaining ingredients, process to consistency of coarse paste. Store in container with tight-fitting lid. Will keep refrigerated 3 to 4 weeks. Freezes well.

Yield: about 2 cups

New Mexico has one of the lowest incidences of heart disease. Researchers believe this is due to the high consumption of chile peppers which are grown and eaten there—over 55,000 tons annually. Chile peppers also appear to help lower blood fat levels.

Pesto, named for the mortar and pestle that produces the creamiest, most subtle results, is more practically made in a food processor.

Basil and cilantro's pungent, complex flavors are mellowed with the addition of miso. Pepitas are high in zinc, protein and amino acids.

Serve this terrific tasting pesto with Anasazi Bean Burgers [p. 178] or thin with a little water for dipping Baked Tortilla Chips [p. 13].

Howling Coyote Hot Sauce

This sauce is for all of you "hot tamalé" lovers! Make it when your garden is overflowing with tomatoes and peppers.

Capsicum, an ingredient in hot peppers, has been proven beneficial in stimulating both circulation and elimination. Acting as a mild diuretic, it increases kidney cleansing. Cayenne pepper is a natural energy stimulant that, unlike coffee, appears to help reduce blood pressure as well as cholesterol levels.

Spoon a little over Anasazi Bean Burgers [p. 178] or just about anything you want to spice-up.

2 pounds Roma tomatoes, seeded and coarsely chopped
2 pounds beefsteak-style tomatoes, seeded and coarsely chopped
~
4 large cloves garlic, minced
1 1/2 cups white onion, diced
1 1/2 cups green bell pepper, chopped
1 cup orange or yellow bell pepper, chopped
5 fresh haberno or serrano chile peppers, seeded and minced
~
3 tablespoons tomato paste
3/4 teaspoon Vege Sal®
1 teaspoon dried mustard
1/2 teaspoon crushed red pepper flakes
1/4 teaspoon cayenne pepper
1/2 teaspoon celery seeds, crushed
1/2 teaspoon ground allspice
1/4 teaspoon ground mace
1/4 teaspoon ground cloves
1/4 teaspoon ground cinnamon
~
1/4 cup honey
1/2 cup apple cider vinegar

- Submerge tomatoes in boiling water 10 seconds, drain. Plunge into ice water, drain. Skins will rub off easily. Core tomatoes, cut in half crosswise. Hold tomatoes upside down, squeezing gently to remove seeds, coarsely chop. Set aside.
- Prepare garlic, onion and peppers as directed.
- In nonreactive stockpot, combine tomatoes, garlic, onion, peppers and all remaining ingredients, except honey and vinegar, bring mixture to slow boil. Reduce heat, simmer, stirring occasionally, until thick and quantity is reduced by half, about 1 hour. Adjust seasonings, if desired.
- Add honey and vinegar to mixture, stirring to blend, bring to rapid boil. Reduce heat, simmer 15 minutes, stirring frequently. Remove pan from heat, let cool. Store in container with tight-fitting lid. Will keep refrigerated up to 4 weeks.
  Note: to preserve, ladle hot sauce into sterilized pint jars with tight-fitting lids. Process in boiling water bath, 10 minutes. When cool, test for seal. Let stand one week before using. Store in cool, dark place. Will keep up to 1 year.

Yield: 7 1/2 cups

Mellow Yellow Sauce

2 large yellow bell peppers, roasted (p. 3)
~
2 tablespoons unhulled sesame seeds, toasted (p.10)
2 teaspoons sesame oil
8 ounces low-fat firm silken tofu*
1/4 cup mellow white miso
1/4 cup water
3 tablespoons freshly squeezed lemon juice

- Roast peppers as directed.
- In blender, combine roasted peppers and all remaining ingredients, purée until smooth.
- Transfer sauce to medium saucepan, simmer over medium heat, 5 to 8 minutes. Store in container with tight-fitting lid. Will keep refrigerated up to 1 week.

Yield: 2 1/2 cups

---

* Mori-Nu Lite® is excellent iwth only 1 percent fat.

This colorful sauce perks up steamed vegetables; miso adds rich flavor, minus the fat; sesame seeds provide a good calcium boost.

A real treat ladled over mashed potatoes.

Sweet'n Sour Sauce

2 teaspoons kudzu dissolved in
3/4 cup pineapple juice, unsweetened
2 tablespoons natural hoisin sauce
2 tablespoons all-fruit apricot jam
2 tablespoons brown rice syrup
2 teaspoons umeboshi vinegar
1 tablespoon rice vinegar
1/4 to 1/2 teaspoon crushed red pepper flakes, to taste

- In small nonreactive sauce pan, combine all ingredients, bring mixture to boil, stirring frequently until thickened, 1 to 2 minutes. Store in container with tight-fitting lid. Will keep refrigerated up to 2 weeks.

Yield: 1 cup

Bold and spicy-sweet, this sauce shines when combined with stir-fried vegetables served over brown rice or Asian noodles. It also satisfies all five tastes put forth in the Chinese five element theory—pungent, sweet, sour, bitter and salty.

Gingery Plum Sauce

1 pound very ripe purple plums
1 teaspoon crystallized ginger, finely chopped
$^1/_3$ cup dark amber maple syrup
~
4 teaspoons kudzu dissolved in
2 tablespoons freshly squeezed lemon juice

This vivid magenta-color sauce is excellent with Asian dishes such as Far East Noodle Salad [p. 149] or for dipping spring rolls.

Plums are a good source of vitamin A and potassium.

- Cut plums in half lengthwise, twist apart and remove pits, cut halves into small pieces.
- In small bowl, combine kudzu and lemon juice, whisk until completely dissolved. Set aside.
- In medium nonreactive saucepan, combine plums, ginger, and maple syrup. Stir kudzu mixture into plums, bring to boil. Cook, stirring constantly until thickened, 2 to 3 minutes. Remove pan from heat, let cool 10 minutes.
- Transfer mixture to blender, process until smooth. Store leftovers in container with tight-fitting lid. Will keep refrigerated up to 2 weeks.

Yield: 2 cups

Sunny Citrus Sauce

Serve this sparkling, saffron-colored sauce over Mediterranean Cabbage Rolls [p. 121], French Toast Mimosa [p. 56] or brown basmati rice with chunks of fresh pineapple and sautéed green pepper.

$^3/_4$ cup freshly squeezed orange juice (about 3 juice oranges)
$^1/_2$ teaspoon fresh ginger root, peeled and coarsely grated
$^1/_4$ teaspoon Five Spice powder
$^1/_4$ teaspoon saffron threads
1 tablespoon honey
~
1 teaspoon kudzu dissolved in
3 tablespoons freshly squeezed lime juice

- In small nonreactive saucepan, combine all ingredients, except kudzu and lime juice, bring to boil. Reduce heat, simmer, 2 to 3 minutes. Dissolve kudzu in lime juice, gradually add to sauce, stirring until thickened, 1 to 2 minutes.

Yield: 1 cup

Alfrézo Sauce

10 ounces low-fat firm silken tofu
2 teaspoons extra-virgin olive oil
1/4 cup raw cashew pieces, finely ground
2 tablespoons unbleached flour with germ
1 cup rice milk
2 teaspoons Gomasio (p. 67)
1 1/2 teaspoons garlic, minced
2 tablespoons nutritional yeast flakes
1 teaspoon herbal seasoning (p. 66)
1/8 teaspoon white pepper
~
1/3 cup parmesan-style cheese alternative, grated

- In blender, combine all ingredients, except parmesan, process until smooth and creamy.
- Transfer mixture to medium saucepan, bring to boil over medium heat, stirring constantly. Reduce heat, simmer until thickened, 2 to 3 minutes.
- Remove pan from heat, stir in parmesan and ladle over your favorite pasta.

Yield: 2 1/4 cups

A guiltless, dairy-free sauce so rich in taste you'll think you're eating the real thing!

Be adventuresome. Using this sauce as a base, create an enticing variation by adding 3/4 cup Basil Spinach Pesto [p. 78] to the Alfrézo sauce.

Tomato "Cream" Sauce

3 large Roma tomatoes (about 12 ounces)
2 tablespoons water
~
1 1/4 cups Alfrézo Sauce (recipe above)
1 tablespoon fresh basil, finely chopped or 1 teaspoon dried
2 tablespoons fresh tarragon, snipped
1/4 to 1/2 teaspoon sea salt, to taste
1/8 teaspoon freshly ground pepper
1 to 2 tablespoons unbleached flour with germ

- Submerge tomatoes in boiling water 10 seconds, drain. Plunge into ice water, drain. Skins will rub off easily. Core tomatoes, coarsely chop.
- In blender, combine tomatoes and water, process until smooth. Strain mixture through mesh sieve, over bowl, discard solids.
- In medium nonreactive saucepan, prepare Alfrézo Sauce as directed. Note: recipe makes 2 1/4 cups, refrigerate remainder.
- Add puréed tomatoes, basil and next 4 ingredients to sauce, stirring to blend, bring to boil. Reduce heat, simmer, stirring frequently until thickened, 4 to 5 minutes.

Yield: about 3 1/4 cups

A terrific, dairy-free version of a popular sauce served in many Italian restaurants.

Holiday Gravy

Celebrate the holidays with food you feel good about.

Mouth-watering, great-tasting gravy full of good nutrition minus the fat and cholesterol of traditional meat-based gravies.

The multi-grain baking mix adds flavor and makes a thicker, fluffier gravy than flour or corn starch.

Ladle over mashed potatoes, stuffing or assorted grains—anyway you eat it, you're gonna love it!
Note: if desired, can be made the day before and refrigerated until ready to reheat.

4 cups mushroom stock (p. 8)
2 tablespoons mirin
2 tablespoons liquid aminos
1 1/2 teaspoons dried sage
1/2 teaspoon dried thyme
1/2 teaspoon dried basil
1/4 teaspoon dried marjoram
1/4 teaspoon Vege Sal®
1/8 teaspoon white pepper
1/2 teaspoon dried rosemary leaves, crushed
~
4 to 6 tablespoons Multi-Grain Baking Mix (p. 9)
3 tablespoons traditional brown miso

- In a 2-quart saucepan, combine 3 1/2 cups stock (reserve 1/4 cup) and all remaining ingredients, except flour and miso, bring to boil. Reduce heat, simmer 5 minutes.

- Make a roux by combining the baking mix with 1/2 cup reserved stock and miso. Whisk roux gradually into gravy mixture, return to boil. Reduce heat, simmer, whisking constantly until thickened, 3 to 4 minutes.

Yield: 4 cups

Toasted Cumin Black Bean Sauce

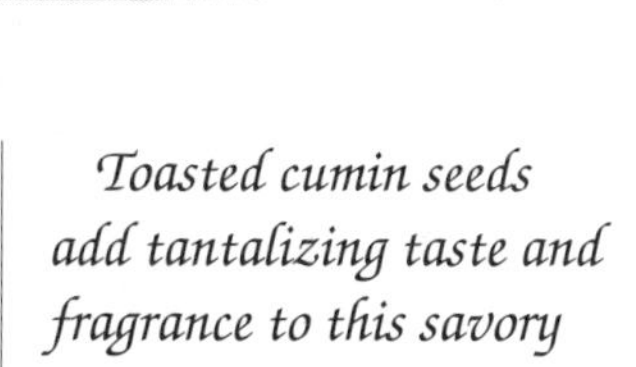

1¾ cups vegetable stock (p. 8)
1½ cups white onion, coarsely chopped
4 large cloves garlic, minced
~
2 tablespoons cumin seeds, crushed and toasted (p.10)
1 tablespoon fresh summer savory, chopped or 1 teaspoon dried
½ teaspoon hot pepper sauce
4 cups cooked black beans
~
2 tablespoons red hatcho miso
2 tablespoons water

- In large wide-bottomed skillet, bring ½ cup stock (reserve remainder) to boil, sauté onion and garlic until soft, 3 to 4 minutes.
- Add 1 cup reserved stock and all remaining ingredients, except miso, to onion mixture, stirring to blend. Cook beans, over medium heat, stirring occasionally until creamy, about 15 to 20 minutes. Reduce heat to lowest setting. Combine miso and water, stir into beans, cover until ready to serve. Note: If beans begin to look dry, add remaining ¼ cup stock.

Yield: 4 to 6 servings

Toasted cumin seeds add tantalizing taste and fragrance to this savory sauce.

It seems I'm always discovering exciting new ways to use this versatile sauce whether ladled over brown rice [a complete protein], over orzo [see p. 126] or topping a baked potato. Go ahead—be creative!

Horsey Sauce

1 cup yogurt, dairy-free
2 tablespoons prepared horseradish
½ teaspoon herbal seasoning (p. 66)
1 teaspoon Dijon-style mustard

- In small nonreactive bowl, combine ingredients, stirring to blend. Store in container with tight-fitting lid. Will keep refrigerated up to 4 days.

Yield: 1 cup

A snap to prepare, this tangy sauce is great for dipping crudités [raw veggies], dressing a sandwich or topping a baked yam.

Herbed Pomadoro Sauce
with Roasted Garlic

1 whole bulb garlic, roasted
2 teaspoons extra-virgin olive oil
~
2 pounds Roma tomatoes, seeded and coarsely chopped
2 cups crushed tomatoes
1/2 teaspoon sea salt
1/4 to 1/2 teaspoon freshly ground pepper, to taste
3 tablespoons fresh basil, minced
2 tablespoons fresh oregano, minced
1 tablespoon fresh thyme, minced
1 teaspoon fresh rosemary leaves, crushed
1/8 teaspoon natural liquid hickory smoke
3 to 4 teaspoons brown rice syrup, to taste

In late summer, when home grown tomatoes and fresh herbs are abundant, prepare several batches of this delicioso sauce to freeze. Then, whenever you need sauce for that favorite recipe, simply thaw and voilá—tantalizing low-fat sauce, ready in a jiffy.*

A rich tasting all-purpose sauce with slightly smoky overtones. Roasted garlic mellows the taste giving the sauce an intense, concentrated flavor.

Serve over Gnocchi and Garbanzos [p. 152] or ladle lavishly over your favorite veggie pizza for a special treat. Manja!

** Fresh herbs are a must here—no substituting please.*

- Preheat oven to 400° F.
- Prepare garlic for roasting by removing as much of the "papery" skin as will rub off easily without peeling. Slice 1/4 to 1/2 inch off top of garlic bulb, making sure to expose all clove tips. Place whole bulb in small garlic roaster or baking dish, drizzle oil over top, cover.
- Bake garlic until soft and fragrant, 45 minutes to 1 hour. Remove dish from oven, uncover. When cool enough to handle, gently squeeze cloves from skins, mash cloves. Set aside.
- Submerge Romas in boiling water 10 seconds, drain. Plunge into ice water, drain. Skins will rub off easily. Core tomatoes, coarsely chop. Set aside.
- Crush rosemary leaves in mortar bowl with pestle (or between two spoons) to release fragrant oil.
- While garlic is roasting, add rosemary and all remaining ingredients to large nonreactive saucepan, bring to boil. Reduce heat, simmer, stirring occasionally, 30 to 40 minutes. Remove pan from heat. Stir roasted garlic into sauce.

Yield: about 6 cups

Sedona Sauce

with Roasted Sweet Peppers

10 ounces red bell peppers, roasted (p. 3)
10 ounces yellow bell peppers, roasted (p. 3)
~
4 large cloves garlic
1 1/4 cups Savory Garlic Broth (p. 8)
2 cups carrot, peeled and diced
~
1 tablespoon extra-virgin olive oil
1/8 teaspoon white pepper
2 1/2 tablespoons mellow white miso

- Prepare and roast peppers as directed.
- Peel garlic, blanch cloves in small, nonreactive saucepan, cover with water, bring to boil, simmer 1 to 2 minutes. Drain, repeat process two more times. Note: the more garlic is blanched, the milder it becomes taking away its bite. Mince garlic. Set aside.
- In medium nonreactive saucepan, bring broth to boil, add carrot and blanched garlic, cover. Reduce heat, simmer until tender, 12 to 15 minutes.
- Meanwhile, peel roasted peppers, remove and discard stems and seeds. Chop peppers into small pieces.
  Note: chopping the peppers instead of puréeing helps retain their distinctive color.
- In food processor or blender, combine carrot/garlic mixture, oil, white pepper and miso, process until smooth, transfer to medium bowl.
- Stir chopped peppers into mixture. Cover, let sauce stand 30 minutes to allow flavors to meld. Store in container with tight-fitting lid. Will keep refrigerated up to 5 days. Sauce will thicken as it stands, thin by adding more broth, a little at a time, to achieve desired consistency.

Yield: about 4 cups

The color of this sauce reminds me of Sedona sunsets—burnished-orange gold. Its smoky-sweet flavor is a refreshing departure from traditional marinara sauce.

Peppers and carrots are loaded with vitamin C and antioxidant carotenoids which appear to neutralize carcinogens and protect cell structures.

Terrific over steamed vegetables or pasta. Garnish with fresh nasturtiums [an edible flower] and sprigs of fresh cilantro or dill for a beautiful presentation.

Figgy Cranapple Chutney

One taste and you'll be making this luscious chutney a holiday tradition at your house.

Beneficial compounds in cranberries block bacteria that cause urinary tract infections. Cranberries have a fair amount of vitamins A and C.

Dried figs are an excellent energy food, rich in potassium, calcium, magnesium, iron, copper and manganese.

Apples are high in fiber, vitamins A and C, potassium, calcium, magnesium and phosphorus. The pectin in apples has a detoxifying quality to it and is used in many colon-cleansing formulas.

4 cups fresh cranberries
1 1/2 cups natural apple cider or juice
1/2 to 3/4 cup honey, to taste
2 whole cinnamon sticks
~
1 cup Calmyrna figs, chopped
1 1/2 cups apple, peeled, seeded and coarsely chopped
juice of 1 medium freshly squeezed orange
zest of 1 orange
juice of 1 medium freshly squeezed lemon
zest of 1 lemon
1 tablespoon agar flakes
~
3 tablespoons mirin
3/4 cup coarsely chopped walnuts, toasted (p.10)

- In a 2-quart nonreactive saucepan, combine cranberries and next 3 ingredients, cook over medium heat, stirring occasionally, until cranberries begin to pop, 7 to 10 minutes (mixture will be frothy).
- Scrub orange and lemon, remove zest with zester tool or shred with a fine-holed grater. Cut fruit in half crosswise, and juice.
- Stir figs and next 6 ingredients into cranberries, simmer, stirring occasionally, until mixture begins to thicken, 3 to 5 minutes. Remove and discard cinnamon sticks.
- Add mirin and nuts to mixture, stirring to blend, transfer to medium serving bowl. Cover, chill 1 to 2 hours before serving. Store leftovers in container with tight-fitting lid. Will keep refrigerated up to 3 weeks.

Yield: 6 cups

Desserts

"Your choice of diet can influence your long-term health prospects more than any other action you might take."

C. Evert Koop
Former Surgeon General

Apple Spice Cake
with Cinnamon Glaze

1 cup cinnamon apple butter (p. 65)
1/3 cup dark amber maple syrup
1/2 cup apple juice concentrate, undiluted
1 teaspoon pure vanilla extract
2 teaspoons expeller-pressed canola oil
~
1 cup whole wheat pastry flour
3/4 cup unbleached flour with germ
3 teaspoons egg replacer powder
1 teaspoon baking soda
1 tablespoon aluminum-free baking powder
2 teaspoons ground cinnamon
1/2 teaspoon freshly ground nutmeg
1/4 teaspoon ground cloves
1/4 teaspoon sea salt
2 teaspoons flax seed, ground
~
1/2 cup walnuts, coarsely chopped
1/2 cup raisins
~
1 1/2 tablespoons kudzu
1 cup amasake
1 teaspoon ground cinnamon
1 teaspoon pure vanilla extract
1 tablespoon brown rice syrup

- Preheat oven to 350° F. (325° F for glass). Lightly oil and flour 9 inch metal baking pan.
- In small bowl, combine apple butter and next 4 ingredients, stirring to blend.
- In large bowl, whisk dry ingredients together.
- Combine wet and dry ingredients, beating until smooth and no lumps remain (do not over mix), fold in nuts and raisins. Pour batter into prepared pan.
- Bake until toothpick inserted in center comes out clean, 30 to 35 minutes. Transfer to wire rack, let cool 20 minutes.
- Meanwhile, prepare glaze. In small saucepan, combine kudzu and amasake, whisking to dissolve, add cinnamon, vanilla and rice syrup, stirring to blend. Bring mixture to boil, stirring constantly until thickened, 2 to 3 minutes. Remove pan from heat, let cool slightly. Drizzle glaze over cake, chill 1 hour before serving.

Yield: 6 servings

This heavenly aromatic cake will satisfy your sweet tooth naturally.

Apples are powerful blood purifiers containing 50 percent more vitamin A than oranges to help ward off colds and other infections. Vitamin A is essential to eye health.

Aromatic spices are good digestive aids, assisting in assimilation of complex carbohydrates.

Apricot Glazed Carrot Cake

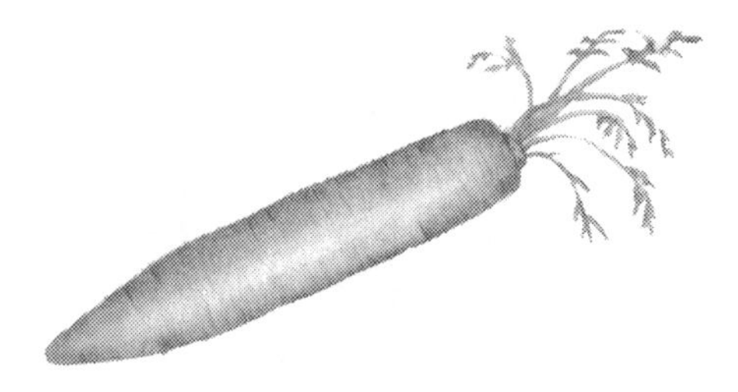

8 ounces dried unsulphured apricots, diced*
½ cup boiling water
~
⅔ cup prune purée (p. 4)
1 tablespoon apple cider vinegar
1½ teaspoons pure vanilla extract
½ cup dark amber maple syrup
4 cups carrot, peeled and coarsely grated
~
2¼ cups unbleached flour with germ
2 cups whole wheat pastry flour
1½ tablespoons aluminum-free baking powder
1 tablespoon baking soda
1 tablespoon egg replacer powder
¼ teaspoon sea salt
1½ teaspoons ground cinnamon
½ teaspoon ground mace
~
¾ cup walnuts, coarsely chopped, optional
~
2 teaspoons kudzu
½ cup all-fruit apricot jam

Light in texture yet rich in taste. This moist cake stands on its own merit but scores high with the addition of the luscious apricot glaze standing-in for traditional fat-laden cream cheese frosting.

Apricots and carrots are a match made in heaven—delivering a big antioxidant punch.

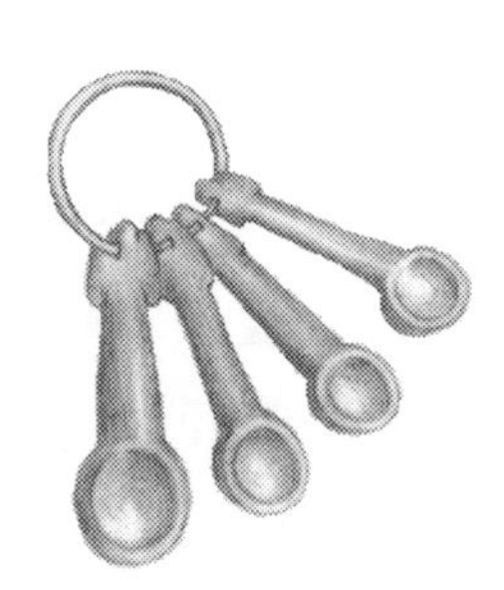

- Preheat oven to 350° F. Lightly oil and flour 9 inch spring-form pan.
- In small bowl, combine apricots and boiling water, let soak 15 minutes to plump. Drain any remaining liquid.
- In separate bowl, combine apricots, prune purée and next 4 ingredients, beating to blend.
- In large bowl, whisk dry ingredients together.
- Combine wet and dry ingredients, beating until smooth and no lumps remain, fold in nuts. Pour batter into prepared pan.
- Bake until toothpick inserted in center comes out clean, 50 to 60 minutes. Transfer cake to wire rack, let cool 20 minutes before removing from pan. Run a knife carefully around sides of pan to loosen cake; release the spring and remove pan sides. Leave cake on bottom for serving.
- Meanwhile, prepare glaze. In small saucepan, combine kudzu and jam, whisking to dissolve. Bring mixture to boil, stirring constantly until thickened, 2 to 3 minutes. Remove pan from heat, let cool slightly. Drizzle glaze over cake, chill 1 hour before serving.

Yield: 12 to 14 servings

---

* Available in natural food stores.

Celebration Cake

18 ounces cream cheese-style alternative*
1 teaspoon expeller-pressed canola oil
2 teaspoons pure vanilla extract
¼ teaspoon Frontier® natural butter flavoring*
1 tablespoon vanilla flavor rice milk
2 tablespoons liquid fruit sweetener
3 teaspoons agar flakes
~
¾ cup unsweetened coconut, toasted
1 tablespoon apple cider vinegar
20 ounces unsweetened crushed pineapple, in juice
1 teaspoon pure vanilla extract
~
¾ cup date sugar
⅓ cup dark amber maple syrup
1¼ cups whole wheat pastry flour
2 cups unbleached flour with germ
1 tablespoon aluminum-free baking powder
2 teaspoons baking soda
1 tablespoon egg replacer powder
~
¾ cup pecans, coarsely chopped

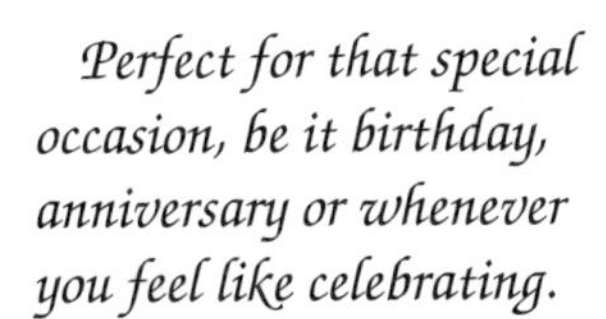

Perfect for that special occasion, be it birthday, anniversary or whenever you feel like celebrating.

Transformed from a family recipe loaded with dairy, fat and refined sugar, this heart-healthy rendition "takes the cake" on decadence!

- In medium bowl, prepare frosting, combine cream cheese and next 6 ingredients. Beat frosting, with electric mixer, on high until smooth, about 1 to 2 minutes. Cover, chill 1 hour.
- Preheat oven to 350° F. Lightly oil and flour two 9 inch round cake pans.
- Toast coconut in small heavy-bottomed skillet, over medium heat, stirring constantly until fragrant and golden, 2 to 3 minutes.
- In small nonreactive bowl, combine vinegar and next 3 ingredients.
- In large bowl, whisk ¼ cup toasted coconut (reserve remainder) and dry ingredients together.
- Combine wet and dry ingredients, beating until blended, fold in nuts (batter will be stiff). Spoon batter into prepared pans.
- Bake until toothpick inserted in center comes out clean, 35 to 40 minutes. Transfer pans to wire rack, let cool 10 minutes. Carefully remove cake from pans, cool completely before frosting.
- Spread ¼ of frosting between layers, frost sides and top with remainder. Sprinkle reserved coconut over top. Chill cake 1 hour before serving.

Yield: 8 to 10 servings

* Available in natural food stores and some well-stocked supermarkets.

Chocolate Surprise Cake

Chocolate decadence guaranteed to "wow" and delight all you chocolate lovers.

Researchers have recently discovered that chocolate is rich in potent antioxidants called phenolics, the same class of antioxidants as those found in red wine.

The mouth-watering chocolate icing is made with tofu. Surprise!

This irresistible, good-for-you cake has a rich, moist ,fudgy texture. Zucchini and prune purée lend moistness, fiber and vitamins, cinnamon adds exotic flavor notes and nutmeg brings out the flavor of the chocolate.

For special occasions, dress it up by adding a border of toasted almond pieces [about 3/4 cup] around perimeter of cake, garnish center with a fresh orange twist.

Variation: love the flavor of cool mint and chocolate? Simply add 1/2 teaspoon pure peppermint extract to cake batter and omit the cinnamon.

1 cup chocolate chips (barley malt sweetened)
1/3 cup low-fat caffeine-free cocoa* (no added sweeteners)
1 tablespoon expeller-pressed canola oil
2 tablespoons agar flakes
1/4 cup vanilla-flavor rice milk
8 ounces low-fat firm silken tofu
2 teaspoons pure vanilla extract
1/4 teaspoon Frontier® natural butter flavoring
1/3 cup dark amber maple syrup

~

1 cup unpeeled zucchini, coarsely grated
1 tablespoon apple cider vinegar
3/4 cup prune purée (p. 4)
1 cup vanilla flavor rice milk
2 teaspoons pure vanilla extract
1/4 cup barley malt syrup
1/4 cup dark amber maple syrup

~

1 1/4 cups whole wheat pastry flour
1 cup unbleached flour with germ
1 tablespoon aluminum-free baking powder
2 teaspoons baking soda
1 tablespoon egg replacer powder
3/4 cup low-fat caffeine-free cocoa* (no added sweeteners)
1/2 teaspoon ground cinnamon
1/4 teaspoon freshly ground nutmeg

- Prepare frosting in double boiler by combining chocolate chips, cocoa, oil, agar flakes and rice milk, cook over medium heat, stirring occasionally, until chips melt. In food processor or blender, combine chocolate mixture, tofu, vanilla, butter flavoring and maple syrup, process until smooth. Chill icing 2 to 3 hours before frosting cake.
- Preheat oven to 350° F. Lightly oil and flour bottom and sides of 9 inch spring-form pan.
- Scrub zucchini and remove ends. Grate zucchini over large bowl. Combine zucchini and all remaining wet ingredients, beating until blended.
- In separate bowl, whisk dry ingredients together. Combine wet and dry ingredients, beating until smooth and no lumps remain. Pour batter into prepared pan.
- Bake until toothpick inserted in center comes out clean and cake springs back when pressed with finger, 45 to 50 minutes. Transfer cake to wire rack, let cool 25 minutes. Chill cake, in pan, 1 to 2 hours.
- Run a knife carefully around sides of pan to loosen cake, release the spring and remove pan sides. Leave cake on pan bottom for serving. Frost sides and top of cake.

Yield: 8 to 10 servings

---

* Wonder Slim® makes an excellent one.

Hawaiian Gingerbread

1/3 cup macadamia nuts,* coarsely chopped
7 freshly cut pineapple rings
~
1/2 cup prune purée (p. 4)
1/2 cup amasake
1/2 cup plain yogurt, dairy-free
1/2 cup unsulphured molasses
1 cup plus 2 tablespoons dark amber maple syrup
1 tablespoon apple cider vinegar
~
2 cups whole wheat pastry flour
1 cup amaranth flour
2 teaspoons aluminum-free baking powder
1 tablespoon egg replacer powder
1 teaspoon ground cinnamon
1 teaspoon ground ginger
1/2 teaspoon ground cloves
1/4 teaspoon dry mustard
1/4 teaspoon sea salt

- Preheat oven to 375° F. Lightly oil and flour bottom and sides of 9 inch spring-form pan.
- Scatter nuts over bottom of prepared pan, lay pineapple rings over top.
- In medium bowl, cream prune purée and next 5 ingredients together.
- In large bowl, whisk dry ingredients together.
- Combine wet and dry ingredients, beating until smooth and no lumps remain. Pour batter over pineapple.
- Bake until tooth pick inserted in center comes out clean, 55 to 60 minutes. Transfer cake to wire rack, let cool 20 minutes. Run a knife carefully around sides of pan to loosen cake; release the spring and remove pan sides and bottom before serving.

Yield: 8 to 10 servings

Gingerbread teams up with tangy-sweet pineapple to create this unusual upside-down cake.

Pineapple contains the digestive enzyme bromelain, which scientists have discovered can thin blood and prevent blood clots from forming, not to mention helping increase circulation.

The aromatic ginger compliments the dark, sweet crumb of this wonderfully moist cake.

Aromatic spices and bromelain are excellent digestive aids.

---

* If macadamias aren't available, substitute pecans.

Pumpkin Maple "Cheese" Cake

A velvety-smooth pumpkin filling teams up with a scrumptious maple-pecan, graham cracker crust to fool even the most sophisticated palate!

Crust

1¼ cups natural cinnamon graham crackers* (about 4 ounces)
½ cup pecans
½ cup whole wheat pastry flour
2 tablespoons expeller-pressed canola oil
3 tablespoons apple juice
2 tablespoons dark amber maple syrup

- Preheat oven to 350° F. Lightly oil and flour bottom and sides of 9 inch spring-form pan.
- Break crackers into pieces. In food processor, combine crackers, pecans and flour, process to fine crumbs. With processor running, gradually add oil, juice and maple syrup through feed tube, process until blended and mixture clumps together, transfer to prepared pan. Spread crust evenly in bottom of pan pressing up along sides, about 1½ inches (the back of a metal spoon works well for this).
- Bake crust 20 minutes. Transfer pan to wire rack, cool completely before filling.

---
* Hains® are delicious.

Filling

2 cups vanilla flavor yogurt, dairy-free
1 1/2 cups pumpkin purée
10 ounces low-fat firm silken tofu*
2 teaspoons pure vanilla extract
3 tablespoons egg replacer powder
2 1/2 teaspoons ground cinnamon
1/2 teaspoon ground ginger
1/4 teaspoon ground cloves
1/2 teaspoon freshly ground nutmeg
1 cup dark amber maple syrup
3 teaspoons agar flakes
2 tablespoons honey
~
12 unbroken pecan halves for garnish

- Reduce oven temperature to 300° F. Fill a metal baking pan with water, and set on oven floor.

- In food processor, combine all ingredients, process until smooth and thoroughly blended (stop motor periodically to scrape down sides with rubber spatula). Pour filling into cooled crust.

- Bake "cheese" cake until puffy, about 2 hours. Halfway through baking time, remove pan from oven. Arrange pecan halves, flat side down, around perimeter (space evenly so each slice will have one pecan), pressing gently into filling. Return "cheese" cake to oven for remainder of baking time, when done, center should be soft but shouldn't wobble. Transfer pan to wire rack, when **completely** cool, drape plastic wrap loosely over pan. Chill "cheese" cake 2 to 3 hours.

- Before serving, carefully run a knife around sides of pan to loosen; release spring and remove sides of pan. Leave cake on pan bottom for serving. Will keep refrigerated several days.

Yield: 12 servings

Silken tofu stands in nicely for the cream cheese. [It can be your secret. No one will ever guess because it's sooooo decadent tasting.]

Tofu is a soy-based food that can be used in virtually any type of recipe. Soy offers the highest quality protein of any plant food containing all 8 essential amino acids [which the body can't produce] and appears to offer women important protection against breast cancer, thanks to the abundance of phytoestrogens, especially genistein.

Helpful Tip: prepare "cheese" cake early in the day to allow time to fully chill.

---
* Mori-Nu Lite® is excellent with only 1 percent fat.

Almond Sun Cookies

½ cup almond butter
½ cup cinnamon apple butter (p. 65)
3 tablespoons honey
2 teaspoons pure vanilla extract
¼ teaspoon pure almond extract
1 teaspoon lemon zest
½ cup apple juice
2 teaspoons expeller-pressed canola oil

~

1½ cups whole wheat pastry flour
¾ cup oat bran
1 teaspoon aluminum-free baking powder
1 teaspoon baking soda
3 teaspoons egg replacer powder
¼ teaspoon sea salt
¼ teaspoon ground cloves
½ teaspoon ground cardamom
1½ teaspoons ground cinnamon

~

1 cup raw sunflower seeds, toasted (p.10)

- Preheat oven to 350° F. Lightly oil two air-cushioned baking sheets (see Glossary).
  Note: omit oil if using non-stick baking sheets.
- In large bowl, cream almond butter and next 7 ingredients together.
- In separate bowl, whisk dry ingredients together.
- Combine wet and dry ingredients, beating until thoroughly blended, fold in sunflower seeds.
- Drop dough by rounded tablespoons onto baking sheets, flatten with fork.
- Bake until bottoms are golden, 8 to 10 minutes. Remove cookies from oven, transfer to wire racks.

Yield: 3 dozen cookies

Kids and adults alike will enjoy these crunchy cookies. Easy-to-prepare, they make a nutritious after-school snack. Pack some in your kids lunch box—they'll love you for it.

Apple butter adds moistness and tenderness of crumb; almond butter binds ingredients together. Almonds are a good source of protein and their fat content is less than most nuts, high in linoleic acid, vitamin E and calcium.

Cranberry Nut Gems

4 ounces reduced-fat* soft tofu
1/2 cup honey
2 tablespoons freshly squeezed orange juice
1 teaspoon orange zest
2 teaspoons pure vanilla extract
2 teaspoons expeller-pressed canola oil
~
3/4 cup unbleached flour with germ
1/2 cup amaranth flour
2 teaspoons aluminum-free baking powder
1 teaspoon baking soda
1/4 teaspoon sea salt
1/2 teaspoon freshly ground nutmeg
1/2 teaspoon ground cardamom
1 teaspoon ground cinnamon
~
1 cup fresh or frozen cranberries, coarsely chopped
1/2 cup Brazil nuts, coarsely chopped

- Preheat oven to 375° F. Lightly oil two air-cushioned baking sheets. Note: omit oil if using non-stick baking sheets.
- In blender, combine tofu and next 5 ingredients, process until smooth.
- In medium bowl, whisk dry ingredients together.
- Combine wet and dry ingredients, beating until thoroughly blended, fold in cranberries and nuts.
- Drop dough by rounded teaspoonfuls onto baking sheets.
- Bake until puffy and bottoms are golden, 7 to 9 minutes. Remove cookies from oven, transfer to wire racks.

Yield: 3 dozen cookies

You'll love these light little morsels with their tantalizing sweet-tart flavor. Consider making a double batch—they'll disappear quickly!

Cranberries are an intestinal antiseptic, high in fiber, containing vitamins A and C as well as calcium, magnesium and silicon.

Brazil nuts are a good quality source of protein, rich in calcium, magnesium, manganese, copper, potassium, selenium, zinc and iron.

---

* White-Wave® makes an excellent one.

Honey Drop Cookies

Bananas and zucchini team up to give these chewy cookies a sweet, moist tenderness. A healthy, energy-packed treat, high in fiber, protein and vitamins.

Zucchini, a variety of summer squash, has a cooling thermal nature, containing a fair amount of calcium, magnesium and iron.

Bananas are high in potassium. Without potassium, cells, especially those in the heart muscle, will not function properly.

3/4 cup unpeeled zucchini, coarsely grated
3/4 cup banana purée
1/3 cup honey
1/4 cup soy milk
2 teaspoons expeller-pressed canola oil

~

2/3 cup oat flour*
1/2 cup oat bran
1 cup whole wheat pastry flour
2 teaspoons aluminum-free baking powder
1 teaspoon baking soda
1/4 teaspoon sea salt
1 1/2 teaspoons ground cinnamon
1/2 teaspoon ground cloves
1/4 teaspoon ground mace
1/2 teaspoon freshly ground nutmeg

~

2/3 cup raw almonds, coarsely chopped

- Preheat oven to 350° F. Lightly oil two air-cushioned baking sheets. Note: omit oil if using non-stick baking sheets.
- Scrub zucchini and grate over large bowl. Combine banana purée and next 3 ingredients with zucchini, beating until blended.
- In medium bowl, whisk dry ingredients together.
- Combine wet and dry ingredients, beating until blended, fold in nuts.
- Drop dough by rounded teaspoonfuls onto baking sheets.
- Bake until bottoms are golden and firm to touch, 10 to 12 minutes. Remove cookies from oven, transfer to wire racks.

Yield: 3 dozen cookies

---

* If oat flour isn't available, use rolled oats and grind to fine powder. (A coffee grinder or spice mill works well for this).

Chewy Molasses Energy Cookies

½ cup prune purée (p. 4)
⅔ cup unsulphured molasses
½ cup apple juice concentrate, undiluted
⅓ cup soy milk
2 teaspoons pure vanilla extract
1 tablespoon expeller-pressed canola oil
~
1 cup whole wheat pastry flour
1 cup unbleached flour with germ
1 cup amaranth flour
1 cup oat bran
¾ cup rolled oats
¾ cup date sugar
2 tablespoons carob powder
2 teaspoons ground cinnamon
1 teaspoon freshly ground nutmeg
1 teaspoon ground allspice
1 teaspoon ground ginger
1 teaspoon flax seeds, ground
¼ teaspoon sea salt
3 teaspoons aluminum-free baking powder
1 teaspoon baking soda
1 tablespoon egg replacer powder
~
¼ cup unhulled sesame seeds
½ cup raw sunflower seeds
⅔ cup dates, chopped
1 cup raisins
½ cup almonds, coarsely chopped

These chewy, dense treats are great for hiking or anytime you're low on energy and in need of a boost!

Freeze some for later. Will keep up to 6 months.

- Preheat oven to 325° F. Lightly oil two air-cushioned baking sheets. Note: omit oil if using non-stick baking sheets.

- In large bowl, combine prune purée and next 5 ingredients, beating to blend.

- In medium bowl, whisk dry ingredients together. Combine wet and dry ingredients, beating until thoroughly blended (dough will be stiff).

- Roll tablespoons of dough into balls, press into rounds, 2 inches apart on baking sheets.
  Helpful tip: moisten fingertips with water to prevent dough sticking.

- Bake until bottoms are golden and firm to touch, 8 to 10 minutes (do not overbake). Remove cookies from oven, transfer to wire racks.

Yield: 5 dozen cookies

Coconut Apricot Balls

1 large unpeeled seedless orange (such as navel)
8 ounces dried unsulphured apricots*
1/3 cup liquid fruit sweetener (see Glossary)
1/2 cup almonds, blanched (p.10)
~
3/4 cup coconut, unsweetened

Great anytime, especially nice for holiday gift-giving. These jeweled, sweet treats are sensational.

Simple to prepare using only 5 ingredients. All work is done with a food processor.

Apricots are loaded with vitamins A and C, minerals, fiber and protein.

Helpful Tip: chilling apricots in freezer 1 hour before processing makes them chop more uniformly.

- Scrub and cut orange in half crosswise. Cover and refrigerate one half for later use. Cut remaining half into chunks.
- In food processor, combine orange chunks and apricots, process to coarse consistency (do not over process). Using pulse-chop feature, add liquid fruit sweetener to fruit mixture, process just until blended, transfer to medium bowl.
- Using pulse-chop feature, add blanched almonds to food processor, process to coarse consistency, about 12 to 15 pulses. Stir almonds into orange/apricot mixture. Cover, chill, in freezer, 1 hour.
- Line two lip-edged baking sheets with waxed or parchment paper. Set aside.
- Place coconut in pie plate. Shape orange/apricot mixture into 1 inch balls and roll in coconut to coat. Arrange balls on baking sheet (mixture will be moist). Let air-dry, uncovered, overnight. Store in covered container, with loose-fitting lid, in cool dark place. Will keep 2 to 3 weeks.

Yield: 4 dozen

---

* Available in natural food stores and some supermarkets.

Orange Apricot Bars with Cardamom

Exotic cake-like bars scented with cardamom and studded with morsels of chewy apricots for a taste-sensation that's out of this world.

2/3 cup dried unsulphured apricots*
1/2 cup freshly squeezed orange juice
1/3 cup all-fruit orange marmalade
1/4 cup prune purée (p. 4)
2 teaspoons expeller-pressed canola oil
3 drops pure orange oil or 1/2 teaspoon pure orange extract
~
3/4 cup unbleached flour with germ
3/4 cup amaranth flour
1/2 cup date sugar
1/4 teaspoon ground mace
1/2 teaspoon ground cardamom
1 teaspoon aluminum-free baking powder
1 teaspoon baking soda
1 tablespoon egg replacer powder

- Preheat oven to 350° F. Lightly oil and flour 11 by 7 inch baking dish.
- In large nonreactive bowl, combine apricots and next 5 ingredients, beating to blend.
- In medium bowl, whisk dry ingredients together.
- Combine wet and dry ingredients, stirring just until blended.
- Spoon mixture into prepared dish; using rubber spatula, push batter into corners.
- Bake until toothpick inserted in center comes out clean, 25 to 30 minutes. Transfer baking dish to wire rack, cool 20 minutes, cut into bars.

Yield: 12 bars

* Available in natural food stores and some supermarkets.

Pie Crusts

The secret to making a flaky crust lies in adding vinegar and chilling the dough before rolling it out. Natural butter flavoring gives it a rich "buttery" taste.

Variation: use finely-ground oats in place of the whole wheat pastry flour.

Helpful Tip: to prevent dough sticking to rolling pin, use a special knit sleeve made for rolling pins or dust pin frequently with flour.

Whole Wheat Crust

1 2/3 cups whole wheat pastry flour
1 cup unbleached flour with germ
1/8 teaspoon sea salt
~
2 tablespoons expeller-pressed canola oil
2 tablespoons apple cider vinegar
1/2 cup apple juice
1/4 teaspoon Frontier® natural butter flavoring

- In food processor fitted with metal blade, combine flours and salt.
- While motor is running, add oil and all remaining ingredients through feeder tube. Stop motor when dough comes together in a ball.
- Wrap dough in plastic wrap, freeze 1 to 2 hours.
- Divide dough in half, shape dough into ball and flatten with palm of hand on lightly floured work surface. Working from center to edge, roll dough into a 10 inch circle, about 1/8 inch thick.
- Using a pastry scraper or cake spatula, slide under edge of crust to loosen from work surface. Drape crust carefully over rolling pin, transfer to pie plate and trim edge to within 1/2 inch of plate, fold overage under and flute edge.

Yield: 2 (9 inch) crusts

Almond Date Crust

1 1/2 cups raw almonds, blanched (p.10)
1 cup pitted dates, chopped
2 tablespoons whole wheat pastry flour
1/4 cup apple juice

Try pairing this crunchy, sweet crust with a no-bake fruit filling for a tantalizing dessert loaded with live enzymes.

- Preheat oven to 300° F.
- In food processor fitted with metal blade, grind almonds to fine powder, transfer to small bowl. Set aside.
- Combine dates, flour and **half** of apple juice in processor, blend to paste consistency. While motor is running, gradually add ground almonds through feeder tube, process until dough comes together in a ball. If dough appears dry, add remaining juice, a little at a time.
- Transfer mixture to lightly oiled pie plate. Moisten fingertips and pat crust evenly along sides and bottom.
- Turn oven **off,** leave crust in oven until dry and set, about 30 minutes.

Yield: 1 (9 inch) crust

Canadice Grape Pie

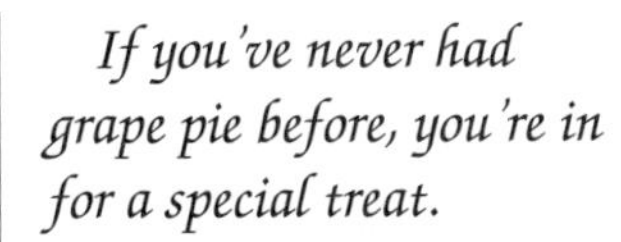

Whole Wheat Crust (p. 104)

~

4 cups purple grapes (such as Concord)
1 cup dark amber maple syrup
1/2 cup prune purée (p. 4)
2 teaspoons freshly squeezed lemon juice
3 drops pure orange oil or 1 1/2 teaspoons orange zest
3 1/2 tablespoons tapioca, finely ground*
1/2 teaspoon ground cinnamon

~

1/3 cup unbleached flour with germ
1/3 cup rolled oats
3 tablespoons blanched almonds, toasted (p.10) and finely chopped
2 tablespoons date sugar
2 tablespoons apple juice concentrate, undiluted
1/2 teaspoon ground cinnamon
1/2 teaspoon freshly ground nutmeg

~

1 tablespoon expeller-pressed canola oil

- Prepare **half** of crust, 2 to 3 hours ahead, as directed.
- Preheat oven to 400° F. Lay crust in pie plate and prick sides with fork. Bake crust 6 to 8 minutes, transfer to wire rack, let cool.
- Meanwhile, prepare filling by gently squeezing grapes into 2 quart nonreactive saucepan (reserve skins). Bring grapes to boil, over medium heat. Reduce heat, simmer 2 to 3 minutes. Remove pan from heat. Using back of wooden spoon, press grapes through mesh sieve, over large mixing bowl, discard seeds.
- Combine reserved skins and all remaining ingredients with grapes, stirring to blend. Pour filling into crust.
- In small bowl, prepare crumb topping, whisk flour and next 6 ingredients together. Using pastry blender or fork, cut oil into topping until mixture resembles large peas, scatter topping evenly over filling.
- Bake 10 minutes, lower temperature to 350° F. Bake an additional 25 to 30 minutes. Transfer pie to wire rack, let cool 30 minutes before cutting.

Yield: 1 (9 inch) pie

If you've never had grape pie before, you're in for a special treat.

I was inspired to create this luscious pie named for the picturesque hamlet of Canadice located in the Finger Lakes Region of New York State, famous for its many lakes, vineyards and wineries.

Fall is harvest time for a variety of grapes. September heralds the annual Grape-Fest where one can delight in sampling freshly squeezed grape juice, home made jellies and prize-winning pies.

Put the kids to work squeezing the grapes out of their skins—they'll have fun and it will free you up to work on the rest of the pie.

Grapes are a good tonic for building and purifying the blood, high in manganese, potassium and vitamins A and C.

---

* Helpful Tip: a coffee grinder works well for this.

Banana Coconut "Cream" Pie

Growing up, my favorite treat was my Grandma Kuhn's coconut cream pie. In this redo, I've replaced the heavy cream, eggs and refined sugar without compromising the delectable creamy-rich flavor. Somehow I feel she would approve.

Nutritious silken tofu, made from soybeans, is the base for the filling. Soy contains a high amount of genistein, a phytochemical compound having estrogenic-activity. Extensive studies conducted on genistein show promise of protection against osteoporosis and other menopausal symptoms, and may reduce the risk of breast cancer.

Almond Date Crust (p. 104)
~
1/2 cup unsweetened white grape juice concentrate, undiluted
1/8 teaspoon saffron threads
3 tablespoons agar flakes
~
20 ounces low-fat firm silken tofu*
3 large ripe bananas
2 tablespoons freshly squeezed lemon juice
1 teaspoon lemon zest
1/3 cup honey
2 teaspoons pure vanilla extract
1/2 teaspoon Frontier® natural coconut flavoring
1/2 teaspoon ground cinnamon
1/4 teaspoon freshly ground nutmeg
~
1/3 cup unsweetened coconut, toasted
~
1/3 cup all-fruit currant jelly for topping

- Prepare crust 1 to 2 hours ahead as directed.
- Preheat oven to 300° F. Bake as directed. Transfer crust to wire rack, let cool.
- In small saucepan, bring grape juice and saffron to boil, reduce heat. Gradually add agar to juice, whisking to dissolve, simmer, stirring constantly until thickened, about 1 to 2 minutes. Remove pan from heat. Set aside.
- Add tofu and **two** bananas to blender, process until partially blended. Combine all remaining ingredients, except coconut and jelly, process until smooth.
- Slice remaining banana. Layer banana slices over bottom of crust, pour filling over top.
- Toast coconut in small heavy-bottomed skillet, over medium heat, stirring constantly until fragrant and golden, 2 to 3 minutes, sprinkle coconut over filling.
- Chill pie 3 to 4 hours until set. Dot pie with jelly before serving. Note: if currant jelly isn't available, substitute all-fruit black cherry jam.

Yield: 8 servings

* Mori-Nu Lite® is excellent with only 1 percent fat.

Plum Empanadas

Whole Wheat Crust (p. 104)
~
8 ounces dried prune-plums, pitted
1/2 cup water
1/2 cup date sugar
1 tablespoon freshly squeezed lemon juice
1 teaspoon ground cinnamon
1 teaspoon pure vanilla extract
~
1 tablespoon apple juice concentrate, undiluted
2 teaspoons honey
2 teaspoons cinnamon

- Prepare crust as directed, omit last step. Set aside.
- In food processor or blender, combine prune-plums and next 5 ingredients, process until smooth.
- Preheat oven to 375° F. Lightly oil two lip-edged baking sheets.
  Note: omit oil if using non-stick pans.
- Using a cookie cutter or glass, cut dough into 4 inch rounds. Repeat procedure using remaining dough.
  Note: dough scraps can be re-rolled; however, more than once and dough will be tough.
- Prepare glaze by combining apple juice and honey in a one cup measure, whisking to blend.
- Spoon one tablespoon filling into center of one circle. Fold dough in half to form crescent shape. Using tines of fork, press edges of dough together to seal empanadas. Repeat procedure with remaining circles. Arrange empanadas on baking sheets, brush tops with glaze, sprinkle with cinnamon.
- Bake until golden, 18 to 20 minutes. Transfer empanadas to wire rack, let cool slightly. Serve warm.

Yield: 18 to 20 empanadas

Empanadas are small Spanish turnovers traditionally made with yeasted dough. However, this version uses time-saving whole wheat pie crust with impressive results.

Prune-plums, high in fiber and iron, are a smaller variety of the common plum used to make dried prunes.

Variation: substitute dried apricots for the plums, omit the vanilla and add 1/2 teaspoon pure almond extract.

Strawberry Glazed Tart

Almond Date Crust (p. 104)

~

1 quart fresh ripe strawberries, chilled
4 ripe (but firm) kiwi, chilled

~

1 1/4 cups unsweetened strawberry* juice concentrate, undiluted
2 tablespoons kudzu

Delicious, colorful, refreshing. A perfect ending to a summer meal, full of live-energy enzymes.

Strawberries are unique members of the berry family in that their seeds grow on the outside of the fruit.

Strawberries are high in vitamin C, potassium and iron. Kiwi are high in vitamin C and potassium.

- Prepare crust 1 to 2 hours ahead as directed.
- Preheat oven to 300° F. Bake as directed. Transfer crust to wire rack, let cool.
- Rinse and hull strawberries, drain in colander. Peel kiwi, slice into 1/2 inch rounds (reserve 6 kiwi rounds). Cut remaining rounds into quarters.
- Combine strawberries and kiwi in large bowl, keep refrigerated while preparing glaze.
- In small saucepan, combine strawberry juice and kudzu, whisking to dissolve, bring mixture to boil. Reduce heat, simmer until thickened and clear, 2 to 3 minutes. Remove pan from heat, let cool 10 minutes.
- Drain any juice that has collected in bowl with fruit. Using rubber spatula, gently fold glaze into fruit. Spoon filling into crust and garnish with reserved kiwi rounds, cover with plastic wrap. Chill 2 to 3 hours before serving.

Yield: 8 servings

---

* If strawberry juice isn't available, substitute raspberry juice.

Kona Banana Bake

6 large ripe (but firm) bananas
1/4 cup freshly squeezed lime juice
~
3/4 cup all-fruit orange marmalade
1/2 teaspoon ground cinnamon
1/4 cup water
1/3 cup dried currants
1/3 cup dried papaya, diced
~
1/3 cup raw macadamia nuts, chopped and toasted (p.10)

- Preheat broiler.
- In medium bowl, cut bananas in half crosswise, then lengthwise. Arrange halves in a 13 by 9 inch glass baking dish, pour lime juice over top. Set aside.
- In small saucepan, combine marmalade and next 4 ingredients, simmer 5 minutes, pour sauce over bananas.
- Position oven rack 4 to 6 inches from broiler. Broil until bubbly, 6 to 8 minutes. Check frequently to be sure fruit doesn't burn.
- Spoon banana bake into stemmed glasses or pretty dessert dishes, garnish with macadamias. Best when eaten warm.

Yield: 4 to 6 servings

I created this sophisticated, yet simple, dessert reminiscent of Hawaii's Kona Coast during one of my stays on the Big Island.

The ambrosial blend of banana, currant and papaya complement the bright citrus notes of lime and orange. Macadamias are the "icing on the bake!"

Bananas are high in iron, selenium, magnesium and potassium. Magnesium is an essential mineral vital for pumping potassium into cells. Without potassium, cells, especially those in the heart muscle, will not function properly.

Blueberry Peach Crisp

A real crowd pleaser. This easy-to-prepare, delectable dessert always wins rave reviews. Perfect for those late-summer days when peaches and blueberries are abundant.

*Later, when autumn leaves turn to gold, try making this irresistible variation: substitute 6 cups sliced apples for the peaches, 1 cup dried currants [or apricots] for the blueberries and cinnamon apple butter [p. 65] for the jam and increase kudzu to 1½ tablespoons. Bake at 375° F. until apples are tender, 45 to 50 minutes. Dress it up and top with a scoop of frozen, non-dairy vanilla dessert.**

** Rice Dream®, by Imagine Foods is excellent. Available in natural food stores.*

4 cups very ripe, fresh peaches, peeled and sliced
3 cups fresh blueberries
2 tablespoons freshly squeezed lemon juice
2 teaspoons ground cinnamon
¼ teaspoon ground mace
~
1 tablespoon kudzu
¾ cup all-fruit peach or blueberry jam
¼ teaspoon pure almond extract
~
1½ cups fruit-juice sweetened blueberry or peach granola

- Preheat oven to 350° F. Lightly oil 11 by 7 inch glass baking dish.
- In medium nonreactive bowl, combine peaches and next 4 ingredients, tossing to coat.
- In small saucepan, combine kudzu and jam, whisking to blend. Bring mixture to simmer, stirring until thickened and clear, 2 to 3 minutes. Remove pan from heat, stir in almond extract. Pour sauce over fruit, tossing to coat, transfer fruit to prepared dish.
- In food processor or mini-chopper, pulse-chop granola several times to break up any large chunks (do not over process). Scatter granola over fruit.
- Bake until peaches are tender, 30 to 35 minutes. Serve warm or room temperature.

Yield: 6 servings

Peach Melba Croustade

3 tablespoons fresh or leftover mashed potatoes
1 teaspoon rapid-rise yeast
1 tablespoon honey
½ cup + 2 tablespoons warm soy milk (105°-115°)
1 cup whole wheat pastry flour
¾ cup unbleached flour with germ
¼ teaspoon sea salt
~
2 tablespoons freshly squeezed lemon juice
¼ cup liquid fruit sweetener
½ teaspoon freshly ground nutmeg
4 cups ripe peaches, peeled, pitted and thinly sliced (5 to 6 large)
2 cups fresh red raspberries (1 pint)
~
1 tablespoon kudzu
¾ cup unsweetened raspberry concentrate, undiluted
¼ teaspoon pure almond extract
~
1 tablespoon apple juice concentrate, undiluted
1 teaspoon liquid fruit sweetener
3 tablespoons slivered almonds, toasted (p. 10)

- In medium bowl, combine mashed potatoes, yeast, honey and soy milk, let stand 5 to 10 minutes until yeast begins to "work". Stir flour and salt into mixture. Knead dough 5 minutes on lightly floured work surface. Add flour, a little at a time, to prevent sticking, if necessary. Transfer dough to large, lightly oiled, nonmetallic bowl. Cover with damp dish towel, let rise in draft free place until double in size, about 30 minutes.

- In medium nonreactive bowl, combine lemon juice, liquid fruit sweetener, nutmeg and peaches, tossing to coat. Gently fold raspberries into mixture with rubber spatula. Set aside.

- Preheat oven to 375° F. Lightly oil deep-sided pie plate.

- In small saucepan, combine kudzu and raspberry concentrate, whisking to blend, cook over medium heat, stirring constantly until thickened, about 2 to 3 minutes. Remove pan from heat, whisk almond extract into glaze. Fold glaze gently into fruit with rubber spatula.

- On lightly floured work surface, roll dough out from center into 12 inch circle. Drape crust over rolling pin, carefully transfer to prepared pie plate allowing dough to drape over sides. Spoon filling into crust. Gently gather crust up and over filling leaving a 2 inch diameter opening in center, so filling is visible and steam can escape. Cover opening with foil to prevent filling drying out.

- Prepare glaze by combining apple juice and liquid fruit sweetener in a one cup measure, whisking to blend. Brush glaze over crust, sprinkle almonds over top. Bake until golden, 30 to 35 minutes.

Yield: 8 servings

A sparkling finale to a special dinner.

My passion for peaches and raspberries inspired this heavenly summer dessert. The fruit is encased in a croustade [a yeasted crust]. Making the crust is easy and foolproof, requiring only one short rise.

Peaches are a good source of potassium and vitamins A and C. Raspberries are high in vitamin C, calcium, magnesium and iron.

Tropical Dream Tapioca

1/2 cup tapioca
1 1/2 cups amasake
1/2 cup vanilla flavor rice milk
1/2 cup coconut milk (p. 4)
2 tablespoons dark amber maple syrup
1 tablespoon egg replacer powder
3 teaspoons agar flakes
1/8 teaspoon sea salt
~
1/4 cup dried papaya or mango, diced
1/2 cup raw macadamia nuts, chopped and toasted (p.10)
~
1/4 teaspoon Frontier® natural coconut flavoring
2 teaspoons pure vanilla extract
~
fresh mint leaves

- In medium saucepan, combine tapioca and next 7 ingredients, let stand 5 minutes.

- Prepare papaya and macadamias as directed.

- Bring tapioca to boil, over medium heat, stirring constantly. Reduce heat, simmer until thickened, about 15 to 20 minutes. Remove pan from heat, whisk coconut flavoring, vanilla, papaya and macadamias into pudding, let stand 15 minutes. Stir pudding, ladle into stemmed glasses or pretty dessert dishes, cover with plastic wrap. Chill 2 hours before serving. Garnish with mint leaves.

Yield: 6 to 8 servings

The tropical taste may induce daydreams of a faraway island paradise.

You will never think of tapioca in quite the same way again after you've tried this winning twist on an old favorite. The magical ingredients are amasake, coconut milk and macadamia nuts. Dried papaya infuses the pudding with a delicate apricot color.

A perfectly luscious finale. Special enough to serve guests.
*Helpful Tip: if you don't have time to make your own coconut milk, be sure to purchase a good quality low-fat brand containing no added sweeteners or preservatives.**

** Thai Kitchen® makes a good one.*

Orange Quinoa Pudding
with Almonds

1 1/2 cups quinoa
3 cups vanilla flavor rice milk
1/4 teaspoon sea salt
~
1/3 cup dark amber maple syrup
3 tablespoons agar flakes
~
2 teaspoons pure vanilla extract
3 drops pure orange oil or 1 1/2 teaspoons orange zest
2 tablespoons freshly squeezed orange juice
~
orange segments, for garnish
1/3 cup slivered almonds, toasted (p. 10)

This unusual grain pudding has a high nutrition profile with close-to-perfect balance of amino acids. Quick-cooking quinoa, prized for its delicious nutty flavor and unique texture, adds a whole new dimension to this pudding.

- Rinse quinoa (in mesh sieve) under cold running water to remove natural saponins.
- In a 2-quart saucepan, combine quinoa, rice milk and salt, bring to boil. Reduce heat, simmer, stirring occasionally, until mixture starts to thicken, about 20 to 25 minutes.
- Combine maple syrup and agar flakes, whisking to dissolve, gradually add to quinoa mixture, stirring constantly, cook until thickened, 2 to 3 minutes.
- Add vanilla, orange oil and juice to quinoa, stirring to blend, simmer 3 to 4 minutes. Remove pan from heat, let stand 15 minutes.
- Stir pudding, ladle into dessert dishes, cover with plastic wrap. Chill 1 to 2 hours before serving. Garnish with orange segments, sprinkle almonds over top.

Yield: 6 (1/2 cup) servings

* This pudding can easily double as a hot breakfast cereal, delivering a powerhouse of energy to keep you going all morning long. Just toss a handful of currants or raisins into quinoa, heat and enjoy.

Lemon Saffron Granita
with Blueberry Coulis

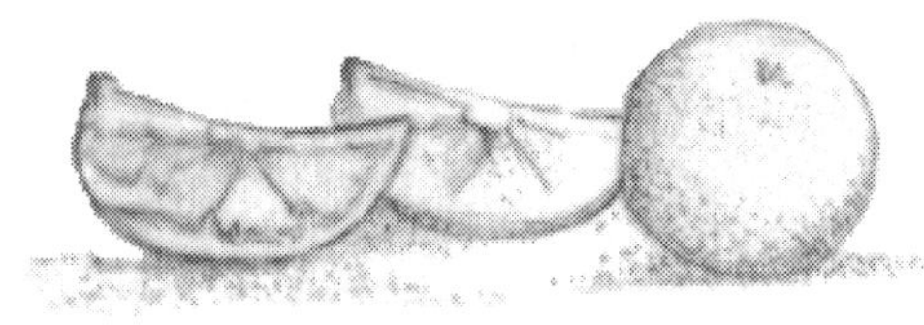

An excellent palate cleanser. This sparkling, frozen dessert is deliciously refreshing with its lemony sweet-tart taste.

The vivid purple-blue of the coulis paints a striking contrast to the saffron-yellow granita.

Italian granitas are low-fat, dairy-free frozen treats similar to sorbet but with a stronger flavor.

The secret to making great granitas is keeping a watchful eye on the syrup as it freezes, then breaking up the crystals before they solidify into sheets. The finished product should look like sequins.

A perfect, light finish to a summer meal.

3 cups water
3/4 cup liquid fruit sweetener
1/4 teaspoon saffron threads, crushed
~
1 cup freshly squeezed lemon juice (about 4 to 5 lemons)
zest from 1 large lemon
3 drops pure lemon oil or 1/2 teaspoon pure lemon extract
~
1 cup fresh blueberries
2 tablespoons liquid fruit sweetener
2 teaspoons freshly squeezed lemon juice
3 tablespoons water
1 tablespoon kudzu

- In medium saucepan, bring water and liquid fruit sweetener to boil. Lightly crush saffron in a mortar bowl with pestle. Remove pan from heat, stir in saffron, let stand 15 minutes. Whisk lemon juice, zest and oil into saffron. Pour mixture into shallow, nonreactive metal pans to 1/4 inch depth, transfer to freezer, check periodically. When layer of ice forms on surface, rake fork over mixture to break apart developing ice crystals which will begin to resemble sequins. Return granita to freezer as quickly as possible.

- Meanwhile, in blender or food processor, prepare coulis by processing blueberries until smooth. Pour mixture into mesh sieve. Press berries through sieve using back of spoon to extract juice, discard skin and pulp.

- Add blueberry juice, liquid fruit sweetener and next 3 ingredients to 1 quart saucepan. Cook, over medium heat, stirring constantly, until slightly thickened, 2 to 3 minutes. Remove pan from heat, let cool 30 minutes.

- Spoon 2 or 3 tablespoons coulis over each dessert dish. Rotate dish to form a pretty crisscross pattern over surface. Spoon 2 or 3 scoops granita over coulis. Serve immediately.

Yield: 4 servings

Coconut Mango Sorbet

2 large ripe mangoes*
~
1/2 cup water
1/3 cup honey
2/3 cup pineapple juice, unsweetened
1/2 cup coconut, unsweetened
1/2 cup coconut milk (p. 4)
2 tablespoons freshly squeezed lime juice
zest of 1 lime
~
10 fresh mint leaves
2 tablespoons orange or coconut liqueur, optional

- Prepare mangoes as directed (p. 5).
- In medium saucepan, combine water and honey. Bring mixture to boil, reduce heat, simmer 5 minutes. Remove pan from heat, pour syrup into heat-resistant measuring cup, transfer to freezer.
- In blender, combine mango with all remaining ingredients, process until smooth. Remove syrup from freezer, add to mango mixture, beating until smooth.
- Pour mixture into large, shallow, nonreactive metal pan to depth of 1 inch, freeze until firm, about 3 to 4 hours. Beat mixture **every hour** until frozen. Before serving, thaw slightly. Cut into chunks, transfer to blender, process 2 to 3 seconds, no more. Serve in stemmed glasses, garnish with mint leaves, drizzle liqueur over top, if desired.

Yield: 5 (1 cup) servings

---

* Variation: substitute papaya for the mango. Reserve and freeze papaya seeds to make Island Dressing (p. 72).

We all crave desserts but don't want the "bad-for-me" baggage that goes with it!

Sorbets [French] use no milk, only fruit juices or fruit purées.

This luscious sorbet tastes so sinful, you'll find it hard to believe it's all-natural, non-dairy, fat-free and sugar-free. Only the intense flavor of the fruit shines through in every mouth-watering spoonful.

Razzle Berry Mousse

½ cup apple juice concentrate, undiluted
3 tablespoons agar flakes
~
3 cups fresh or frozen raspberries
10 ounces low-fat* firm silken tofu
⅔ cup all-fruit raspberry jam
2 tablespoons dark amber pure maple syrup
~
fresh whole raspberries, for garnish
fresh mint leaves, for garnish

Quick and easy.

Whip up this light'n luscious raspberry dessert with none of the guilt of traditional fat-laden mousse.

Silken tofu adds rich creaminess, filling in nicely for heavy cream. Tofu is a high-protein soy food with no cholesterol, low in fat.

So go ahead—razzle and dazzle 'em with this heavenly pink treat. They'll never guess it's good for them too!

- In a 1-quart saucepan, bring apple juice to simmer over medium heat, add agar, whisking to dissolve. Cook until mixture begins to thicken, 1 to 2 minutes. Set aside.
- In food processor or blender, combine raspberries and next 3 ingredients, process only until small chunks of raspberry are visible. Note: if using frozen raspberries, do not thaw.
- Combine raspberry mixture and thickened syrup, stirring to blend.
- Spoon mousse into stemmed glasses, garnish with fresh whole raspberries and mint leaves. Chill 1 to 2 hours before serving.

Yield: 6 servings

---
* Mori-Nu Lite® is excellent with only 1 percent fat.

Entrées

"Nothing will benefit human health and increase the chances for survival of life on Earth as much as the evolution to a vegetarian diet."

Albert Einstein

Mandarin Orange Stir Fry
with Apricots and Snow Peas

1 pound reduced-fat* extra-firm tofu, drained
~
3/4 cup vegetable stock (p. 8)
1/3 cup freshly squeezed orange juice
1 tablespoon low-sodium tamari sauce
1 tablespoon brown rice syrup
2 teaspoons curry powder (p. 66)
1/2 teaspoon Five Spice powder
1/4 to 1/2 teaspoon crushed red pepper flakes, to taste
~
2 cloves garlic, minced
1 large red bell pepper, cut into 3/4 inch strips
2 large carrots, diagonally sliced
1 cup dried unsulphured apricots, chopped
1 medium onion, cut into 1/2 inch slivers
8 ounces snow pea pods, diagonally halved
1/2 cup slivered almonds
~
2 teaspoons toasted sesame oil
2 teaspoons kudzu
~
Spicy Udon Noodles (p. 202)

- Squeeze tofu gently to drain, cut into 1/2 inch cubes.
- Combine 1/3 cup stock (reserve remainder) and next 6 ingredients in shallow pan. Marinate tofu 30 minutes, turn periodically.
- Meanwhile, prepare garlic and next 5 ingredients as directed. Place each ingredient in separate bowl. Set aside.
- Prepare Spicy Udon Noodles as directed.
- In wok (or deep-sided skillet), heat sesame oil and reserved stock on high until small bubbles appear. Using slotted spoon, transfer tofu to wok, reserve marinade. Braise tofu, turning frequently, until puffy and golden on all sides, 3 to 4 minutes.
- Add garlic, cook 1 minute, stirring constantly. Add pepper and carrot, cook, 2 to 3 minutes. Add apricots and onion, cook 2 minutes. Add snow peas and almonds, cook 1 minute. Stir after each addition.
- Add kudzu to reserved marinade, whisking until dissolved, gradually add to wok, stirring constantly, until thickened and clear, 1 to 2 minutes. Remove wok from heat. Ladle stir-fry over noodles. Serve warm.

Yield: 4 servings

Colorful and delicious with a taste of the Orient in every bite.

Make this exotic but simple stir-fry anytime—always a hit.

Udon noodles, prevalent in the southern tip of Japan, are nutritious, chewy and satisfying. Made from high-gluten wheat flour, these noodles soak up sauce and hold it well.

---
* White Wave® makes an excellent one.

Kealakekua Stir Fry

Saffron Scented Rice (p. 187)

~

3/4 cup pineapple juice, unsweetened
2 tablespoons natural hoisin sauce
1 tablespoon liquid aminos
3 teaspoons brown rice syrup
1 tablespoon kudzu
1 teaspoon Five Spice powder

~

1 jumbo sweet onion (such as Maui or Walla Walla), cut into bite-size chunks
2 medium yams, peeled and cut into bite-size chunks
1 large red bell pepper, cut into bite-size chunks
2 cups broccoli stems, diagonally sliced into bite size chunks
2 cups papaya, peeled and cut into bite-size chunks
2 cups fresh pineapple, cut into bite-size chunks

~

1/3 cup vegetable stock (p. 8)
1 tablespoon expeller-pressed canola oil
3 cloves garlic, minced
1 tablespoon ginger root, peeled and coarsely grated
3 tablespoons raw macadamia nuts, coarsely chopped and toasted (p. 10)

You'll find few meals quicker to prepare than a stir-fry.

This tropically inspired version was created in honor of my friends on The Big Island of Hawaii. Bursting forth with color and tantalizing taste, it packs a nutritional punch.

- Prepare Saffron Scented Rice as directed. Cover to keep warm.
- In small bowl, whisk pineapple juice and next 5 ingredients together. Set aside.
- Prepare vegetables and pineapple as directed. Place each ingredient in separate bowl. Set aside.
- In wok (or deep-sided skillet), heat oil and stock on high until small bubbles appear. Add garlic and ginger root, cook 30 seconds, stirring constantly, to prevent burning. Add onion, yam and pepper, cook 1 to 2 minutes. Add broccoli, cook 2 minutes. Stir after each addition.
- Add pineapple juice mixture to wok, cook, stirring constantly, until thickened and clear, 1 to 2 minutes. Add papaya, pineapple chunks and macadamias, cook 1 minute. Remove wok from heat. Serve immediately.

Yield: 4 to 6 servings

Mediterranean Cabbage Rolls

2 tablespoons low-sodium tamari sauce
$2\frac{1}{2}$ cups vegetable stock (p. 8)
$\frac{1}{2}$ cup freshly squeezed orange juice
1 cup whole wheat couscous
~
$\frac{1}{2}$ cup slivered almonds
$\frac{1}{2}$ cup dried currants*
$\frac{1}{2}$ cup pitted dates, chopped
$\frac{3}{4}$ teaspoon Five Spice powder
$\frac{1}{4}$ teaspoon white pepper
~
Sunny Citrus Sauce (p. 82)
1 large head green cabbage

- Preheat oven to 350° F. Lightly oil 13 by 9 inch baking dish.
- In medium saucepan, bring tamari, stock and orange juice to boil. Reduce heat to lowest setting, stir in couscous. Cover, simmer 5 minutes. Remove pan from heat, let stand until liquid is absorbed, about 5 minutes. Uncover and fluff with fork.
- Stir almonds and next 4 ingredients into couscous.
- Prepare Sunny Citrus Sauce as directed. Set aside.
- In stockpot, bring 4 quarts water to rolling boil, cover, reduce heat. Cut 14 to 16 leaves from base of cabbage, remove any tough core areas, blanch leaves in boiling water until semisoft and pliable, about 4 minutes; drain, plunge leaves into ice water, 10 seconds, transfer to colander.
- Spoon $\frac{1}{3}$ cup filling into center of one leaf. Roll up burrito-style, folding ends under, as you roll, to prevent filling from escaping. Repeat procedure with remaining leaves. Arrange rolls, seam side down, in prepared dish, pour sauce over top. Cover.
- Bake until tender, 30 to 40 minutes.
Note: rolls are done when fork pierces leaf easily.

Yield: 6 to 8 servings

A new treatment for an old favorite. Currants, dates and almonds team up with a piquant citrus sauce for tantalizing taste appeal.

Cabbage is a nutritious member of the crucifer family—a group of vegetables with anticancer properties, rich in chlorophyll, folic acid and vitamin C.

Serve with a side of Beets Normandy [p. 193] or Lemon-Dill Green Beans [p. 194] and Honey Wheat Rolls [p. 40] for a highly satisfying cold weather meal.

---
* If currants aren't readily available, substitute raisins.

Lemon Tempeh Picatta
with Capers

Tempeh replaces the meat in this mouth-watering meatless version of veal picatta. Tempeh is high in vitamins, calcium and Omega-3 fatty acids, yet low in fat with zero cholesterol.

Round out the meal with a side of Saffron Scented Rice [p. 187] and Sautéed Greens with Apples and Currants [p. 194].

1 tablespoon extra-virgin olive oil
2 teaspoons liquid aminos
2 8-ounce packages tempeh, thawed and cut into 1/2 inch strips
~
2 large lemons
~
1/2 cup whole wheat bread flour
1 teaspoon Gomasio (p. 67)
1/2 teaspoon freshly ground pepper
~
1 1/4 cups Savory Garlic Broth (p. 8)
3 large cloves garlic, pressed
~
3 tablespoons capers, drained and chopped
1 tablespoon brown rice syrup
1 tablespoon kudzu
~
1/4 cup fresh flat-leaf Italian parsley, chopped

- In large wide-bottomed skillet, bring oil and liquid aminos to simmer over medium heat. Braise tempeh until golden, 2 to 3 minutes each side, transfer to platter. Cover to keep warm.
- Scrub lemon, remove rind and pith (white part) with sharp paring knife. Working over bowl to catch juice, cut lemon segments from surrounding membranes, chop segments into small pieces, add to lemon juice. Set aside.
- In shallow dish, combine flour, Gomasio and pepper, whisking to blend. Coat braised tempeh with flour mixture, shake off excess. Set aside.
- In same skillet, bring 1/2 cup broth to boil (reserve remainder). Reduce heat, sauté garlic, stirring constantly, until lightly brown, 2 to 3 minutes. Add reserved broth to skillet, stirring and scraping up any browned bits in bottom of skillet. Add lemon juice and pieces, capers, brown rice syrup and kudzu, stirring to blend. Cook, stirring constantly, until sauce is thickened and clear, 1 to 2 minutes.
- Spoon sauce over tempeh, sprinkle parsley over top. Serve warm.

Yield: 6 servings

Black Bean Enchiladas Grānde

½ cup vegetable stock (p. 8)
1 large white onion, coarsely chopped
1 large yellow or green bell pepper, diced
2 large ribs celery, diced
3 large carrots, diced
1 medium jalapeño chile pepper, finely chopped
1 large mild green chile pepper, finely chopped

~

¼ to ½ teaspoon crushed red pepper flakes, to taste
2 teaspoons ground cumin
1 teaspoon chili powder
½ teaspoon Vege Sal®
1 tablespoon unbleached flour with germ
3 cups cooked black beans
1½ cups cooked brown rice
24 10-inch whole wheat flour tortillas

~

1½ cups Jack or cheddar-style cheese alternative, grated
½ cup rice milk

~

1 cup Border Salsa (p. 76)
1 cup Salsa Verde (p. 77)

- Preheat oven to 350° F. Lightly oil two 13 by 9 inch baking dishes.
- In large wide-bottomed skillet, bring stock to boil. Reduce heat, sauté onion and next 5 ingredients until tender, 5 to 7 minutes. Remove pan from heat. Note: if you prefer less heat in your enchiladas, remove seed ribs from the chile peppers.
- Combine seasonings, flour, beans and rice with sautéed veggies, stirring to blend. Spoon ⅓ cup filling into center of one tortilla. Roll up, burrito-style, folding ends under, as you roll, to prevent filling from escaping. Repeat procedure with remaining tortillas. Arrange enchiladas, seam side down, in prepared pan, mist lightly with water to prevent tortillas drying out and breaking apart. Set aside.
- In a 1-quart sauce pan, combine cheese and rice milk, cook over medium heat, stirring frequently, until cheese melts. Remove pan from heat. Pour cheese sauce over enchiladas, spoon salsas over sauce. Cover.
- Bake 30 minutes. Uncover, bake an additional 10 minutes.

Yield: 24 enchiladas*

* This recipe can serve a crowd or a small group of people. Leftovers freeze well.

A favorite recipe, frequently requested in my cooking classes.

Savory black beans are an excellent source of fiber, iron, calcium and potassium.

Assembly will be a snap if you have salsa, beans and rice already prepared.

Accompany with South of the Border Skillet Cornbread [p. 42] for a meal that will have them shouting olé!

Asparagus Risotto
with Mushrooms and Fennel

A special dish to make when you're out to impress. The extra effort will elicit plenty of complements.

Caution: don't attempt to prepare this dish if you're in a hurry.

The secret to making great risotto is gradually adding hot stock to the rice. Constant stirring produces the creaminess for which risotto is well known.

Asparagus is a favorite spring vegetable; the tips are actually little flowers. Asparagus contains good amounts of vitamins A and C, folic acid [an important B vitamin] and potassium.

Serve with Berry-Green Salad and Raspberry Walnut Vinaigrette [p. 164].

6½ cups vegetable stock (p. 8)
½ cup onion, diced
½ cup celery, diced
8 ounces asparagus, trimmed and cut into 2 inch pieces
1 cup fennel, cut into 2 inch slivers (white part only), reserve fronds
3 cups crimini mushrooms, sliced (about 9 ounces)
~
16 ounces arborio rice
2 tablespoons fresh thyme leaves, snipped or 2 teaspoons dried
¼ teaspoon sea salt
1½ teaspoons herbal seasoning (p. 66)
¼ teaspoon white pepper
~
2 tablespoons mellow barley miso mixed with
¼ cup mirin or apple juice concentrate, undiluted
~
¼ cup reserved fennel fronds (lacy leaves), chopped
½ cup parmesan-style cheese alternative, grated
¾ cup cashew pieces, toasted (p.10)

- In large wide-bottomed skillet, bring ½ cup stock to boil (reserve remainder), sauté onion, celery, asparagus, fennel and mushrooms until soft and mushrooms release their juices, 5 to 8 minutes. Set aside.
- In stockpot, bring reserved stock to boil. Ladle 4 (of 6) cups stock into a large measuring cup, set aside. Add 2 cups stock, rice and next 4 ingredients to stockpot. Return to boil, gradually pour the 4 cups stock into rice, stirring constantly. Cook, maintaining a slow boil, until creamy but still somewhat firm, about 20 minutes.
- Gradually add miso-mirin mixture to risotto, stirring constantly, until blended. Remove pan from heat.
- Add fennel fronds, parmesan and cashews to risotto, stirring to blend, transfer to paella pan or large serving dish. Serve immediately.
  Note: risotto will set up as it stands, thin by adding small amount of stock or water.

Yield: 4 servings

Moroccan Tagine
with Couscous

3 cups Savory Garlic Broth (p. 8)
3 large cloves garlic, minced
2 cups onion, coarsely chopped
1 large green bell pepper, cut into 1 inch pieces
1 1/2 cups fennel, cut into 1 inch pieces (white part only)

~

12 ounces Roma tomatoes, seeded and coarsely chopped (about 3 large)
1 cup fresh green beans, cut into 2 inch pieces
2 cups peeled sugar pumpkin or butternut squash, cut into 1 inch cubes
3/4 cup dried currants
2 tablespoons freshly squeezed lime juice
1 tablespoon sweet Hungarian paprika
3 whole cinnamon sticks
1/2 teaspoon ground coriander
1/2 teaspoon ground ginger
1/2 teaspoon tumeric
1/2 cup yellow split peas
2 cups cooked garbanzo beans

~

1 1/2 cups whole wheat couscous
2 tablespoons liquid aminos
3 cups Savory Garlic Broth (p. 8)

~

3 tablespoons freshly squeezed lemon juice
2 tablespoons Harissa (p. 68), optional
3 tablespoons fresh cilantro, chopped

- In stockpot, bring 1/2 cup broth (reserve remainder) to boil. Reduce heat, sauté garlic, onion, pepper and fennel until soft, 4 to 6 minutes, add 2 cups reserved broth, tomatoes and next 11 ingredients to sautéed veggies, stirring to blend. Transfer mixture to 4 quart clay cooker. Soak cooker lid in water 10 minutes. Cover and transfer cooker to **cold** oven (do not preheat).

- Set oven at 350° F. Bake until tender and veggies test done when pierced with fork, about 50 to 60 minutes.

- Fifteen minutes before you are ready to eat, combine couscous, liquid aminos and remaining 3 cups broth in large saucepan, bring to boil. Reduce heat to lowest setting. Cover, simmer until liquid is absorbed, 5 to 7 minutes. Uncover, fluff with fork, transfer couscous to large serving bowl.

- Remove cooker from oven. Open lid slowly, away from you, to allow steam to escape. Discard cinnamon sticks, stir lemon juice and Harissa into stew. Note: if gravy seems thin, add flour, a little at a time, until desired consistençy is achieved.

- Ladle stew over couscous, garnish with cilantro.

Yield: 4 to 6 servings

A tagine is a colorful Moroccan stew. In this recipe the unexpected flavor of lime, paprika and cinnamon give it a fascinating flavor—wonderfully fragrant and satisfying.

Serve with toasted whole grain pita triangles or Chapati bread [p. 36]. Perfect for cold winter nights.

Helpful Tip: this dish can also be cooked in a crockpot, if you happen to have one of these gems sitting around. For crockpot cookings, sauté veggies [see first step], combine with next 10 ingredients, in crockpot. Cook on low setting until tender, about 6 to 7 hours.

Black Bean Primavera
with Saffron Orzo

A hearty, satisfying dish with complex flavors for all you black-bean lovers!

Saffron is one of the most expensive spices in the world due to the labor-intense cultivation of this lightly fragrant, unique spice. The rich, golden threads are actually the stigma of the autumn crocus. It takes 150,000 crocus stigma [at only 3 per bloom] to produce 1 kilo of saffron. Saffron aids in the digestion of starches.

Accompany with a salad of mixed greens and Cilantro Lime Vinaigrette [p. 69].

Toasted Cumin Black Bean Sauce (p. 85)

~

4½ cups water
¼ teaspoon saffron threads
½ teaspoon Vege Sal®
2½ cups orzo pasta

~

3 small (2 inch diameter) unpeeled zucchini, cut into ½ inch rounds
2 cups broccoli flowerettes
1½ cups cauliflower flowerettes
1½ teaspoons herbal seasoning (p. 66)

~

1 medium red or yellow bell pepper, thinly sliced
12 fresh cilantro sprigs

- Prepare Toasted Cumin Black Bean Sauce as directed. Cover, keep warm.
- In a 2-quart saucepan, bring water to boil. Remove pan from heat, stir saffron and Vege Sal into water. Cover, let stand 6 minutes, return to boil, add orzo, re-cover. Reduce heat, simmer until liquid is absorbed, 12 to 15 minutes.
- Steam veggies until crisp-tender, about 6 to 8 minutes. Drain, sprinkle herbal seasoning over veggies.
- Ladle bean sauce over orzo, top with ½ cup steamed veggies. Garnish with strips of pepper and cilantro sprigs.

Yield: 4 to 6 servings

Chayote Kamut Medley
with Toasted Cashews

3 chayote squash (about 1 1/4 pounds)
~
2/3 cup vegetable stock (p. 8)
1 tablespoon low-sodium tamari sauce
1 cup red onion, coarsely chopped
1 medium orange bell pepper, cut into 1/2 inch pieces
3 cups crimini mushrooms,* sliced (about 9 ounces)
2 tablespoons fresh tarragon, snipped or 2 teaspoons dried
1/4 to 1/2 teaspoon Vege Sal®, to taste
1/4 teaspoon freshly ground pepper
~
1 cup cheddar-style cheese alternative, grated (about 6 ounces)
1/4 cup soy milk
~
5 cups cooked kamut (p. 7)
2/3 cup cashew pieces, toasted (p. 10)

- Peel chayote, cut in half lengthwise. Remove and discard pit, cut chayote into 1/4 inch thick slices.
  Note: if chayote are small and young, peeling is not necessary.
- In large wide-bottomed skillet, bring stock and tamari to boil. Reduce heat, simmer chayote, onion, pepper and mushrooms until mushrooms release their juices, about 5 to 8 minutes, add seasonings, simmer 1 minute. Remove pan from heat. Cover, set aside.
- In small saucepan, combine cheese and soy milk; cook mixture, over medium heat, stirring frequently, until cheese melts. Set aside.
- Preheat oven to 350° F. Lightly oil 4 quart baking dish.
- Combine sautéed veggies, cheese sauce and kamut, stirring to blend, transfer to prepared dish. Sprinkle toasted cashews over top, cover.
- Bake 20 to 25 minutes.

Yields: 6 servings

* If criminis aren't available, substitute white button mushrooms.

This tantalizing dish encompasses fusion cooking at its best.

Chayote, native to Central America, is a pale green, pear-shaped squash with a sweet flavor and firm texture. Known in Louisiana as mirliton, chayote is commonly used in Creole cooking.

Kamut [Egyption for "wheat"] dates back to the pyramids. Less allergenic then common wheat with a slightly buttery flavor, chewy texture and pleasant aroma, kamut contains more protein and minerals than modern bread wheat and grows three times larger. Cooked, it resembles oversized grains of rice.

Hickory Grilled Portabellas

Portabellas are jumbo mushrooms that can grow to the size of a salad plate! These delectable giants have a deep, meatlike flavor and substantial texture that holds up well to grilling.

Mushrooms are a good source of germanium, an element that improves cellular oxygenation and enhances immunity. They are also fairly high in protein, iron and selenium.

Serve with Lemon Pineapple Kebobs Maui [p. 131] and jasmine rice for an irresistibly delicious meal.*

** Available in Asian markets and well-stocked supermarkets.*

2 teaspoons ginger root, peeled and coarsely grated
3 large cloves garlic, crushed
1/3 cup low-sodium tamari sauce
1/3 cup apple juice concentrate, undiluted
2 teaspoons dark amber maple syrup
1/8 teaspoon natural liquid hickory smoke, optional
1/4 teaspoon freshly ground pepper
1/3 cup water
2 teaspoons toasted sesame oil
1 tablespoon traditional brown miso
~
4 large portabella mushrooms (5 to 6 inches across)
1 cup hickory chips,* soaked

- Combine ginger root and next 9 ingredients, whisking to blend. Set aside.
- Wipe mushroom caps with damp paper towel to remove dirt. Remove stems, cutting carefully around base with tip of paring knife. Grasp stem where it attaches to cap and, using a twisting motion, turn stem clockwise until it detaches; discard or reserve stems for grilling.
- In shallow wide-bottomed baking pan or lip-edged baking sheet, lay caps flat, gill side up; pour marinade over portabellas, let stand 45 minutes, turn halfway through marinating time.
- Twenty minutes before grilling, soak hickory chips in cold water. When grill is hot, drain any remaining water that chips have not absorbed.
- Heat gas or charcoal grill on high. Remove grilling rack. When coals are hot, spoon chips over coals (coals will start to "smoke"), reposition rack. Using tongs, arrange portabellas on rack, gill side up, baste with marinade, cook 3 to 4 minutes. Turn, baste and cook, 3 to 4 minutes. To seal in heat and smoky flavor, keep grill covered, opening only to turn or check portabellas. *If cooking indoors, arrange portabellas on broiler pan, position 4 to 6 inches from broiler. Proceed same as for grilling. Watch mushrooms closely, baste periodically (do not overcook).*

Yield: 4 servings

* Sold in specialty stores and some supermarkets.

Artichoke Stuffed Portabellas

½ cup sun-dried tomatoes, diced
¾ cup boiling water
~
2 teaspoons extra-virgin olive oil
¾ cup sweet onion (such as Vidalia or Walla Walla), diced
2 teaspoons garlic, minced
2 tablespoons fresh basil, finely chopped
1 teaspoon Italian seasoning (p. 68)
3 cups white button mushrooms, diced (about 9 ounces)
~
14 ounces water-packed artichokes, drained and chopped
½ cup natural onion crackers, crumbled
3 tablespoons parmesan-style cheese alternative, grated
¼ teaspoon freshly ground pepper
~
1½ tablespoons liquid aminos
⅓ cup vegetable stock (p. 8)
2 tablespoons mirin
6 large portabella mushrooms (5 to 6 inches across)

Frequently requested in my cooking classes, this tantalizing entrée is elegant enough to serve your most honored guests.

Serve with Maple Roasted Yams [p. 200] and a medley of mixed greens with Herbal Vinaigrette [p. 70].

Helpful Tip: can be prepared in advance and refrigerated until ready to cook.

- In small bowl, pour boiling water over sun-dried tomatoes, let soak 15 minutes to reconstitute. Drain any remaining liquid.
- Wipe mushroom caps with damp paper towel to remove dirt. Remove stems, cutting carefully around base with tip of paring knife. Grasp stem where it attaches to cap and, using a twisting motion, turn stem clockwise until it detaches; discard or reserve stems for grilling. Set aside.
- In wide heavy-bottomed skillet, heat oil, sauté onion and garlic, 2 to 3 minutes. Add basil, Italian seasoning and diced mushrooms, cook until mushrooms release their juices, 5 to 8 minutes. Remove pan from heat.
- Stir sun-dried tomatoes, artichokes and next 3 ingredients into sautéed veggies, transfer to medium bowl. Set aside.
- Preheat oven to 350° F. Lightly oil lip-edged baking sheet.
- In same skillet, bring liquid aminos, stock and mirin to slow boil. Reduce heat, sauté caps, gill side up, 3 to 4 minutes. Turn, sauté, 3 to 4 minutes. Arrange caps, gill side up, on prepared baking sheet.
- Spoon filling into caps, mounding over top. Cover with foil.
- Bake 20 to 25 minutes. Serve immediately.

Yields: 6 servings

Zesty Glazed Neat Loaf

If you were a meatloaf lover in a former life, be prepared to fall in love all over again. This sensational, meatless version of an old favorite uses tahini [made from sesame seeds] to replace the traditional egg which helps bind the loaf together. Tahini is high in calcium.

Don't let the long list of ingredients intimidate you—you'll be ready to eat in no time. If desired, can be prepared in advance and refrigerated until ready to bake.

Serve hot with Oven Roasted Potatoes [p. 200] and Lemon Dill Green Beans [p. 194] for a dinner right out of your past! Leftovers make great sandwiches for your kids lunch box—or yours.

2 teaspoons extra-virgin olive oil
2 tablespoons liquid aminos
1 cup onion, diced
2/3 cup celery, diced
2/3 cup carrot, diced

~

1/3 cup raw cashew pieces, ground
1/3 cup raw sunflower seeds, ground
1/2 cup whole grain bread crumbs
1/2 cup texturized vegetable protein granules
1 1/2 cups cooked brown rice
3 tablespoons barley miso
1 teaspoon dried sage
1 teaspoon dried basil
1/2 teaspoon chili powder
1/2 teaspoon dried thyme
1 teaspoon celery seeds
1/4 teaspoon freshly ground pepper
2 teaspoons Gomasio (p. 67)
2 tablespoons tahini
1/4 cup gluten flour*
3 tablespoons unbleached flour with germ
1/4 cup vegetable stock (p. 8)

~

1/3 cup Howling Coyote Hot Sauce (p. 80) or Zesty Ketchup (p. 75)
1 tablespoon whole grain mustard
1 to 2 teaspoons prepared horseradish, to taste

- Preheat oven to 350° F. Lightly oil one standard 9 inch loaf pan.
- In medium heavy-bottomed skillet, bring oil and liquid aminos to boil. Reduce heat, sauté onion, celery and carrot until tender, 4 to 6 minutes.
- In mini-chopper or coffee grinder, grind cashews and sunflower seeds.
- In large bowl, combine sautéed veggies, cashew/sunflower mixture and next 16 ingredients. Pat mixture evenly into prepared pan.
  Note: if mixture appears dry, add more stock, a little at a time, until mixture binds together.
- In small bowl, combine Howling Coyote Hot Sauce, mustard and horseradish, whisking to blend. Using back of spoon, spread glaze evenly over top, cover loaf with foil.
- Bake 45 minutes. Transfer pan to wire rack, let cool 15 minutes before cutting.

Yield: 6 servings

* Available in natural food stores and some well-stocked supermarkets.

Lemon Pineapple Kabobs Maui

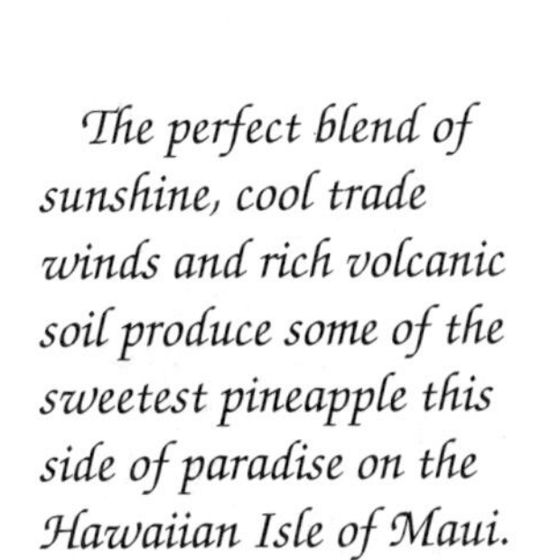

shish kabob skewers (bamboo or metal)
~
1 tablespoon lemon zest
3 tablespoons freshly squeezed lemon juice
3 tablespoons mirin
¼ cup water
2 tablespoons extra-virgin olive oil
2 teaspoons garlic, minced
2 tablespoons mellow white miso
1½ tablespoons balsamic vinegar
1 tablespoon brown rice syrup
½ teaspoon freshly ground pepper
2 tablespoons fresh lemon thyme* leaves, snipped
~
1 ripe pineapple, cut into bite-size chunks
2 cups fennel, cut into bite-size chunks
2 cups peeled yams, cut into bite-size chunks
16 large ripe cherry tomatoes

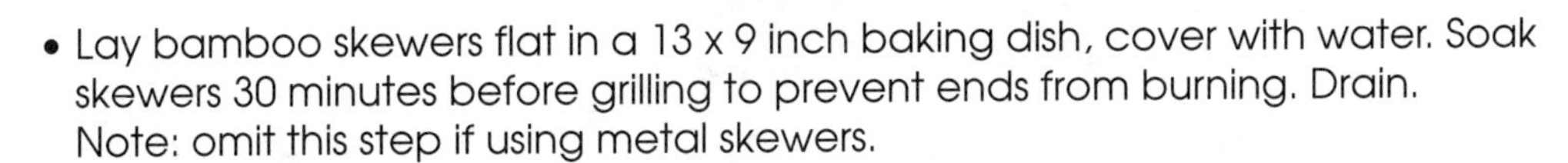

The perfect blend of sunshine, cool trade winds and rich volcanic soil produce some of the sweetest pineapple this side of paradise on the Hawaiian Isle of Maui.

A real palate pleaser. This colorful presentation is redolent with the tantalizing tastes of pineapple and lemon.

Serve with Green Papaya Rice [see sidebar p. 187] and a salad of crisp greens with Island Dressing [p. 72] for a memorable summer meal. For the grand finale, enjoy a piece of Hawaiian Gingerbread [p. 95].

- Lay bamboo skewers flat in a 13 x 9 inch baking dish, cover with water. Soak skewers 30 minutes before grilling to prevent ends from burning. Drain. Note: omit this step if using metal skewers.
- In a 2-cup measure, whisk lemon zest and next 10 ingredients together for marinade. Set aside.
- Prepare fennel, yams and pineapple as directed (reserve pineapple juice). Steam fennel and yams until crisp-tender, about 4 to 6 minutes (do not over cook), transfer to colander, drain.
- In large shallow pan, combine pineapple, fennel, yams and cherry tomatoes, pour marinade over top. Cover, refrigerate 1 hour, stirring occasionally. Alternately thread pineapple and veggies onto skewers.
- Heat gas or charcoal grill on high. Arrange kabobs on grill rack, close lid, grill over medium-hot coals, 4 minutes. Turn kabobs, baste with remaining marinade. Close lid, continue grilling kabobs until tender, about 4 to 5 minutes. Serve warm.
  If cooking indoors, arrange kabobs on lip-edged baking sheet, baste with remaining marinade. Position kabobs about 4 to 6 inches from broiler, cook, 3 to 4 minutes. Turn, continue broiling until tender, about 3 to 5 minutes. Caution: watch closely to prevent kabobs charring.

Yield: 4 to 6 servings

* Lemon thyme has a distinct lemon flavor and aroma. If lemon thyme isn't available, substitute regular thyme.

Pecan Lime "Chick" Fingers

Kids and adults alike will love these crispy "fingers". Great for dipping with Sweet 'n Sour Sauce [p. 81] or Herbed Pomadoro Sauce [p. 86].

Tofu is made from fresh cooked soybean curd. Recent studies show soy's soluble fiber appears to lower blood cholesterol levels while helping regulate glucose levels. Soy provides complete protein without the saturated fat and cholesterol that accompany animal protein. A good source of iron, phosphorus and potassium, soy contains almost 25 percent more calcium by weight than dairy milk. Freezing [the tofu] gives it a chewier, denser texture.

Nutritional yeast, rich in B vitamins, helps bind the marinade to the tofu.

2 16-ounce blocks reduced-fat* extra-firm tofu, thawed and drained

~

1 teaspoon garlic, minced
3 tablespoons freshly squeezed lime juice
2 tablespoons water
1/3 cup liquid aminos
3 tablespoons apple juice concentrate, undiluted
1 tablespoon honey mustard
1 tablespoon dark amber maple syrup
1 teaspoon toasted sesame oil
1/4 teaspoon freshly ground pepper
3 tablespoons nutritional yeast flakes
1/2 teaspoon dried thyme
1/2 teaspoon dried basil

~

1/2 cup whole grain cracker crumbs, crushed
3 tablespoons stone ground yellow whole grain cornmeal
1/3 cup pecans, ground
1/4 to 1/2 teaspoon Vege Sal®, to taste
1 1/2 tablespoons fresh flat-leaf Italian parsley, chopped or 1 1/2 teaspoons dried
2 teaspoons Cajun seasoning, optional

~

extra-virgin olive oil (in spray bottle) for misting

- The night before, transfer frozen tofu to refrigerator to thaw. When completely thawed, squeeze tofu gently to drain. Cut each block in half lengthwise. Position wire rack over lip-edged baking sheet to catch drips. Weigh tofu down with heavy-bottomed pan to drain any remaining water, about 30 minutes.

- Prepare marinade by combining garlic and next 11 ingredients, whisking to blend.

- Slice tofu (on short end) into 1 inch "fingers." Lay "fingers" single layer, in shallow wide-bottomed pan, pour marinade over top. Cover pan with plastic wrap, marinate 30 minutes, turning tofu several times.
  Note: tofu will absorb liquid like a sponge.

- Preheat oven to 375° F. Spray wire rack with oil. Position rack over lip-edged baking sheet, to catch drips as "fingers" bake.

- In pie plate, toss cracker crumbs and next 5 ingredients together.

- Dredge "fingers" in cracker mixture, transfer to wire rack, mist lightly with oil.

- Bake 30 to 40 minutes, turn "fingers" half way through baking time, mist lightly with oil.

Yield: 6 to 8 servings

---

* White Wave® makes an excellent one.

Pueblo Tortilla Casserole

2 cups white onion, coarsely chopped
2 cups Roma tomatoes, coarsely chopped
1 medium red bell pepper, diced
1 medium yellow bell pepper, diced
1 tablespoon ground cumin
½ teaspoon Vege Sal®
4 cups cooked black beans
1 cup Border Salsa (p. 76)

~

12 6-inch corn tortillas
1 cup Jack-style cheese alternative, grated
3 cups romaine lettuce, shredded
2 tablespoons fresh cilantro, chopped

~

2 large beefsteak-style tomatoes, sliced ½ inch thick
6 scallions, diagonally sliced (include some green)
½ cup pitted black olives, sliced

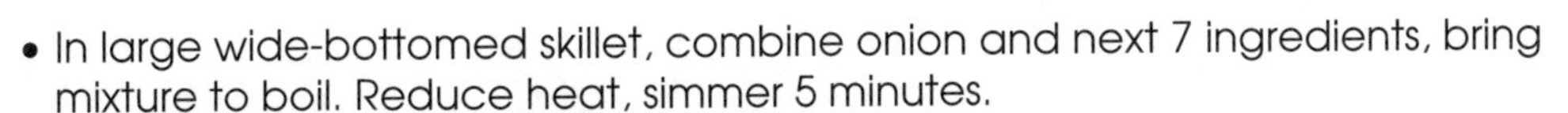

- In large wide-bottomed skillet, combine onion and next 7 ingredients, bring mixture to boil. Reduce heat, simmer 5 minutes.
- Preheat oven to 350° F. Lightly oil 13 by 9 inch casserole dish.
- Spread ⅓ of bean mixture over bottom of prepared dish. Lay ½ of tortillas over beans, overlapping to fit. Scatter lettuce and ½ of cheese over tortillas. Spread another ⅓ of bean mixture over cheese followed by remaining tortillas. Top with remaining beans, cheese and cilantro. Cover dish.
- Bake 30 to 35 minutes. Remove casserole from oven. Garnish with tomatoes, scallions and olives; cut casserole into squares. Serve warm.

Yield: 6 servings

Irresistible—like eating a taco, casserole-style.

Black beans are high in iron, calcium, potassium, phosphorus, protein and fiber.

Serve with a medley of crisp mixed greens, drizzled with Cilanto-Lime Vinaigrette [p. 69] and South of the Border Skillet Cornbread [p. 42].

Ratatouille Ragout
with Fresh Herbs

A tasty way to utilize that bumper crop of tomatoes and zucchini. Soba noodles lend substance to this classic stew—an unlikely marriage, but one that works quite well.

Fresh herbs are a must here. Local farm markets should have a good selection if you don't have the time, space or inclination to grow your own.

Serve with crusty sourdough bread. Rataouille is also terrific ladled over a baked potato.

½ pound soba noodles*
~
2 teaspoons extra-virgin olive oil
1½ cups onion, slivered
2 tablespoons garlic, minced
~
4 cups unpeeled zucchini, cut into bite-size chunks
1 large yellow bell pepper, cut into bite-size chunks
1 large green bell pepper, cut into bite-size chunks
4 large beefsteak-style tomatoes (about ½ pound)
3 tablespoons mirin
1½ cups tomato sauce
1 teaspoon Gomasio (p. 67)
1 teaspoon Italian seasoning (p. 68)
2 teaspoons fresh summer savory, snipped
1 teaspoon fresh oregano, snipped
2 tablespoons fresh basil, snipped
2 teaspoons fresh tarragon, snipped
~
3 tablespoons parmesan-style cheese alternative, grated

- In stockpot, bring 4 quarts water to rolling boil. Partially cook noodles, about 6 minutes, using slotted spoon, transfer noodles to colander (reserve cooking liquid).

- In medium heavy-bottomed skillet, heat oil, sauté onion and garlic until soft, 3 to 4 minutes. Remove pan from heat. Set aside.

- Prepare zucchini and peppers as directed. Bring reserved cooking liquid back to boil. Submerge tomatoes in boiling liquid 10 seconds, drain. Plunge into ice water, drain. Skins will rub off easily. Core tomatoes and invert, squeezing gently to remove seeds. Cut tomatoes into bite-size chunks.

- Combine noodles, sautéed and raw veggies, mirin and next 7 ingredients in 4 quart clay cooker, tossing to blend. Soak cooker lid in water, 10 minutes. Cover, transfer cooker to cold oven (do not preheat).

- Set oven at 400° F. Bake until veggies are tender and test done when pierced with a fork, about 45 to 60 minutes.

- Transfer cooker to hot pad. Open lid slowly, away from you, to allow steam to escape. Dish noodles into large, wide soup bowls, ladle rataouille over top, sprinkle with parmesan. Serve warm.

Yield: 6 servings

---

* If soba noodles aren't available, substitute udon noodles or spinach fettuccine.

Potatoes El Greco

2 teaspoons fresh rosemary leaves, crushed

~

1 tablespoon tahini
1/4 teaspoon Frontier® natural butter flavoring*
2 tablespoons freshly squeezed lemon juice
1/2 cup unbleached flour with germ
1 teaspoon Dijon-style mustard
1/2 teaspoon Vege Sal®

~

2 1/4 cups soy milk
1 teaspoon ground cumin
1/2 teaspoon freshly ground pepper
3 tablespoons mellow white miso

~

1 cup onion, diced
3 pounds unpeeled Butter Finn or Yukon Gold potatoes, thinly sliced (about 12 cups)
1 mild green chile pepper, seeded and chopped
2 teaspoons extra-virgin olive oil

- Crush rosemary leaves in mortar bowl with pestle (or between two spoons) to release fragrant oil.
- In a 2-quart saucepan, combine tahini and next 4 ingredients, bring to simmer, stirring constantly.
- Whisk soy milk and next 2 ingredients into tahini mixture, cook, stirring frequently, until sauce thickens and begins to boil, about 6 to 8 minutes. Remove pan from heat, add miso, whisking to blend. Cover, set aside.
- Scrub potatoes well. Prepare onion and potatoes as directed.
- Preheat oven to 375° F. Lightly oil a 4-quart baking dish.
- Arrange potatoes, single layer, over bottom of prepared dish, follow with layer of onion. Alternate layers using remaining potato and onion. Pour sauce over potatoes and along sides of dish.
- In small heavy-bottomed skillet, sauté chile pepper in oil, 2 to 3 minutes. Scatter chopped chile over potatoes. Cover dish.
- Bake 60 minutes. Uncover, bake until tender and top is crisp and golden, about 20 to 30 minutes. Transfer dish to wire rack, let stand 10 minutes before serving.

Yield: 6 servings

---

* Available in natural food stores and some supermarkets.

A new twist on an old favorite—scalloped potatoes.

Tahini, natural butter flavoring and miso give the sauce its rich "buttery" taste without the added saturated fat and cholesterol.

Potatoes are considered one of the most completely nourishing foods if eaten with skin intact. [When leaving the skin intact, use organically grown potatoes, if available.] Potatoes are expansive in nature and are excellent for combating stress.

Rosemary contains a number of potent antioxidants.

Serve with Pineapple Glazed Carrots [p. 198] and Honey-Wheat Rolls [p. 40] for a meal that will leave you satisfied long after dinner has ended.

Roasted Veggie Medley
with Garlic Polenta

4 large carrots
4 medium beets
4 medium parsnips
4 medium potatoes
1 jumbo sweet (such as Vidalia or Walla Walla) onion
2 heads garlic
~
2 teaspoons fresh rosemary leaves, crushed
3 tablespoons extra-virgin olive oil
1/3 cup fresh flat-leaf Italian parsley, chopped
1 tablespoon fresh thyme leaves, snipped or 1 teaspoon dried
1 teaspoon Italian seasoning (p. 68)
1/2 teaspoon Vege Sal®
1/2 teaspoon freshly ground pepper

Root vegetables are underground storehouses of nutrients, high in fiber and an excellent source of energy.

Roasting is a fast method that seals in the vegetable juices, caramelizing their exterior sugars. Vitamins and flavor remain in the food instead of leaching out into the cooking liquid as they do when braised or boiled.

- Peel all vegetables. Slice carrots diagonally into 2 inch pieces. Cut beets in half, then into quarters, cut potatoes in half crosswise, then into quarters. Cut onion in half crosswise, then into wedges. Separate garlic cloves from heads and peel.
- Preheat oven to 450° F. Lightly oil large roasting pan. Move rack to lowest position.
- In prepared pan, arrange veggies in rows, leaning against each other (don't overcrowd). Scatter garlic cloves over veggies and around sides of pan.
- Crush rosemary leaves in mortar bowl with pestle (or between two spoons) to release fragrant oil.
- Drizzle olive oil over veggies and sprinkle with rosemary, parsley, thyme, Italian seasoning, Vege Sal and pepper.
- Roast veggies until lightly browned on top, about 25 minutes. Turn, reduce oven temperature to 375° F. Continue roasting, turning every 15 minutes until tender and test done when pierced with fork, 45 to 60 minutes.

Garlic Polenta

5 cups Savory Garlic Broth (p. 8)
2 teaspoons Gomasio (p. 67)
1½ cups whole grain stone ground yellow cornmeal
2½ tablespoons extra-virgin olive oil
½ teaspoon herbs de Provence (see Glossary)
2 tablespoons fresh oregano, minced
¼ teaspoon freshly ground pepper

- Forty-five minutes before you are ready to eat, start preparing polenta. In 3 quart heavy-bottomed saucepan, bring broth and Gomasio to boil, gradually add cornmeal in a slow, steady stream, whisking to blend. Cook over medium heat, stirring constantly, until polenta starts to thicken, about 2 minutes.
- Reduce heat to low-simmer, cover saucepan. Cook, stirring every 10 minutes, until polenta begins to pull away from sides of pan, about 40 minutes. Stir oil, herbs and pepper into polenta, transfer to medium serving bowl. Serve immediately.
- Transfer roasted veggies to hot pad or large serving bowl.

Yield: 4 to 6 servings

Polenta is a staple of northern Italian cooking. The secret to sweet polenta lies in buying whole grain cornmeal as fresh as possible. Yellow cornmeal contains a fair amount of vitamin A.

Serve this satisfying meal on a wintery Sunday evening. It will warm you from the inside out. Accompany with a medley of fresh salad greens, Herbal Vinaigrette [p. 70] and E-Z Tarragon Rolls [p. 41].

Stuffed Peppers Ranchero

Easy Tex-Mex fare at its best.

These nutritious peppers loaded with protein, calcium, vitamins and fiber are stuffed with a chewy and satisfying seven-grain, black-bean filling topped with tantalizing salsa. Make extra to freeze. Will keep up to 4 months.

Serve with a side of Oven-Roasted Potatoes [p. 200] or Beanz'n Greens [p. 197], minus the beans.

1 envelope Kashi® breakfast pilaf (see Glossary)
2 1/3 cups vegetable stock (p. 8)
6 medium red, yellow or orange bell peppers (or use 2 of each for a colorful presentation)

~

2 large ribs celery, diced
1 cup onion, diced
1/3 cup vegetable stock (p. 8)

~

1 1/2 cups cooked black beans
1 1/2 cups Roma tomatoes, diced
1 cup fresh or frozen corn kernels
1/4 to 1/2 teaspoon hot pepper sauce, to taste
1 teaspoon Gomasio (p. 67)
2 teaspoons chili powder
2 teaspoons ground cumin
2 tablespoons fresh cilantro, chopped

~

1 1/2 cups Border Salsa (p. 76)
1 cup Jack-style cheese alternative, grated

- Rinse kashi briefly (in mesh sieve) to remove any dust. In medium saucepan, bring 2 cups stock (reserve remainder) to boil, add kashi. Cover, reduce heat and simmer, until stock is absorbed, 30 to 35 minutes. Remove pan from heat.

- Meanwhile, in stockpot, bring 4 quarts water to boil. Cut peppers in half lengthwise, cut out and discard stem and seed ribs. Blanch peppers in boiling water, 3 to 4 minutes. Drain well in large colander.

- Preheat oven to 375° F. Lightly oil shallow roasting pan. Arrange peppers, cut side up, in prepared pan. Set aside.

- In small heavy-bottomed skillet, bring reserved stock to boil. Reduce heat, sauté celery and onion until soft and tender, 4 to 6 minutes.

- Combine kashi, black beans and next 7 ingredients, stirring to blend. Add 1/2 of salsa (reserve remainder) and sautéed veggies to mixture. Spoon filling into pepper shells, top with remaining salsa and cheese. Cover.

- Bake until tender, 30 to 40 minutes.

Yield: 6 servings

Scorned Woman Chili
with Cornmeal Dumplings

2 cups white onion, coarsely chopped
5 large cloves garlic, crushed
1 large green bell pepper, coarsely chopped (about 6 ounces)
1 large red bell pepper, coarsely chopped (about 6 ounces)
1 haberno chile pepper, finely chopped*
2 large ribs celery, coarsely chopped
4 medium carrots, diced (about 1 pound)
3 small (2 inch diameter) unpeeled zucchini, diced (about 12 ounces)
~
1 cup vegetable stock (p. 8)
2 cups cooked Anasazi beans
3 cups cooked black beans
1½ cups cooked red kidney beans
5 cups crushed tomatoes
2 cups beefsteak-style tomatoes, quartered and seeded
7 ounces chipotle chile peppers in adobo sauce (see Glossary)
1½ cups fresh or frozen corn kernels
1 cup texturized vegetable protein granules
⅔ cup natural apple cider
2 to 3 teaspoons brown rice syrup, to taste
¼ teaspoon natural liquid hickory smoke, optional
¼ cup liquid aminos
2 tablespoons chili powder
¼ to ½ teaspoon ground cinnamon, to taste
1 tablespoon ground cumin
2 teaspoons cumin seeds, toasted (p.10)
¼ teaspoon crushed red pepper flakes
~
Cornmeal Dumplings (p. 191)

- Prepare onion and next 7 ingredients as directed.
- In 6 quart pan, bring stock to boil. Reduce heat, sauté prepared veggies until soft, 6 to 8 minutes.
- Combine all remaining ingredients with veggies, simmer 20 minutes.
- Meanwhile, prepare cornmeal dumplings as directed.
- Ladle chili into large, wide soup bowls, spoon dumplings over top. Serve piping hot.

Yield: 4 quarts

* Wear rubber gloves when handling to avoid burning sensitive skin. Keep hands away from eyes. For milder chili, remove seed ribs.

Chili—everybody loves it!

The fiery flavors of New Mexican cuisine shine in this mouth-watering meatless chili which exhibits the quintessential qualities of traditional chili–thick, highly seasoned and very satisfying.

Don't let the long list of ingredients intimidate you —you'll be ready to eat in less than an hour. Makes enough for a crowd. Freeze extra. Keeps several months.

Variation: for a powerhouse of energy, serve over corn pasta or quinoa.

Thanksgiving Hubbard
with Apricot Sourdough Stuffing

This succulent dish has become the traditional "bird" at our Thanksgiving table.

Hubbards are the giants of the squash family. Some have been known to weigh-in at 30 pounds and up. Easily recognized by their bumpy, blue-gray shell and large size, their bright-orange flesh is delectably sweet and nutty making them a favorite of the winter-squash family. And, like their winter cousins, hubbards are high in fiber, complex carbohydrates and antioxidant carotenoids.

Serve with mashed potatoes and Holiday Gravy [p. 84], Figgy Cranapple Chutney [p. 88], Lemon Dill Green Beans [p. 194] and Honey-Wheat Rolls [p. 40] for a memorable heart-healthy feast.

1 large loaf sourdough bread (about 10 cups)

~

1 8- to 10-pound Hubbard squash
2 tablespoons extra-virgin olive oil
3 teaspoons honey

~

1½ cups onion, diced
2 cups celery, diced
3¾ cups vegetable stock (p. 8)

~

1 tablespoon dried sage
1 teaspoon dried thyme
½ teaspoon Vege Sal®
¼ teaspoon white pepper
1½ cups dried unsulphured apricots,* diced
⅔ cup dried currants
1 cup pine nuts, toasted (p.10)

- The night before, cut bread into 1 inch cubes. Spread bread cubes, single layer, over baking sheet, drape waxed paper loosely over top allowing air to circulate and "stale" bread.
- Preheat oven to 400° F.
- Cut squash in half lengthwise. Using large metal spoon, scoop out seeds and stringy flesh and discard.
- In a 1-cup measure, whisk oil and honey together. Baste perimeter and cavity of each squash half with mixture. Place squash halves on two lip-edged baking sheets, drape foil over top to prevent drying out during baking.
- Bake 45 minutes, halfway through baking time, rotate sheets top to bottom.
- Meanwhile, prepare onion and celery as directed. In large heavy-bottomed skillet, bring ¾ cup stock to simmer (reserve remainder), sauté onion and celery until soft, 4 to 6 minutes. Add seasonings, apricots, currants and pine nuts to skillet, stirring to blend.

---
* Available in natural food stores.

- In a 1-quart saucepan, bring reserved stock to boil. Remove pan from heat.
- In large mixing bowl, combine bread cubes, apricot mixture and hot stock, tossing until bread cubes are evenly moistened.
- Reduce oven temperature to 375° F. Transfer squash to wire racks, spoon stuffing into cavities, cover squash with foil. Continue baking, about 1 hour; halfway through baking time, rotate baking sheets top to bottom. Remove foil last 10 minutes to lightly brown stuffing. Insert fork in squash to test for doneness.

Yield: 10 to 12 servings

Cajun Creole

4 cups cooked brown basmati rice
~
1 16-ounce block reduced-fat extra-firm tofu
1 tablespoon extra-virgin olive oil
~
$1/2$ cup vegetable stock (p. 8)
1 teaspoon garlic, minced
1 cup onion, diced
1 cup celery, diagonally sliced
1 medium orange bell pepper, cut into $1/2$ inch pieces
2 small (2 inch diameter) yellow crook neck squash, cut into $1/2$ inch pieces
~
1 cup fresh or frozen corn kernels
2 cups cooked black-eyed peas
$1\,1/2$ cups Roma tomatoes, coarsely chopped
$1/3$ cup tomato sauce
$1/3$ cup unsulphured molasses
$1/4$ cup water
1 tablespoon low-sodium tamari sauce
2 tablespoons Spice Hunter® Blackened Redfish seasoning*
~
1 large apple, cored, seeded and diced
$1/2$ cup dried currants
2 tablespoons freshly squeezed lime juice

Tempt your taste buds with sweet and pungent flavor notes straight out of New Orleans.

My friend, Steven Jarose, performed his culinary wizardry on this dish which won him first place in a local contest.

- Cook rice. Cover, keep warm while preparing creole.
- Squeeze tofu gently to drain, cut block in half lengthwise. Position wire rack over lip-edged baking sheet to catch drips. Weigh tofu down with heavy-bottomed pan to drain any remaining water, 20 to 30 minutes, cut into $1/2$ inch cubes.
- In large wide-bottomed skillet, heat oil. Braise tofu, turning periodically, until puffy and golden on all sides, transfer to plate. Cover to keep warm.
- In same skillet, bring stock to boil. Combine garlic, onions and celery, sauté until soft, 4 to 6 minutes. Add pepper and squash, sauté additional 4 to 6 minutes.
- Stir in all remaining ingredients, except apple, currants and lime juice. Reduce heat, simmer 15 minutes. Add apple, currants and lime juice to mixture, simmer an additional 5 minutes. Serve over warm rice.

Yield: 4 to 6 servings

* If unable to locate Spice Hunter® Blackened Redfdish seasoning, make your own blend using: 1 tablespoon mild paprika, 1 teaspoon dried oregano, $1/4$ teaspoon ground cloves, $1/2$ teaspoon thyme, $1/4$ teaspoon cayenne pepper and 1 large bay leaf.

Shepherdess Pie

2 teaspoons extra-virgin olive oil
1 cup onion, chopped
~
$1\frac{1}{2}$ cups Roma tomatoes, cut into bite-size chunks
1 cup cauliflower flowerettes
$1\frac{1}{2}$ cups carrot, diced
2 cups squash (winter or summer variety), cut into ½ inch cubes
1 cup fresh or frozen peas
½ cup tomato sauce
1 medium bay leaf, crumbled
2 tablespoons fresh summer savory, snipped or 2 teaspoons dried
1 teaspoon Italian seasoning (p. 68)
¼ teaspoon dried thyme
1 tablespoon liquid aminos
2 tablespoons Multi-Grain Baking Mix (p. 9)
~
3 cups fresh or leftover mashed potatoes
2 tablespoons fresh flat-leaf Italian parsley, snipped
¼ teaspoon freshly ground pepper
½ teaspoon sea salt
1 teaspoon sweet Hungarian paprika

- In small heavy-bottomed skillet, heat oil, sauté onion until soft, 4 to 6 minutes.

- Preheat oven to 375° F. Lightly oil shallow 3-quart baking dish.

- Prepare tomatoes, cauliflower, carrots and squash as directed. Steam veggies, except tomatoes, until crisp-tender, 6 to 8 minutes. Drain. Combine tomatoes, steamed veggies and all remaining ingredients, except mashed potatoes, stirring to blend. Pour mixture into prepared dish. Mix parsley, pepper and salt into mashed potatoes. Using a rubber spatula, spread potatoes over filling, dust with paprika.

- Bake, uncovered, until potatoes appear "dry," 20 to 25 minutes. Place dish under broiler, lightly brown mashed potatoes, about 1 to 2 minutes. Serve hot.

Yield: 4 to 6 servings

Shepherd's Pie, long a favorite of English country folk, brings to mind the warmth and comfort of a simple, hearty meal eaten after a hard days' work.

Always welcomed by kids and adults alike, this meatless, dairy-free version is equally satisfying and delicious. It contains a wide array of vegetables baked in a savory sauce topped with fluffy white mashed potatoes. [You can vary the vegetables according to the season, keeping tomatoes and sauce for your base ingredients].

Serve with warm crusty slices of Seven Grain Bread [p. 43] and Apple Spice Cake with Cinnamon Glaze [p. 91].

Curry In A Hurry

This savory dish combines complex flavors and textures reminiscent of the best Indian curries.

Serve with a side of Cucumber Mint Raita [p. 187] and triangles of Chapati bread [p. 36] for soaking up the intensely-flavored curry sauce.

Helpful Tip: peel and freeze ginger root in resealable freezer bag—makes grating a snap. Will keep several months.

Saffron Scented Rice with Peas (p. 187)
~
½ cup vegetable stock (p. 8)
4 large cloves garlic, crushed
1 cup onion, coarsely chopped
1 tablespoon ginger root, peeled and grated
~
¼ teaspoon ground cinnamon
1 teaspoon ground cumin
2 teaspoons mild paprika
2 to 3 teaspoons curry powder (p. 66), to taste
¼ teaspoon sea salt
¼ teaspoon hot pepper sauce
2 tablespoons low-sodium tamari sauce
~
2 teaspoons tamarind concentrate (see Glossary)
¼ cup red curry paste*
1 cup coconut milk (p. 4)
1 cup rice milk
~
1 tablespoon expeller-pressed canola oil
2 cups cauliflower flowerettes
1½ cups carrot, diagonally sliced
1 cup peeled potatoes, cut into ½ inch cubes
1 medium red bell pepper, cut into ½ inch pieces
1 cup green beans, cut into 1 inch pieces
1½ cups Roma tomatoes, coarsely chopped
⅔ cup cooked garbanzo beans
½ cup cashew pieces, toasted (p.10)

- Prepare rice as directed. Cover, keep warm while preparing curry.
- In large heavy-bottomed skillet, bring stock to boil. Reduce heat, sauté garlic, onion and ginger root until soft, 4 to 6 minutes. Add cinnamon and next 6 ingredients to mixture, stirring to blend.
- In small bowl, combine tamarind concentrate, curry paste, coconut and rice milk, whisking to blend, add to onion mixture, simmer 4 to 6 minutes. Set aside.
- Meanwhile, prepare cauliflower, carrot, potatoes and pepper as directed. Steam veggies, except pepper, until crisp-tender, about 6 to 8 minutes.
- In wok (or deep sided pan), heat oil, on high, until small bubbles appear, add cauliflower, carrot and potatoes, cook 2 to 3 minutes, add pepper, cook 2 to 3 minutes. Stir beans, tomatoes, garbanzos and curry/onion sauce into veggies, cook 1 minute, add cashews, stirring to blend. Serve over warm rice.

Yield: 6 to 8 servings

* Available in Indian markets, natural food stores and some supermarkets.

Stuffed Tomatoes Provencale

6 large beefsteak-style tomatoes
1 1/4 cups cooked quinoa
~
1/2 cup vegetable stock (p. 8)
2/3 cup leeks, thinly sliced (include some green)
2/3 cup yellow bell pepper, diced
~
2 tablespoons fresh basil, snipped
2 tablespoons fresh thyme leaves, snipped
1 teaspoon Gomasio (p. 67)
1/2 teaspoon Italian seasoning (p. 68)
1/8 teaspoon white pepper
2 tablespoons freshly squeezed lemon juice
2 1/2 tablespoons capers, drained and chopped
~
2 tablespoons extra-virgin olive oil

- Cut 3/4 inch slice from stem end of tomatoes. Invert tomatoes and squeeze gently to remove seeds. Using metal spoon, scoop out most of pulp, chop and set aside. Set wire rack on lip-edged baking sheet to catch drips, invert tomatoes, let drain 10 minutes
- Preheat oven to 350° F. Lightly oil 13 by 9 inch baking dish.
- In small heavy-bottomed skillet, bring stock to boil. Reduce heat, sauté leeks and pepper, stirring frequently until tender, 4 to 6 minutes. Remove pan from heat.
- In large bowl, combine quinoa, sautéed veggies, reserved pulp, basil and next 6 ingredients, tossing to blend.
- Stuff tomatoes, mounding filling over top, transfer to prepared dish, drizzle oil over top.
- Bake tomatoes until tender, about 20 minutes (don't overbake or tomatoes will collapse). Serve chilled, or room temperature, on bed of crisp greens.

Yield: 6 servings

Travelers to the Province region of France have long returned with ecstatic reports on the produce in the markets and food in the many inns and restaurants.

Late summer is an ideal time to make this easy dish when tomatoes are abundant and at their peak of sweetness. If desired, can be prepared ahead and put in oven to bake when guests arrive.

Nutritious quinoa adds a delightful, nutty taste to the filling, accented by the capers' piquant flavor notes.

Serve with Summertime Cucumber Dill soup [p. 219] and grilled whole grain baguettes spread with Basil Spinach Pesto [p. 78].

Three Sisters Stew

The "three sisters"—beans, corn and squash were more than just food to Native Americans. Daily life was steeped in magic and mystery to the early people of the world. These three staples were part of myth and religion as well as food and were revered as "gift givers and caretakers of the People."

Bursting with flavor, this dish makes a quick, satisfying meal, ready in 30 minutes.

Accompany with a side of cooked quinoa [p. 7].

2 teaspoons expeller-pressed canola oil
1 1/2 cups sweet onion (such as Vidalia), coarsely chopped
2 large cloves garlic, minced
~
2 pounds butternut (or other winter variety) squash, peeled, seeded and cut into 1/2 inch cubes
4 large ribs celery, diagonally sliced into 1 inch pieces
1 cup vegetable stock (p. 8)
1/2 teaspoon sea salt
1 1/2 teaspoons ground cumin
1 teaspoon curry powder (p. 66)
1/2 teaspoon dried summer savory
~
1 cup dried Great Northern beans or black-eyed peas, cooked
1 1/2 cups fresh or frozen corn kernels
1/4 cup fresh cilantro, chopped

- In large, wide-bottomed skillet, heat oil. Sauté onion and garlic until soft, 3 to 5 minutes.

- Add squash and next 6 ingredients with sautéed veggies. Cover, cook over medium heat, until squash is tender, 20 to 25 minutes, add all remaining ingredients, simmer 3 minutes. Serve warm in a clay cassolet dish.

Yield: 4 to 6 servings

Pasta

"The doctor of the future will give no medicine but will interest his patients in the care of the human frame, in diet and in the cause and prevention of disease."

Thomas A. Edison

Far East Noodle Salad
with Gingery Plum Sauce

1 cup Gingery Plum Sauce (p. 82)
~
8 ounces udon noodles
~
1 1/2 cups fresh asparagus, cut into 1 inch pieces
1 cup sugar snap or snow peas, diagonally sliced into 1 inch pieces
1 large red or orange bell pepper, cut into 1/2 inch pieces
1/3 cup scallions, diagonally sliced (include some green)
2 tangerines, peeled and sectioned
~
1 1/2 teaspoons sesame oil
2 tablespoons low-sodium tamari sauce
1/4 teaspoon hot pepper sauce
1/3 cup slivered almonds

- Prepare Gingery Plum Sauce as directed, refrigerate until ready to use in salad.
- In stockpot, bring 3 quarts water to boil, break noodles into thirds, add to boiling water, cook until tender, stirring occasionally, 9 to 10 minutes (do not over cook). Using slotted spoon, transfer noodles to colander, (reserve cooking water). Rinse noodles briefly under cold water to prevent sticking and tearing. Drain, transfer to large serving dish. Cover and refrigerate.
- Return water to boil, add asparagus, reduce heat. Cover, cook until crisp-tender, 6 to 8 minutes. Drain immediately, run briefly under cold water to stop cooking process and help asparagus retain its bright color. Set aside.
- Prepare peas, pepper, scallions and tangerines as directed.
- In small bowl, combine plum sauce, sesame oil, tamari and hot pepper sauce, stirring to blend.
- Combine noodles, asparagus, peas, peppers, scallions, tangerines and 3/4 cup plum sauce (reserve remainder), tossing to coat. Chill 1 to 2 hours. Remove salad from refrigerator 20 minutes before serving, sprinkle almonds over top.
  Note: if noodles have absorbed sauce and appear dry, mix remaining plum sauce into salad **before** adding almonds.

Yield: 6 servings

A real winner!

This dish is a potpourri of complex flavors. Udon noodles, made from high-gluten whole wheat flour, are more nutrient-dense and heavier than noodles made from semolina flour. Paired with the almonds, the noodles provide a good amount of protein. Vitamin C scores high in this unusual pasta salad, with a taste of the Orient, thanks to the addition of asparagus, bell pepper, tangerine, and snow peas. The tangy-sweet, magenta-colored plum sauce is its crowning glory.

Serve with toasted whole wheat pita triangles for a special lunch or lite dinner fare.

Pesto Pasta Salad
with Toasted Pine Nuts

Easy picnic fare for those dog days of summer.

A potpourri of flavors delight the palate in this terrific pasta salad. Can be assembled in a flash when you have made-ahead pesto in the freezer.

Serve with a bowl of chilled Summertime Cucumber Dill soup [p. 219] and end the meal on a light note with a dish of mouth-watering Razzle Berry Mousse [p. 116].

1 cup broccoli, cut into small flowerettes
12 ounces lemon-pepper penne rigate pasta*
1 large yellow bell pepper, diced
~
1/2 cup Basil-Spinach Pesto (p. 78)
1/2 cup Herbal Vinaigrette (p. 70)
~
1/2 cup pine nuts, toasted (p.10)

- In large stockpot, bring 4 quarts water to boil, add broccoli, blanch 2 to 3 minutes, remove immediately with slotted spoon (reserve cooking water). Plunge flowerettes into ice water 10 seconds to stop cooking process and help broccoli retain its bright green color. Drain, set aside.
- Return water to boil, add pasta, cook al denté, stirring occasionally, 6 to 8 minutes. Drain, rinse briefly under cold water to prevent pasta from sticking, drain again, transfer to large serving bowl.
- Toss pepper and broccoli with pasta. Set aside.
- In blender, combine pesto and vinaigrette, process just until blended, add to pasta, tossing to coat, fold in nuts.
- Chill salad 1 to 2 hours before serving.

Yield: 6 to 8 servings

* Penne are tube-shaped pasta with diagonal, quill-shaped ends.

Orzo Salad
with Pineapple Salsa

1½ cups orzo pasta
2½ cups water
4 scallions, diagonally sliced (include some green)
½ cup orange bell pepper, diced
~
1 ripe pineapple
3 teaspoons chipotle chile peppers with adobo sauce (see Glossary)
½ mild green chile pepper, seeded and finely chopped
2 tablespoons fresh cilantro, chopped
3 teaspoons brown rice syrup
¼ cup freshly squeezed lime juice
¼ teaspoon ground coriander
½ teaspoon ground cumin

- In large saucepan, bring water to rolling boil, add orzo, reduce heat. Cover, simmer until liquid is absorbed, 12 to 15 minutes. Remove pan from heat, uncover, let cool.
- Prepare scallions and bell pepper as directed. Remove peel and eyes from pineapple, cut in half lengthwise, then into 1 inch chunks (reserve 1½ cups).
- Add pineapple chunks, chipotle and green chiles to food processor, pulse-chop until mixture is consistency of crushed pineapple, about 8 to 10 pulses. Transfer pineapple salsa to small bowl, add cilantro and next 4 ingredients, stirring to blend.
- In large serving bowl, combine orzo, reserved pineapple chunks, scallions, pepper and salsa, stirring to blend. Chill 1 hour before serving. If pasta appears dry, add unsweetened pineapple juice, a little at a time.

Yield: 6 servings

This tantalizing salad is typical of Hawaii's crossroads of many cultures.

Hawaii is one of the largest growers of pineapple in the world. Pineapples are high in bromelain, a digestive enzyme, that appears to have anti-inflammatory action in the body, as well as a good amount of the trace mineral manganese. Also present are vitamins A and C, potassium, calcium and selenium.

The intense fragrance and flavor of the pineapple is accented by the smoky overtones from the chipotles.

Puttanesca Insalate

This enticing pasta salad has a taste of the sunny Mediterranean in every bite.

Tomatoes contain lycopene, an antioxidant nutraceutical which may decrease risk of colon and bladder cancers.

Allicin, found in leeks, helps lower LDL cholesterol.

Serve with Seven Grain Bread [p. 43]. Manja!

16 ounces tomato-basil or garlic-parsley angel hair pasta

~

4 large beefsteak-style tomatoes, seeded and diced
2 cloves garlic, minced
1/2 cup leeks, thinly sliced (white part only)
1/2 cup fresh basil leaves, snipped
1/4 cup fresh flat-leaf Italian parsley, snipped
3 tablespoons capers, drained and chopped
1 teaspoon Italian seasoning (p. 68)
1/4 to 1/2 teaspoon Vege Sal®, to taste
3 tablespoons extra-virgin olive oil
3 tablespoons red wine vinegar
1/2 cup parmesan-style cheese alternative, grated

- In stockpot, bring 4 quarts water to boil, add pasta, cook al denté, stirring occasionally, 3 to 4 minutes. Transfer pasta to colander, rinse briefly under cold water to prevent sticking, drain thoroughly.
- In large serving bowl, combine pasta, tomatoes and all remaining ingredients, tossing to coat. Serve chilled or at room temperature.

Yield: 4 servings

Gnocchi and Garbanzos
with Herbed Pomadoro Sauce

This easy-to-prepare dish has only 3 ingredients. If you have frozen Pomadoro Sauce on hand, you can be eating in less than 30 minutes.

These little potato-filled pasta dumplings will make you forget all about the meatballs.

Round out the meal with a medley of leafy greens and crusty sourdough rye bread.

2 1/2 cups Herbed Pomadoro Sauce with Roasted Garlic (p. 86)
2 cups cooked garbanzo beans
1 pound fresh or frozen natural potato-filled gnocchi

~

fresh parsley sprigs

- Prepare Pomadoro Sauce as directed.
- In stock pot, bring 4 quarts water to boil, add gnocchis. Cook until gnocchis float to surface, 8 to 10 minutes. Drain, return to pan. Stir garbanzos and gnocchi together, transfer to large serving bowl.
- Ladle sauce over gnocchis, garnish with parsley sprigs. Serve immediately.

Yield: 4 servings

Tomato Zucchini Bolognése

1 pound spinach fettuccine
~
1 cup Roma tomatoes, seeded and cut into bite-size pieces
1 cup crushed tomatoes
1/2 cup tomato sauce
1/2 cup rice milk
1 tablespoon unbleached flour with germ
1 tablespoon honey mustard
1 tablespoon liquid aminos
1 tablespoon mirin
1/4 teaspoon hot pepper sauce
1 teaspoon Italian seasoning (p. 68)
~
3 cloves garlic, minced
1/4 cup shallots, peeled and finely chopped
4 small (2 inch diameter) unpeeled zucchini, cut into matchstick julienne
1 large yellow bell pepper, cut into matchstick julienne
~
3 teaspoons sesame oil
1/2 cup Savory Garlic Broth (p. 8)
1 tablespoon fresh oregano, snipped
2 tablespoons fresh basil, snipped
3 tablespoons fresh chives, snipped
~
1/3 cup pine nuts, toasted (p.10)

- In stockpot, bring 4 quarts water to boil, add fettuccine, cook al denté, stirring occasionally, 6 to 8 minutes. Drain, return to pot. Cover to keep warm.

- In large saucepan, combine Roma tomatoes and next 9 ingredients, bring mixture to boil. Reduce heat, simmer 15 minutes, stirring occasionally. Remove pan from heat, cover to keep warm.

- Prepare garlic, shallots, zucchini and pepper as directed.

- Heat oil and broth in wok (or deep sided skillet), over high heat, until small bubbles appear. Add garlic, cook 1 to 2 minutes, stirring constantly to prevent burning. Add shallots, zucchini and bell pepper, cook 3 to 4 minutes, stirring occasionally. Stir oregano, basil and chives into mixture, cook 1 minute. Remove pan from heat immediately.

- Combine fettuccine and sauce with stir-fried veggies, tossing to blend, transfer to large pasta bowl, sprinkle pine nuts over top. Serve immediately.

Yield: 4 servings

A taste-tempting dish that pairs pasta with stir-fried vegetables. A terrific way to utilize summers bumper crop of peppers, tomatoes and zucchini.

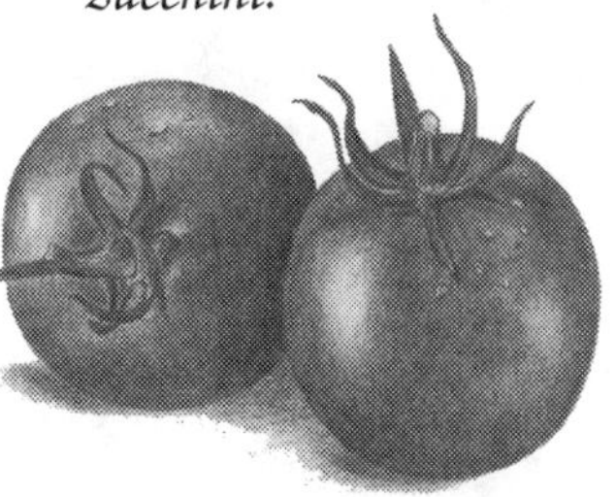

Helpful Tip: pick zucchini while they're small for optimal taste, tenderness and smaller seeds.

Amazing Grains
with Pasta, Greens and Mushrooms

Exotic, nutritious and satisfying.

Kashi is a blend of seven whole grains, high in protein, calcium, fiber and iron, and low in calories. Sesame oil, dark pasta and mushrooms add depth to create a unique dish with rich, earthy flavor.

Kale is a hardy cold-weather green, whose flavor becomes sweeter with a touch of frost, exceptionally high in calcium, magnesium, potassium, iron and vitamins A and C.

For a hearty meal, serve with Ginger Sesame Broccoli [p. 202] and crusty rye or pumpernickel bread.

1 envelope Kashi®* breakfast pilaf (see Glossary)
2½ cups mushroom stock (p. 8)
~
16 ounces whole wheat or spelt rotini pasta
~
8 cups fresh kale
3 medium leeks, diagonally sliced (include some green)
3 large cloves garlic, minced
12 ounces assorted mushrooms (such as crimini, shitake and oyster*), coarsely chopped
2 teaspoons toasted sesame oil
~
3 tablespoons liquid aminos
½ teaspoon dried thyme
1 teaspoon dried summer savory
¼ teaspoon freshly ground pepper
~
2 tablespoons unhulled sesame seeds

- Rinse kashi briefly (in mesh sieve) to remove any dust. In medium saucepan, bring 2 cups stock to boil (reserve remainder), add kashi. Cover, simmer, over medium heat, until stock is absorbed, 30 to 35 minutes. Remove pan from heat.

- In stockpot, bring 4 quarts water to boil, add rotini, cook al denté, stirring occasionally, 7 to 9 minutes. Drain, return to pot. Cover to keep warm.

- Rinse kale thoroughly to dislodge any dirt or sand particles, repeat, if necessary. Remove and discard any large, tough stems. Pile several leaves on top of each other, roll tightly into cigar shape, slice crosswise into ½ inch ribbons.

- Prepare leeks, garlic and mushrooms as directed.

- In large heavy-bottomed skillet, heat oil and reserved stock. Sauté leeks, garlic and mushrooms until soft and mushrooms release their juices, 5 to 7 minutes. Add kale, liquid aminos and next 3 ingredients, stirring to blend. Cover, simmer on low, stirring frequently, until greens are tender, 10 to 15 minutes. If necessary, add a little stock or water during cooking to maintain liquid in bottom of pan.

- Combine kashi and sautéed veggies, stirring to blend, transfer to large serving dish, sprinkle with sesame seeds. Serve warm.

Yield: 6 servings

---

* Almost always available these days in the produce section of well-stocked supermarkets.

Caponata Stuffed Shells

Caponata (p. 23)
~
Herbed Pomadoro Sauce (p. 86)
~
24 jumbo pasta shells
1/3 cup mozzarella-style cheese alternative, grated
1/3 cup parmesan-style cheese alternative, grated

- In stockpot, bring 5 quarts water to rolling boil, add shells, one at a time, while stirring bottom of pot with wooden spoon, continue stirring gently from bottom to prevent shells sticking. Return to boil, cook shells about 8 minutes, carefully transfer to colander, rinse briefly with cold water to stop cooking process.
- Preheat oven to 350° F. Lightly oil 13 by 9 inch glass baking dish. Note: if using metal pan, increase temperature to 375° F.
- Ladle thin layer of sauce over bottom of prepared dish. Stuff shells carefully with about 2 tablespoons caponata per shell. Arrange shells, seam side down, over sauce. Ladle remaining sauce over shells, top with cheeses, cover.
- Bake 35 minutes, uncover, bake an additional 5 minutes to lightly brown cheese.

Yield: 6 to 8 servings

Delicioso!

Caponata, a traditional Italian antipasto, is elevated to new heights in this savory rendition. The sauce and filling can be prepared 1 to 2 days in advance making final assembly a snap.

Perfect with a medley of mild and bitter greens, Herbal Vinaigrette [p. 70] and Savory Sunflower Bread [p. 44].

Penne Four Pepper Pasta

Go ahead, tempt your taste buds!

This colorful, zesty stir-fry combines four different peppers in a tantalizing pineapple-ginger sauce that blends harmoniously with the lemon-pepper pasta. Loaded with vitamin C and beta carotene.

12 ounces lemon-pepper penne* rigate pasta
~
3 cloves garlic, minced
2 cups fennel, sliced into 1/2 inch strips (white part only)
2 medium red bell peppers, sliced into 1/2 inch strips
2 medium yellow bell peppers, sliced into 1/2 inch strips
2 medium green bell peppers, sliced into 1/2 inch strips
2 mild green chile peppers, seeded and sliced into 1/2 inch strips
1/2 cup pineapple juice, unsweetened
2 tablespoons freshly squeezed lemon juice
3/4 cup vegetable stock (p. 8)
1 tablespoon kudzu
1 tablespoon brown rice syrup
2 tablespoons mellow white miso
1 tablespoon low-sodium tamari sauce
1/4 teaspoon crushed red pepper flakes
2 teaspoons fresh ginger root, peeled and grated
~
1 tablespoon extra-virgin olive oil
2 tablespoons unhulled sesame seeds

- In stockpot, bring 3 quarts water to boil, add penne pasta, cook al denté, stirring occasionally, 6 to 8 minutes. Drain, return to pot. Cover to keep warm.
- Prepare fennel and peppers as directed.
- Whisk pineapple juice and next 8 ingredients together. Set aside.
- Heat oil in wok (or deep sided skillet), over high heat, until small bubbles appear. Add garlic, cook 1 to 2 minutes, stirring constantly to prevent burning. Add fennel and peppers, cook 2 to 3 minutes. Gradually add pineapple juice mixture to veggies, cook stirring constantly, until thickened and clear, 1 to 2 minutes. Combine pasta and peppers, tossing to blend, transfer to large pasta bowl, sprinkle sesame seeds over top. Serve warm.

Yield: 6 servings

* Penne are tube-shaped pasta with diagonal, quill-shaped ends.

Pasta Monterey

1 cup sun-dried tomatoes
1 1/4 cups boiling water
~
1 pound tricolor fusilli pasta
~
1 pound rhubarb chard*
1/2 cup mushroom or vegetable stock (p. 8)
8 cloves garlic, crushed
4 ounces shitake mushrooms, coarsely chopped
8 ounces white button mushrooms, quartered
14 ounces water-packed artichoke hearts, drained and quartered
2/3 cup pitted black olives, cut in half lengthwise
2 1/2 tablespoons extra-virgin olive oil
1 tablespoon fresh oregano, snipped or 1 teaspoon dried
2 tablespoons fresh basil, snipped or 2 teaspoons dried
1/4 teaspoon hot pepper sauce
1/2 teaspoon Vege Sal®
1 teaspoon Italian seasoning (p. 68)
~
1/2 cup toasted pine nuts (p.10)

- In medium bowl, pour boiling water over tomatoes, let soak 15 minutes to reconstitute. Drain any remaining liquid.

- In stockpot, bring 4 quarts water to boil, add fusilli (if using long fusilli, break strands in half), cook al denté, stirring occasionally, 7 to 8 minutes. Drain, return to pot. Cover to keep warm.

- Wash chard thoroughly to dislodge any dirt or sand particles, repeat, if necessary. Cut out and discard any large, tough stems. Pile several leaves on top of each other, roll tightly into cigar shape, slice crosswise into 1/2 inch ribbons.

- In large wide-bottomed skillet, bring 2 quarts water and 1/4 teaspoon sea salt to rapid boil, add chard. Cover, blanch 3 minutes, stirring occasionally, drain well. In stockpot, combine chard and fusilli, tossing to blend. Cover to keep warm.

- In large wide-bottomed skillet, bring stock to boil. Reduce heat, sauté garlic and mushrooms until soft and mushrooms release their juices, 4 to 6 minutes.

- Combine sun-dried tomatoes, sautéed veggies, artichokes and all remaining ingredients, except pine nuts, with fusilli, tossing to blend. Transfer to large serving bowl, sprinkle pine nuts over top. Serve warm.

Yield: 6 to 8 servings

A real attention-getter!

The inspiration for this recipe came from my friend Jo-Ann Alibrandi. The taste and textures are reminiscent of California cuisine—colorful, sunny, healthy and delicious.

Contrasting flavors of sun-dried tomatoes and artichokes add pizzazz.

Chilled, this dish transforms into a delightful summer salad.

---

* If rhubarb chard isn't readily available, substitute green chard or spinach.

Confetti Roll-Ups
with Alfrézo Sauce

12 whole wheat lasagna noodles

~

$^{3}/_{4}$ cup onion, diced
5 cloves garlic, minced
1 medium red bell pepper, diced
1 cup carrot, diced
1$^{1}/_{2}$ tablespoons liquid aminos
$^{1}/_{2}$ cup vegetable stock (p. 8)
10 ounces frozen spinach, thawed
2 teaspoons Italian seasoning (p. 68)
$^{1}/_{4}$ teaspoon sea salt
$^{1}/_{4}$ teaspoon freshly ground pepper

~

2 cups Alfrézo Sauce (p. 83)
16 ounces reduced-fat firm tofu
6 ounces mozzarella-style cheese alternative, grated
2 teaspoons mild paprika

Elegant enough for entertaining, easy enough for a midweek meal, these confetti-flecked rollups can be assembled the day before and refrigerated until ready to bake.

With protein-rich tofu standing in for riccota cheese, you can fool even the most discriminating palate. Tofu is the easily-digestible curd from cooked soy beans, high in calcium, complex carbohydrates and isoflavones [also known as phytoestrogens], a plant form of the female hormone estrogen. Research has shown soy foods contain potent antioxidants as well as tumor-preventing properties.

- In stockpot, bring 5 quarts water to boil, add noodles, cook until tender, stirring occasionally, 7 to 8 minutes. Drain, immerse noodles in cold water until ready to assemble to prevent sticking and tearing.
- Preheat oven to 375° F. Lightly oil 13 by 9 inch baking dish.
- Prepare onion, garlic, pepper and carrot as directed. Drain spinach thoroughly, chop into small pieces.
- In large heavy-bottomed skillet, bring liquid aminos and stock to boil. Reduce heat, sauté onion, garlic, pepper and carrot, 3 to 4 minutes. Add spinach and next 3 ingredients, stirring to blend. Cover, cook until spinach is wilted, about 3 to 4 minutes. Remove pan from heat. Set aside.
- Prepare Alfrezo Sauce as directed. Ladle thin layer sauce over bottom of prepared dish.
- Squeeze tofu gently to drain. Place tofu in mesh sieve, let drain over bowl, 15 minutes, squeeze again. Crumble with fork or hands into sautéed veggies.
- Drain noodles in colander, pat dry with paper towel. Spread one noodle out over work surface, place $^{1}/_{2}$ cup filling at one end, roll up, jelly-roll style. Arrange rollups, seam side down, in dish. Repeat procedure with remaining noodles.
- Ladle remaining sauce over rollups, top with cheese and paprika. Cover.
- Bake until hot and bubbly, about 40 minutes, uncover last 5 minutes.

Yield: 6 servings

Wild Mushroom Stroganoff

16 ounces kamut fettuccine*
1½ cups Alfrézo Sauce (p. 83)
~
8 ounces crimini or white button mushrooms
4 ounces shitake mushrooms
12 ounces sliced portabella mushroom caps
¼ cup mushroom or vegetable stock (p. 8)
1 tablespoon low-sodium tamari sauce
4 cloves garlic, minced
~
4 tablespoons fresh chives, snipped
2 teaspoons fresh tarragon, snipped or ½ teaspoon dried
2 teaspoons fresh rosemary leaves, crushed or ½ teaspoon dried
¼ teaspoon freshly ground pepper
2 tablespoons sweet Hungarian paprika
3 tablespoons traditional brown miso dissolved in 2 tablespoons mirin or apple juice
~
fresh parsley sprigs
1 large red bell pepper, cut into ½ inch strips

- In stockpot, bring 5 quarts water to boil, add fettuccine, cook al denté, stirring occasionally, 7 to 8 minutes. Drain, return to pot. Cover to keep warm.
- Meanwhile, prepare Alfrézo Sauce as directed. Cover to keep warm.
- Remove and discard ends of criminis and shitakes, coarsely chop.
- In large wide-bottomed skillet, bring stock and liquid aminos to boil. Reduce heat, sauté garlic, stirring constantly, until soft, 2 to 3 minutes.
- Crush rosemary leaves in mortar bowl with pestle (or crush between two spoons) to release fragrant oil. Set aside.
- Combine mushrooms and garlic, cook until mushrooms release their juices, 5 to 7 minutes. Add herbs, seasonings, miso mixture and Alfrézo Sauce to mushrooms, simmer 8 to 10 minutes. Remove pan from heat.
- Combine stroganoff and fettuccine, tossing to blend, transfer to large pasta bowl. Garnish with parsley and red pepper. Serve warm.

Yield: 6 servings

* Shiloh Farms® makes an excellent one. If unable to locate kamut fettuccine, substitute whole wheat fettuccine.

Wild mushrooms and dark pastas are perfect earthy partners. This deceptively rich, low-fat dairy-free version of a classic will add warmth to a chilly winters' night.

Mushrooms are a good source of germanium, a trace mineral that improves cellular oxygenation and enhances immunity, also fairly high in protein, iron and selenium.

Fragrant rosemary and tarragon are perfect accents for the rich, earthy mushrooms.

Serve with a side of steamed broccoli and slices of crusty Seven Grain Bread [p. 43].

Salads

"The greatest thing in this world is not so much where we are, but in what direction we are moving."

Oliver Wendell Holmes

German Potato Salad
(A Warm Salad)

12 cups small unpeeled red potatoes
~
2 teaspoons expeller-pressed canola oil
1 cup vegetable stock (p. 8)
3/4 cup onion, diced
3/4 cup celery, diced
~
1 tablespoon kudzu dissolved in
1/2 cup balsamic vinegar
1/4 cup brown rice syrup
1/8 teaspoon natural liquid hickory smoke
2 teaspoons celery seeds, crushed
1/2 teaspoon dry mustard powder
1/4 teaspoon sea salt
1/4 teaspoon freshly ground pepper
~
2 tablespoons soy bacon bits*
2 tablespoons fresh flat-leaf Italian parsley, chopped
2 teaspoons sweet Hungarian paprika

- In stockpot, bring 5 quarts water to boil. Cook potatoes until done but firm, about 10 to 14 minutes (test periodically to avoid overcooking), drain in colander. When cool enough to handle, cut potatoes into slices, transfer to lightly oiled 3-quart baking dish.
- In small heavy-bottomed skillet, heat oil and 1/2 cup stock (reserve remainder), add onions and celery, sauté until soft and translucent, 4 to 6 minutes. Set aside.
- In medium saucepan, combine reserved stock, kudzu, vinegar and next 6 ingredients, bring to boil, cook, stirring constantly, until thickened, about 2 to 3 minutes. Remove pan from heat.
- Stir sautéed onions and celery into sauce. Using rubber spatula, fold sauce and bacon bits into potatoes, garnish with parsley and dust with paprika. Serve warm.

Yield: 6 servings

* Lightlife Foods® makes a delicious bacon substitute, 100 percent natural, vegetarian, and low in sodium with zero cholesterol.

A family favorite that's always popular at gatherings. Here I've made it heart-healthy for the nineties, eliminating the saturated fat and cholesterol while keeping the same delicious taste. I hope you enjoy it as much as I do.

Potatoes reward the body with a big boost of potassium. Eaten with their skins intact, they provide a good dose of vitamin C and fiber and are low in calories, fat-free and satisfying.*

Accompany with a side of steamed carrots and Mom's Baked Beans [p. 192]. For dessert, serve up a dish of Blueberry Peach Crisp [p. 110].

** Purchase organically grown potatoes, if available.*

Berry Green Salad
with Raspberry Walnut Vinaigrette

Bursting with flavor and color. An unusual combination of ingredients complement each other beautifully in this composed summer salad.*

Spinach is high in vitamin A, potassium, magnesium, calcium and iron. One cup of raw spinach contains nearly 2 mg. of iron.

Raspberries are also a good source of iron, vitamin C and calcium.

Walnuts are considered "brain food", high in protein, iron, and potassium with a moderate amount of vitamins A, C, E and biotin.

Sesame seeds are an abundant source of calcium, copper, magnesium and potassium.

** A composed salad is a carefully arranged salad with beauty and eye appeal.*

1½ cups fresh red raspberries*
2 tablespoons balsamic vinegar
2 tablespoons raspberry vinegar
1½ tablespoons brown rice syrup
¼ teaspoon dry mustard powder
2 tablespoons walnut oil
3 tablespoons walnuts, toasted (p.10)

~

6 cups fresh spinach (about 5 ounces)
1 head Boston or butter bibb-style lettuce
4 leaves red-leaf lettuce
1 small red onion, thinly sliced into rings

~

2 tablespoons unhulled sesame seeds

- In blender, combine ½ cup raspberries (reserve 1 cup) and next 6 ingredients, process until blended, chill vinaigrette 1 hour.
- Rinse spinach, lettuce and radicchio thoroughly to dislodge any dirt or sand particles, repeat, if necessary. Remove spinach stems. Spin dry or pat with paper towel. Reserve whole lettuce leaves. Tear spinach and radicchio into bite-size pieces,
- Lay Boston lettuce leaves (2 per serving) on individual salad plates. Arrange spinach and red-leaf lettuce in crescent shape on lettuce, place several whole raspberries in bow of crescent. Refrigerate. Before serving, drizzle with vinaigrette, sprinkle sesame seeds over top.

Yield: 8 servings

---

* If red raspberries aren't available, substitute strawberries. Use only fresh fruit.

Broccoli Salad
with Pineapple Dressing

1 cup ripe pineapple, cut into 1/2 inch cubes
1/3 cup red bell pepper, diced
4 cups broccoli stems and flowerettes, coarsely chopped
1/3 cup raw sunflower seeds, toasted (p.10)
~
2/3 cup Dijon Eggless Mayo (p. 74)
2 tablespoons honey
2 tablespoons pineapple juice, unsweetened

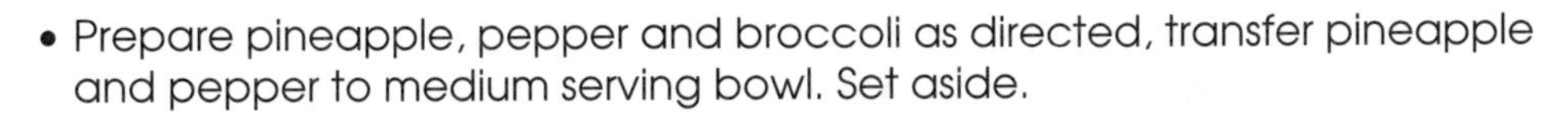

- Prepare pineapple, pepper and broccoli as directed, transfer pineapple and pepper to medium serving bowl. Set aside.
- In large saucepan, bring 3 quarts water to rolling boil, add broccoli, blanch 2 to 3 minutes. Drain broccoli, plunge into ice water 10 seconds to stop cooking process and help retain its bright green color, drain again. Combine broccoli, pineapple, pepper and sunflower seeds, tossing to blend.
- In small bowl, whisk mayo, honey and pineapple juice together, fold into broccoli mixture. Chill 2 hours to allow flavors to meld, stir before serving.

Yield: 4 servings

A delicious way to get your daily dose of vitamins and minerals.

Broccoli, a cruciferous vegetable, is chock full of antioxidant beta carotene and vitamin C that fight cancer, cataracts and heart disease, as well as strengthen the immune system.

Pinwheel Salad

Cilantro Lime Vinaigrette (p. 69)
~
4 ripe beefsteak-style tomatoes, cut into wedges
2 chayote squash, peeled, pitted, and cut into wedges

- Prepare vinaigrette, chill 1 hour before using.
- Prepare tomato and chayote as directed. Set tomatoes aside.
- Steam chayote just until crisp-tender, about 5 to 7 minutes, drain and plunge into ice water 10 seconds to stop cooking process, drain again.
- Alternate wedges of tomato and chayote, pinwheel fashion, on individual salad plates, pour vinaigrette over top. Serve room temperature or chill salads 1 hour.

Yield: 4 servings

Vibrant with plenty of eye appeal.

This quick and easy salad will get you out of the kitchen fast! Perfect for those summer days when it's so hot the air shimmers.

Serve with a cup of chilled Garden Gazpacho [p. 212] or Summertime Cucumber Dill Soup [p. 219]. End on a cool note with Lemon Saffron Granita [p. 114].

Sweet 'n Sour Salad

2 cups fresh or frozen peas
2 cups cooked Great Northern beans
1 small red onion, diced
1 medium orange bell pepper, diced
1 pound cooked beets, cut into matchstick julienne

~

1/3 cup rice vinegar
3 tablespoons balsamic vinegar
2/3 cup apple juice concentrate, undiluted
1/4 to 1/2 teaspoon Vege Sal®, to taste
1/4 teaspoon white pepper
1/2 teaspoon dry mustard powder

- In large bowl, toss peas with next 4 ingredients. Set aside.

- In 2 cup measure, combine rice vinegar and all remaining ingredients, whisking to blend. Pour vinaigrette over bean mixture, refrigerate 1 to 2 hours, or overnight, to allow flavors to meld. Stir salad before serving.

Yield: 8 to 10 servings

Loaded with pizzazz, this marinated salad boasts a zesty oil-free vinaigrette [the beets give it a rosy hue.]

Peas are high in iron, potassium, calcium, magnesium, vitamins A and C as well as folic acid [an important B vitamin]. Great Northerns contain high levels of thiamine, niacin, pantothenic acid, iron, calcium and potassium. Both peas and beans are members of the legume family.

Beets are an excellent source of iron, potassium, copper and vitamin C. Folic acid, zinc, calcium, manganese, magnesium and phosphorus are also present.

Squaw Salad
(Black Beans and Corn)

3 cups cooked black beans
1½ cups fresh or frozen corn kernels
1 medium orange bell pepper, diced
6 scallions, diagonally sliced (include some green)
2 tablespoons fresh jalapeño chile pepper, seeded and finely chopped
3 medium ribs celery, diagonally sliced
¼ cup fresh cilantro, chopped

~

¼ cup freshly squeezed lime juice
¼ cup apple juice concentrate, undiluted
2 tablespoons extra-virgin olive oil
3 cloves garlic, minced
1 tablespoon ground cumin
½ teaspoon chili powder
1 tablespoon mellow white miso

- In medium serving bowl, toss beans with next 6 ingredients. Set aside.
- In blender, combine lime juice and all remaining ingredients, process until blended.
- Pour vinaigrette over bean mixture, refrigerate 1 to 2 hours, or overnight, to allow flavors to meld, stir before serving.

Yield: 6 servings

Savor the flavor of the Great American Southwest with this zesty black bean salad.

Black beans are high in fiber, calcium, iron, potassium and protein.

American Indians used corn [maize] as a staple food in their diet, cooking it with lime. Rich in vitamin A, potassium and magnesium, corn is mostly carbohydrate with about 20 percent protein content.

Serve with Baked Tortilla Chips [p. 13] and Anasazi Bean Burgers [p. 178]. For dessert, Plum Empanadas [p. 107].

Quinoa Tabouleh

Traditionally, tabouleh is made with bulgur made from wheatberries. However, in this delicious version, quinoa, an ancient Incan grain now grown in the Colorado Rockies, fills in nicely for bulgur.

Nutritionally superior to bulgur, quinoa is a non-glutenous grain with a nutty flavor and is a good alternative for those with wheat intolerance.

Serve on a bed of crisp leafy greens or stuff into a whole grain pita pocket with fresh sprouts and tomato slices.

1 cup quinoa
1 1/2 cups vegetable stock (p. 8)
~
3 tablespoons freshly squeezed lemon juice
2 tablespoons extra-virgin olive oil
1/3 cup scallions, diagonally sliced (include some green)
3/4 cup yellow or green bell pepper, diced
3/4 cup carrot, diced
2 medium beefsteak-style tomatoes, seeded and diced
2 tablespoons fresh mint, chopped
2/3 cup fresh flat-leaf Italian parsley, chopped
1/2 teaspoon Gomasio (p. 67)
1/2 teaspoon ground coriander
1 to 2 teaspoons curry powder (p. 66), to taste

- Rinse quinoa briefly (in mesh sieve) under running water to remove natural saponins.
- In medium saucepan, bring stock to boil. Reduce heat, simmer until liquid is absorbed, 15 to 20 minutes, transfer quinoa to medium serving bowl, fluff with fork, let cool slightly.
- Combine all remaining ingredients with quinoa, tossing to blend, cover, chill 1 to 2 hours. Stir tabouleh before serving.

Yield: 6 to 8 servings

Hasta la Pasta

1 large spaghetti squash (3 to 4 pounds)
~
12 large cherry tomatoes, quartered
1 large orange bell pepper, cut into 2 inch matchstick julienne
2 large leeks, diagonally sliced (include some green)
3 tablespoons capers, drained and chopped
1/3 cup pitted black olives, sliced
~
3 tablespoons extra-virgin olive oil
3 tablespoons rice vinegar
3 teaspoons umeboshi vinegar
2 tablespoons fresh tarragon, snipped

- Cut squash in half lengthwise. Using a large metal spoon, scoop out seeds and discard.
- Preheat oven to 350° F.
- Place squash, cut side up, on lip-edged baking sheet, cover loosely with foil. Bake until squash tests done when pierced with fork, 45 to 60 minutes.
- Allow squash to cool slightly before handling. Grasp squash with potholder or oven mitt (squash will be very hot), rest squash on work surface. Using a fork, begin at top and drag tines down over flesh to remove spaghetti-like strands, continue scraping until only the shell remains. Repeat procedure with remaining half.
- In large serving bowl,* toss squash, tomatoes and next 4 ingredients together, until blended. Set aside.
- In a 2-cup measure, combine all remaining ingredients. Pour vinaigrette over salad, tossing to blend. Chill 1 to 2 hours. Twenty minutes before serving, remove salad from refrigerator, stir to re-blend.

Yield: 6 servings

* Use a glass bowl, if you have one, to show off this colorful salad.

Consistently popular with my cooking classes, this distinctive salad is loaded with taste and eye appeal.

Spaghetti squash, named for its pastalike strands of flesh, is a low-calorie, low-carbohydrate alternative to pasta, high in vitamin A.

In summer and early fall, you'll find fresh tarragon readily available at roadside stands, farmers markets and some supermarkets.

Lemon Couscous Salad

Low-fat foods require less digestion time than do slower metabolizing fatty foods. This low-fat grain salad is guaranteed to give you extra energy for that summer activity like hiking or weeding the garden.

Grains are excellent choices for summer and winter fare—low in fat and high in complex carbohydrates, they support physical activity by stabilizing blood-sugar to provide even, sustained energy.

Whole wheat couscous, with its slightly nutty flavor, contains a good amount of protein and fiber. Cooking the couscous in vegetable stock instead of water, gives it a richer flavor.

Serve this Middle Eastern dish with wedges of Chapati bread [p. 36].

1½ cups whole wheat couscous
2½ cups vegetable stock (p. 8)
~
½ cup pitted green olives, cut in half lengthwise
½ cup radish, thinly sliced
6 scallions, diagonally sliced (include some green)
2 teaspoons lemon zest
~
⅓ cup freshly squeezed lemon juice
1 teaspoon Gomasio (p. 67)
3 tablespoons extra-virgin olive oil
1½ tablespoons ground cumin
1 tablespoon whole grain mustard
¼ teaspoon freshly ground pepper
⅛ teaspoon ground allspice
~
lemon twists

- In medium saucepan, bring stock to boil, add couscous, reduce heat to lowest setting. Cover, cook until liquid is absorbed, 5 to 8 minutes, transfer to large serving bowl, fluff with fork. Combine olives and next 3 ingredients with couscous, tossing with blend.
- In a 2-cup measure, whisk lemon juice and next 6 ingredients together, until blended. Pour vinaigrette over couscous, stir thoroughly. Garnish with lemon twists. Best served at room temperature.

Yield: 6 servings

Dilly Barley Salad

4 cups cooked pearled barley
1/3 cup raw sunflower seeds, toasted (p.10)
1 cup carrot, diced
1/3 cup shallots, finely chopped
1/2 cup dried currants
~
2 tablespoons grapeseed oil
3 tablespoons balsamic vinegar
2 tablespoons liquid aminos
1 teaspoon ground cumin
1/2 teaspoon ground coriander
1 teaspoon mild paprika
~
1/3 cup fresh dill, snipped
2 teaspoons poppy seeds

- In large heavy-bottomed skillet, toast barley, over medium heat, stirring constantly until fragrant, 6 to 8 minutes, cook as directed (p. 7), let cool 30 minutes.
- In large serving bowl, combine barley, sunflower seeds and next 3 ingredients, tossing to blend.
  Note: if currants are hard, soak in boiling water 5 minutes to plump, drain any remaining liquid.
- In blender, combine grapeseed oil and all remaining ingredients, except dill and poppy seeds, process until blended. Add dill and poppy seeds to vinaigrette. Pour vinaigrette over barley mixture, tossing to blend. Chill 1 to 2 hours. Twenty minutes before serving, remove salad from refrigerator, stir to re-blend.

Yield: 4 to 6 servings

Satisfying and nourishing, loaded with sensory delights for the nose, eyes and taste buds.

Dills' piquant flavor and intoxicating fragrance complement the flavor of cumin and coriander perfectly in this chilled main-dish grain salad.

Barley with its chewy, satisfying texture is high in gluten, fiber, carbohydrates, niacin, folic acid, calcium, iron, potassium and magnesium. Less acid-forming than other grains, barley is easily digested.

Orange Wheatberry Salad

with Apricots, Asparagus and Almonds

Here's a terrific main-dish salad brimming with sophisticated flavor—truly a gustatory delight.

Sprouting wheatberries gives them a wonderful chewiness while increasing their digestibility by converting starch into simple sugars. An added benefit to sprouting—vitamins B, C and E are greatly enhanced.

A cornucopia of anticancer compounds, vitamins and minerals abound in the apricots, asparagus, almonds and orange.

Serve with a bowl of Asparagus Velouté soup [p. 206] and welcome Spring with panache.

1 cup sprouted wheatberries,*
3½ cups vegetable stock (p. 8)
~
8 ounces dried unsulphured apricots,* cut into matchstick julienne
½ cup apple juice, warmed
1 pound asparagus (tips and stems), cut diagonally into 2 inch pieces
~
½ cup freshly squeezed orange juice
2 teaspoons orange zest
¼ teaspoon Vege Sal®
¼ teaspoon white pepper
2 tablespoons almond or walnut oil
2 teaspoons brown rice syrup
~
½ cup almond pieces, blanched and toasted (p.10)

- Cook sprouted wheatberries as directed (p. 7).
- Meanwhile, prepare apricots as directed, let soak in warm apple juice 5 minutes to plump. Drain any remaining juice.
- Blanch or steam asparagus 3 to 4 minutes (do not over cook), plunge into ice water 10 seconds to stop cooking process and help retain green color.
- In container, with tight fitting lid, combine orange juice and next 5 ingredients, shake well to blend.
- In large serving bowl, combine wheatberries, apricots, asparagus and almonds, pour dressing over top, tossing to blend. Chill salad 1 hour before serving.

Yield: 4 servings

---

* Available in natural food stores. Begin sprouting the wheatberries **3 days before** you plan to make the salad.

Pockets, Sandwiches and Wraps

"The healing of ourselves is the healing of the whole nation."

Thich Nhat Hanh

Mock Chicken Wraps

2 teaspoons extra-virgin olive oil
8 ounces frozen tempeh, thawed (see Glossary)
~
½ cup celery, diced
½ cup onion, diced
½ cup carrot, diced
~
½ cup Dijon Eggless Mayo (p. 74)
1 teaspoon Dijon-style mustard
2 teaspoons liquid aminos
1 teaspoon celery seeds, crushed
3 teaspoons poultry seasoning
¼ teaspoon freshly ground pepper
~
4 10-inch whole wheat flour tortillas, warmed
1 cup Romaine lettuce, shredded
2 Roma tomatoes, seeded and cut into julienne strips
½ cup Creamy Cucumber Dill Dressing (p. 71)

- Cut tempeh into ½ inch cubes. In medium cast-iron skillet, heat oil over high heat. Reduce heat, braise tempeh until golden on all sides, 4 to 5 minutes, transfer to medium mixing bowl. Set aside.
- Prepare celery, onion and carrot as directed.
- In medium bowl, beat mayo and next 5 ingredients together until blended, stir tempeh and diced veggies into mayo.
- Briefly warm tortillas (both sides) on preheated pancake griddle or in cast-iron skillet. Do not overheat or tortillas will dry out and break apart.
- Assemble wraps by dividing "chicken" mixture between tortillas, add lettuce and tomato, top with dressing. Fold in top and bottom portions of tortilla. Roll up from side to completely enclose filling. Serve immediately.

Yield: 4 servings

Whole wheat flour tortillas are excellent wrappers for this tantalizing mock chicken salad.

Tempeh, a fermented, highly-nutritious soy food is easy to digest, sodium free and high in protein. Some brands may even contain vitamin B-12. Tempehs' meaty texture lends versatility to a variety of dishes.

Great for lunch. Serve with Chile Dilly Carrot Paté [p. 14] and celery sticks, for dipping.

Tofuna Waffle Club

Light golden corn waffles become the "bread" for this intriguing sandwich.

Kelp [a mineral-rich sea vegetable] admirably lends authentic flavor to this mock tuna stand-in.

Tofu [soy bean curd] contains all 8 essential amino acids, and is an excellent source of easily digestible protein, iron, potassium and calcium. Depending on how it's made, tofu can equal milk in calcium content, with the capability of taking on the flavor of whatever it's combined with. Most noted for its isoflavone [a source of phytoestrogens] properties, tofu shows promise of reducing the risk of breast cancer.

For a nourishing lunch, serve this unique club sandwich with carrot and celery sticks on the side.

Helpful Tip: make extra and freeze for quick assembly of these tempting clubs when you're short on time.

16 ounces reduced-fat* firm tofu
2 large ribs celery, diced
4 scallions, finely chopped (white part only)
~
½ cup plus 2 tablespoons Dijon Eggless Mayo (p. 74)
2 teaspoons whole grain mustard
2 tablespoons liquid aminos
1 tablespoon freshly squeezed lemon juice
¾ teaspoon kelp powder
1 teaspoon celery seeds, crushed
1 teaspoon herbal seasoning (p. 66)
2 tablespoons fresh flat-leaf Italian parsley, chopped
~
12 leaves Romaine lettuce, washed and dried
12 slices beefsteak-style tomatoes
¼ cup Dijon Eggless Mayo (p. 74)
~
Golden Corn Waffles (p. 54)
2 teaspoons cumin seeds, crushed
2 tablespoons whole grain mustard

- Squeeze tofu gently to drain. Place tofu in mesh sieve, let drain over bowl, 15 minutes, squeeze again, transfer to medium bowl, crumble with fork or hands, add celery and shallots, stirring to blend.
- Whisk mayo and all remaining ingedients together, fold mixture into tofu. Chill 1 to 2 hours, to allow flavors to meld. Refrigerate any leftovers. Will keep 3 to 4 days.
- Prepare lettuce and tomatoes, refrigerate while cooking waffles.
- Meanwhile, prepare a **double** batch of waffle batter, add cumin and mustard, stirring just until blended. Cook waffles as directed, let cool slightly.
- Assemble clubs by spreading small amount of mayo over 2 waffles. Alternate layers of lettuce, tomato and tofuna on 1 waffle. Repeat, cover with other waffle (good looking side up) and serve immediately.

Yield: 6 servings

* White Wave® makes an excellent one.

Garden of Eat'n Burgers

1/4 cup vegetable stock (p. 8)
2 large cloves garlic, minced
1/2 cup sweet onion (such as Vidalia), diced
1/2 cup green bell pepper, diced
1/3 cup carrot, diced
3 tablespoons natural barbeque sauce*
2 tablespoons liquid aminos
1/4 teaspoon hot pepper sauce

~

1 cup cooked garbanzo beans
1 cup cooked brown rice

~

1/2 cup rolled oats (not instant)
1/3 cup raw sunflower seeds, chopped
2 tablespoons unhulled sesame seeds
2 tablespoons freshly squeezed lemon juice
1 1/2 teaspoons poultry seasoning
2 tablespoons fresh dill, snipped
1/2 to 2/3 cup fresh or leftover mashed potatoes

~

1/3 cup whole grain stone ground yellow cornmeal

- In medium heavy-bottomed skillet, bring stock to boil, add garlic and onion. Sauté, stirring frequently, until soft, about 4 minutes. Add bell pepper, carrot, barbeque sauce, liquid aminos and hot pepper sauce. Reduce heat, cover and simmer until pepper and carrot are tender, about 5 to 7 minutes.
- Mash garbanzos and rice together in medium bowl, or pulse-chop in food processor, until mixture resembles lumpy mashed potatoes.
- In coffee grinder or spice mill, grind oats slightly, soak in 1/2 cup water, 5 minutes. Drain oats in mesh sieve, pressing with back of spoon to remove excess water.
- In large mixing bowl, combine garbanzo mixture, oats, sunflower seeds and all remaining ingredients, except burger buns.
- Preheat oven to 400° F. Lightly oil baking sheet. Note: omit this step if using non-stick baking sheet.
- Shape mixture into 4 inch diameter (1/2 inch thick) patties, adding extra mashed potatoes, if needed, for patties to hold their shape; coat patties in cornmeal, place on prepared baking sheet. Bake until golden, about 15 minutes each side. If you prefer a crispier texture, grill or broil burgers 2 to 3 minutes per side, after baking.

Yield: 8 burgers

These heart-healthy burgers are chock full of wholesome veggies, beans, grains and seeds; mashed potatoes help bind them together.

Make extra to freeze for a quick, nourishing lunch on the run [bake before freezing].

Serve on a Honey-Wheat bun [see side bar p. 40] with your favorite toppings and a side of Pesto Pasta Salad [p. 150].

---

* Annie's™ Smokey Maple Barbeque Sauce is my favorite.

Anasazi Bean Burgers

3 teaspoons extra-virgin olive oil
$\frac{3}{4}$ cup sweet onion (such as Vidalia), diced
2 large cloves garlic, minced
$\frac{1}{2}$ cup orange or yellow bell pepper, diced
1 small jalapeño or serrano chile pepper, seeded and minced

~

1 cup cooked Anasazi* beans, mashed
1 cup cooked quinoa
$\frac{1}{3}$ cup whole grain stone ground yellow cornmeal
2 teaspoons ground cumin
1 teaspoon dried summer savory
1 teaspoon chili powder

~

$\frac{1}{3}$ cup whole grain stone ground yellow cornmeal

These pretty cranberry-color beans with creamy-white spots were named for the Anasazi Indians and the painted ponies they rode. According to legend, the beans were discovered in ancient Anasazi burial chambers. Today they are grown and cultivated in several states.

Anasazis have a sweet flavor and contain a higher amount of protein than some of the more familiar varieties of dried beans.

Serve on a Honey-Wheat Bun [see side bar p. 40] with Southwest Chile Pesto [p. 79] and a side of Squaw Salad [p. 167] for a protein-packed lunch or lite dinner fare.

- In medium heavy-bottomed skillet, heat oil, sauté onion and garlic, stirring frequently, until soft, about 4 minutes, add bell and chile peppers, cook 3 minutes. Remove pan from heat.
- Mash beans and quinoa together in medium bowl, or pulse-chop in food processor until mixture resembles lumpy mashed potatoes.
- Preheat oven to 375° F. Lightly oil baking sheet.
  Note: omit this step if using non-stick baking sheet.
- In large bowl, combine sautéed veggies, bean mixture and all remaining ingredients, except cornmeal, stirring to blend.
- Shape mixture into 4 inch diameter ($\frac{1}{2}$ inch thick) patties, coat in cornmeal, place on prepared baking sheet. Bake until golden, about 15 minutes each side. If you prefer a crispier texture, grill or broil burgers 2 to 3 minutes per side, after baking.

Yield: 6 burgers

* If Anasazi beans aren't available, substitute pinto beans.

Baba Ganouj Pockets

2 large eggplant (about 2½ pounds)
juice of 1 large freshly squeezed lemon
3 to 4 large cloves garlic, minced
¼ cup tahini
2 teaspoons sweet Hungarian paprika
1 tablespoon ground cumin
1 tablespoon liquid aminos
2 tablespoons fresh mint, chopped
1 tablespoon Harissa (p. 68), optional
~
8 whole grain pita pockets

- Preheat broiler. Lightly oil broiler pan.
- Scrub eggplant, cut in half lengthwise. Lay eggplant, cut side down, on prepared broiler pan, broil until skins are charred and puffy, 12 to 14 minutes. Using oven mitts, transfer eggplant to wire rack. When cool enough to handle, scoop pulp and seeds from skins, using large metal spoon.
- In food processor, combine eggplant and all remaining ingredients, process until smooth.
- Spread Baba Ganouj inside pita pockets, stuff with fresh spinach or lettuce, tomato slices and your choice of sprouts.

Yield: 8 servings

A Middle Eastern spread that's a snap to prepare.

Eggplant is mainly carbohydrate, containing zero fat, high in niacin and potassium.

Serve as an appetizer with crudités or crackers.

Garden Patch Bagels
with Creamy Cucumber Dill Dressing

Over a decade ago, Americans began their love affair with the lowly bagel. This recipe elevates it to star status where it really shines.

Tomatoes are the #1 source of lycopene, a red pigment and strong antioxidant that provides overall bodily protection.

Onions are high in quercetin, a bioflavonoid and formidable antioxidant. Studies have shown quercetin to be anti-inflammatory, antiviral, anticancer and antibacterial, as well as helpful in blocking the formation of blood clots.

Avocados are rich in folic acid, a B vitamin that helps rid the body of homocystine. High levels of this amino acid have been linked to heart disease; also high in beta carotene, a potent antioxidant and magnesium, which helps regulate blood pressure and keeps the heart healthy.

Serve with a bowl of chilled Garden Gazpacho soup [p. 212] for a cool, refreshing summer lunch.

1 large beefsteak-style tomato, sliced thick
1 medium red onion, sliced thin
2 ripe (but firm) Haas avocados, sliced thick
4 leaves red leaf lettuce
4 whole grain bagels
~
Creamy Cucumber Dill Dressing (p. 71)
1 cup fresh sprouts (such as aduki, clover, mung or sunflower)

- Prepare tomato and onion as directed.
- Cut avocados in half lengthwise, remove pit. Holding avocado in palm of hand, cut into slices taking care not to cut through shell. Carefully work a tablespoon between avocado and skin to separate slices (if avocado is just ripe enough, this will be easy to accomplish.)
  Helpful Tip: select avocados that are ripe (slightly firm, not mushy) with dark purple-black shells. If avocados are bright green and hard, let ripen on counter 2 to 3 days, before using.
- Rinse and dry lettuce in salad spinner or pat dry with paper towel. Cut bagels in half and toast, if desired.
- Assemble garden bagels by alternating layers of lettuce, tomato and avocado on bottom half of bagel, add a few sprouts. Drizzle dressing over sprouts and top with other bagel half. Cut in half and serve.

Yield: 4 servings

Reuben James

Asian Marinade (p. 74)
8 ounces frozen tempeh, thawed
~
Thousand Island Dressing (p. 71)
~
3 teaspoons extra-virgin olive oil
~
8 thick slices pumpernickel rye bread
1½ cups prepared sauerkraut, drained
2 large beefsteak-style tomatoes, sliced thick
8 pieces mozzarella-style cheese alternative, sliced thin

- Prepare **half** of marinade as directed.
- In a 2-cup measure, prepare dressing as directed. Refrigerate until ready to use.
- Slice tempeh in half crosswise, cut in half again (like cutting a cake into layers), to give you 4 pieces about the size of a slice of bread. Marinate tempeh, 20 minutes.
- In large cast-iron skillet, heat oil, over medium heat, braise tempeh until golden, about 4 minutes each side.
- Assemble reubens by alternating layers of braised tempeh, sauerkraut and sliced tomato on a piece of bread. Drizzle dressing over tomatoes, top with 2 slices of cheese.
- Microwave on high, 30 to 40 seconds, top with other bread slice. Serve immediately.

Yield: 4 servings

Reubens are traditionally made with corned beef. Here tempeh, a fermented, high-protein, low-fat soy food replaces the beef. Marinating tempeh produces a tantalizing flavor.

Accompany with a cup of Potato Leek Pottage [p. 215] or a side of Oven Roasted Potatoes [p. 200]. For dessert, serve up a dish of Orange Quinoa Pudding [p. 113].

Note: if desired, the marinade and dressing can be prepared ahead and refrigerated until ready to use.

Sloppy Josettes

8 Honey Wheat Buns (see side bar, p. 40)
~
2 cups texturized vegetable protein granules (see Glossary)
1 3/4 cups Savory Garlic Broth (p. 8)
~
1 tablespoon extra-virgin olive oil
2 large cloves garlic, minced
1 cup onion, diced
3/4 cup green bell pepper, diced
1 fresh mild green chile pepper, seeded and finely chopped
~
1 1/2 cups Herbed Pomadoro Sauce (p. 86)
1 teaspoon dried basil
1 teaspoon Italian seasoning (p. 68)
1 teaspoon mild chili powder
2 to 3 teaspoons brown rice syrup, to taste
2 tablespoons liquid aminos mixed with
2 tablespoons red hatcho miso

- Make buns ahead, as directed.
- In medium bowl, combine texturized vegetable protein and 1 1/2 cups hot broth (reserve remainder), let soak 15 minutes to reconstitute, drain and reserve any remaining broth. Set aside.
- In large wide-bottomed skillet, heat oil, over medium heat, sauté garlic, onion and peppers until tender, 4 to 6 minutes.
- Add texturized vegetable protein and all remaining ingredients to sautéed veggies, stirring to blend. Bring mixture to boil, reduce heat, simmer 5 minutes. Remove pan from heat.
  Note: if mixture seems thick, add reserved broth, a little at a time, until desired consistency is achieved.
- Split buns in half, arrange open-face on plate, ladle sloppy josette mixture over top. Serve warm.

Yield: 8 servings

A new twist on an old favorite. Kids and adults alike will love this tasty, updated, heart-healthy version.

TVP [texturized vegetable protein], a soy-based food resembling ground meat in chewiness and texture, is terrific here. In addition to providing high-quality protein, soy is a rich source of isoflavone compounds that may reduce your risk of heart disease and some cancers.

Miso, fermented soy-food, is nutritionally superior. Its smooth taste helps mellow the sharp edge of the chile pepper.

Mesquite Summer Grill
with Basil Spinach Pesto

1 cup Zorba The Greek dressing (p. 73)
1½ cups mesquite pods*
~
6 (2 inch diameter) yellow crookneck squash, cut into ½ inch rounds
2 large red bell peppers, cut into ½ inch strips
6 medium portabella mushroom caps, cut into ½ inch slices
1 jumbo sweet onion (such as Maui or Vidalia), cut into thick rounds
~
8 leaves butter bibb or red-leaf lettuce
2 large beefsteak-style tomatoes, sliced
~
2 12-ounce sourdough baguettes**
1½ cups Basil Spinach Pesto (p. 78)

- In a 2-cup measure, prepare dressing as directed. Refrigerate until ready to use.
- Boil mesquite pods for 5 minutes in microwave or on stove top. Drain.
- Meanwhile, prepare squash and next 3 ingredients as directed. Transfer veggies to large shallow pan, pour dressing over veggies and marinate 40 minutes, turning occasionally.
- Heat gas or charcoal grill on high. Remove grilling rack. When coals are hot, place mesquite pods on top of coals (mesquite will start to smolder), reposition rack. Using slotted spoon, transfer marinated veggies to wire grilling basket (reserve marinade). Place basket on grill rack, close lid, cook 4 to 6 minutes. Turn basket, drizzle reserved marinade over veggies, continue grilling until tender, 4 to 6 minutes.
  Note: grilling in a basket makes turning easier and prevents veggies falling through grill rack.
- Assemble sandwiches by cutting baguettes in half lengthwise. Spread pesto over cut side of baguettes. Alternate layers of grilled veggies, lettuce and tomatoes over two baguette halves, top with remaining halves, cut in half crosswise and serve.

Yield: 4 servings

Basil Spinach Pesto is the crowning glory of this exotic grilled summer fare. Mesquite imparts a delicious, spicy-smoked flavor to the vegetables.

The mesquite pod is the fruit of the Mesquite tree which contains a sweet pulp.

Accompany with roasted corn-on-the-cob for an out-of-this-world cookout. End the meal with a slice of Peach Melba Croustade [p. 111] under the stars.

* Sold in hardware stores, home and garden specialty stores, as well as some supermarkets.

** Long loaves of French bread.

Sides

"There is no disease, bodily or mental, which adoption of vegetable diet and pure water has not infallibly mitigated, wherever the experiment has been fairly tried."

Percy Bysshe Shelley, Queen Mab, 1813

Cucumber Mint Raita

3 teaspoons ground cumin
1/2 teaspoon sea salt
2 large cucumbers, peeled, seeded and coarsely grated
2 cups yogurt, dairy-free
2 teaspoons brown rice syrup
pinch cayenne pepper
2 tablespoons fresh mint, minced
2 teaspoons freshly squeezed lemon juice

- In medium bowl, combine all ingredients, stirring to blend. Chill raita 1 hour before serving.

Yield: 4 to 6 servings

Serve with Curry-In-A-Hurry [p. 144] and Saffron Scented Rice [recipe follows].

Saffron Scented Rice
with Peas

2 teaspoons extra-virgin olive oil
1/2 cup onion, diced
3 1/2 cups vegetable stock (p. 8)
2 inch square fresh orange peel
generous pinch saffron threads
~
2 cups uncooked brown basmati rice
1 cup fresh or frozen green peas
1/4 teaspoon ground cinnamon
1/8 teaspoon ground cloves
1/4 teaspoon ground cardamom
1/2 teaspoon sea salt
2 teaspoons brown rice syrup

- In 2 quart saucepan, heat oil, over medium heat, sauté onion until tender, 4 to 5 minutes. Add stock, orange peel and saffron, bring to boil. Reduce heat, simmer, 2 to 3 minute.

- Add rice and all remaining ingredients to pan, stirring to blend. Cover, simmer until rice is tender and liquid is absorbed, 25 to 30 minutes. Discard orange peel, fluff rice with fork. Serve warm.

Yield: 4 to 6 servings

Saffron imparts a delicate yellow color and orange peel lends warm citrus overtones to this delectable rice dish.

Basmati [literally translates to "queen of fragrance"] rice has a wonderful perfumy aroma and nutty flavor.

Variation: make Green Papaya Rice by omitting the orange peel and peas, and adding 1 cup green papaya, peeled, seeded and coarsely chopped.

Quinoa and Wild Rice Avocados

A favorite with my cooking classes—sure to win rave reviews!

The much-maligned avocado is a natural source of lecithin, a brain food. Over 80 percent of its caloric content is easily digested fat in the form of monounsaturated fat which helps lower the buildup of LDL [bad cholesterol]. Avocados are one of the richest sources of the antioxidant glutathione which helps block the absorption of harmful fat in the intestinal tract. The folic acid [a B vitamin] in avocados, helps stimulate red blood cell production.

Quinoa is a complete-protein grain, similar to millet. High in iron and calcium, quick-cooking quinoa is ready in 20 minutes.

Wild rice has a delicate nutty flavor and contains more protein and vitamins than regular rice.

For light summer fare, serve these terrific-tasting avocados for a special luncheon. Accompany with chilled Garden Gazpacho soup [p. 212] or Red Pepper Velouté [p. 217] for cooler weather.

3/4 cup cooked quinoa
3/4 cup cooked wild rice
2 medium Roma tomatoes, seeded and chopped
3 teaspoons ground cumin
2 tablespoons fresh basil, snipped or 2 teaspoons dried
1 tablespoon fresh flat-leaf Italian parsley, snipped
1/2 cup pitted black olives, chopped
2 tablespoons capers, drained and chopped
~
1/2 cup pine nuts, toasted (p.10)
1/2 cup Zorba The Greek dressing (p. 73)
6 ripe (but firm) Haas avocados
~
1 bunch fresh salad savoy or kale, for garnish

- In medium bowl, combine quinoa, rice and next 6 ingredients, stirring to blend.
- Add pine nuts and 1/4 cup dressing (reserve remainder) to quinoa-rice mixture, stirring to blend.
- Peel avocados, cut in half lengthwise, remove and discard pit. Cut 1/4 inch slice off rounded bottom to prevent avocado from sliding off plate. Spoon filling into cavaties, mounding over top. With pastry brush, baste perimeter and sides of avocado with reserved dressing to prevent browning.
- Rinse salad savoy or kale thoroughly to dislodge sand particles, repeat, if necessary. Spin leaves until dry or pat with paper towel, spread out over large platter or serving tray. Set avocados on savoy, cover with plastic wrap. Chill 1 hour before serving.

Yield: 6 servings

Thai Rice Bake
with Lemon Grass and Basil

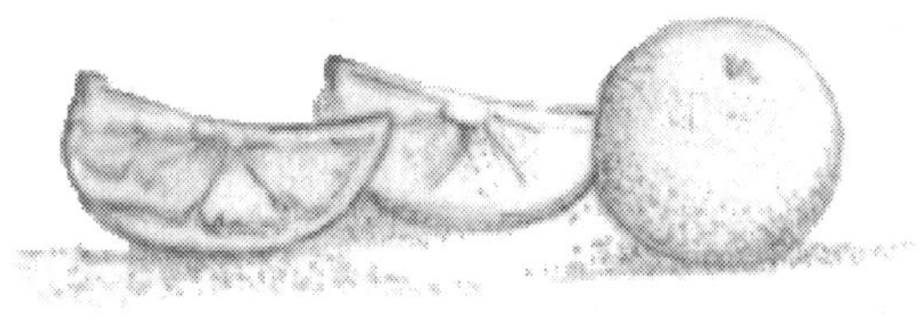

½ cup wild rice
~
2 teaspoons extra-virgin olive oil
⅓ cup leeks, chopped (include some green)
~
1 cup long-grain brown rice
1 medium bay leaf
3 tablespoons fresh Thai basil leaves,* snipped
1 teaspoon lemon grass*
3 tablespoons freshly squeezed lemon juice
2 teaspoons lemon zest
2 teaspoons Spicy Thai® Chili Sauce
¼ teaspoon white pepper
3 cups vegetable stock (p. 8)

- Soak wild rice overnight in tepid water (be sure to cover with plenty of water as wild rice expands considerably when soaked). Drain soaking water. In medium saucepan, partially cook rice in 1½ cups fresh water, about 15 minutes. Drain remaining water.
- Preheat oven to 400° F. Lightly oil a 3-quart casserole dish. Set aside.
- In a 4-quart saucepan, heat oil, over medium heat, sauté leeks until soft, 4 to 6 minutes.
- Rinse brown rice briefly (in mesh sieve) under running water to remove any dust particles.
  Note: rinsing the rice also removes excess starch, yielding rice that is light and fluffy.
- Combine wild and brown rice with sautéed leeks and all remaining ingredients, in prepared casserole dish, cover.
- Bake until rice is tender and liquid is absorbed, 45 minutes to 1 hour. Remove bay leaf, fluff rice with fork. Serve warm or chilled.

Yield: 6 to 8 servings

---

* Available in Asian markets and some supermarkets.

In Bangkok, basil is an integral part of everyday cooking. The leaves of Thai basil have a concentrated lemon fragrance and flavor that comingles clear, sweet lemon with basils' perfume.

Lemon grass is a deliciously delicate and fragrant herb used in a vast array of Thai and Southeast Asian dishes.

Wild rice is actually a grain with twice as much protein as white rice and more niacin, riboflavin, iron and phosphorus than brown rice.

Brown rice is an excellent source of minerals [potassium, phosphorus and magnesium], B vitamins [folacin, niacin and thiamine] and vitamin E. It is also high in fiber which helps prevent colon cancer and boosts the immune system.

Cranberry Wheatberry Pilaf

Special enough for the holidays, this festive whole grain dish is a delicious and satisfying potpourri of flavors and textures. Celery and walnuts add a tantalizing crunchiness.

Wheatberries are whole, unprocessed wheat kernels, high in vitamins A, B, C and E, protein, iron, magnesium, potassium and zinc.

Amaranth contains an excellent balance of amino acids and boasts a higher amount of perfect protein than whole wheat, corn, soybeans or cows milk. High in fiber, amaranth also packs a wallop of calcium.

Terrific with Honey-Glazed Acorn Rings [p. 196], Hickory Grilled Portabellas [p. 128] and E-Z Tarragon Rolls [p 41]. End the meal on a sweet note with a slice of Apricot Glazed Carrot Cake [p. 92].

1/2 cup dried cranberries
1/3 cup dried currants
1/2 cup natural apple cider
~
3 teaspoons walnut oil
1 cup uncooked amaranth
2 1/2 cups cooked wheatberries*
2 3/4 cups vegetable stock (p. 8)
3 tablespoons mellow white miso mixed with
1/4 cup freshly squeezed orange juice
1/2 teaspoon ground cinnamon
~
1/3 cup scallions, chopped (include some green)
2 medium ribs celery, diagonally sliced
1/2 cup walnut pieces, toasted (p.10)

- In small saucepan, combine cranberries, currants and cider, bring to boil, reduce heat. Cover, simmer until fruit has absorbed most of liquid, about 4 to 6 minutes. Drain, set aside.
- Preheat oven to 350° F. Lightly oil a 3-quart casserole dish.
- Rinse amaranth briefly (in mesh sieve) under running water. Shake out excess water. Toast amaranth in large heavy-bottomed saucepan, over medium heat, stirring constantly, until fragrant and seeds begin to pop, about 4 to 6 minutes.
- Combine wheatberries and next 4 ingredients with amaranth, bring mixture to boil. Remove pan from heat, add cranberries and currants, stirring to blend, transfer to prepared dish, cover.
- Bake until liquid is absorbed, about 30 minutes.
- Meanwhile, prepare scallions, celery and walnuts as directed. Set aside.
- Remove dish from oven, add scallions, celery and walnuts, tossing to blend. Serve warm or chilled.

Yield: 4 servings

* Wheatberries can be cooked in advance and refrigerated until ready to use. If frozen, will keep up to 3 months.

Cornmeal Dumplings

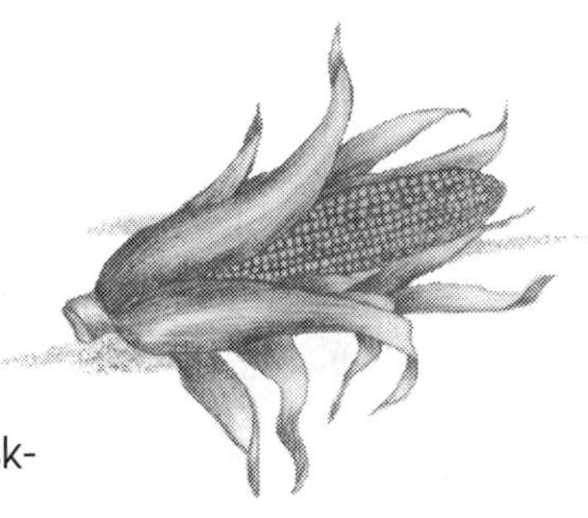

1 cup whole grain stone ground yellow cornmeal
1 teaspoon Gomasio (p. 67)
1 teaspoon aluminum-free baking powder
10 ounces low-fat extra-firm silken tofu

- In medium bowl, combine cornmeal, Gomasio and baking powder, whisking to blend. Set aside.
- Add tofu to blender or food processor, process just until smooth and creamy. In medium bowl, combine tofu and cornmeal mixture, beating until blended.
- Drop batter, by rounded tablespoons, into simmering chili or 4 cups mushroom stock(p. 8). Cover, simmer over medium heat, 10 to 15 minutes. Helpful Tip: to test for doneness, remove a dumpling from pan, cut a small slice off one end, inside should resemble texture of bread.

Yield: 14 dumplings

These savory dumplings go great with Scorned Woman Chili [p. 139].

Acropolis Pilaf

Pasta [orzo] and grain [millet] team up to create a marriage of delicious tastes and textures.

Greek oregano's intense, spicy flavor complements tomato dishes. Known to chefs the world over as "the pizza herb," oregano adds robust flavor and aroma to this savory dish from the sunny Mediterranean.

The ancient Greek philosopher Pythagoras encouraged his followers to eat millet to improve their health and vitality. Millet is high in iron, magnesium, phosphorus, potassium and choline which helps control cholesterol levels. Unlike other grains, millet is alkalizing in nature, making it soothing and easy to digest.

1 cup millet
1 tablespoon liquid aminos
4¼ cups Savory Garlic Broth (p. 8)
1 cup orzo pasta
~
⅓ cup pitted Kalamata olives, chopped
1 cup beefsteak-style tomatoes, seeded and coarsely chopped
3 tablespoons fresh Greek oregano leaves, snipped
2 tablespoons freshly squeezed lemon juice
2 tablespoons extra-virgin olive oil
¼ teaspoon sea salt
½ teaspoon freshly ground pepper
3 tablespoons Basil Spinach Pesto (p. 78)

- Toast millet in large saucepan, over medium heat, stirring constantly, until it gives off a nutlike aroma, 3 to 4 minutes, add liquid aminos and stock, bring to boil, reduce heat. Cover, simmer 15 minutes.
- Stir orzo into millet. Cover, continue simmering until liquid is absorbed, about 10 to 15 minutes. Remove pan from heat, stir in all remaining ingredients, let stand 10 minutes before serving.

Yield: 4 to 6 servings

Mom's Baked Beans

Growing up, these savory beans were one of my favorite comfort foods. Mom's fabulous baked beans were known for miles around. This heart-healthy version, eliminates the bacon and brown sugar from the original recipe while kombu and miso lend flavor and richness to the beans.

Dried beans [members of the legume family] are high in protein, iron, calcium, potassium and fiber and low in fat. Pound for pound and dollar for dollar, legumes are an excellent nutritional value.

Kombu [a sea vegetable] is extremely rich in minerals and helps balance the protein in the beans while increasing their digestibility.

2 cups dried Great Northern beans
6-inch strip kombu
~
1 cup onion, diced
3/4 cup celery, diced
~
1 cup reserved bean liquid
1 tablespoon vegetarian Worcestershire sauce
1/2 cup cinnamon apple butter (p. 65)
2 tablespoons balsamic vinegar
2/3 cup natural chili sauce, honey sweetened
3 teaspoons honey mustard
2 teaspoons celery seeds, crushed
1 1/2 teaspoons dried summer savory
1/8 teaspoon natural liquid hickory smoke, optional
2 tablespoons red hatcho miso
3 tablespoons unbleached flour with germ
2 tablespoons soy bacon bits*

- Soak beans overnight, drain soaking water.
- In large stockpot, bring 6 cups water, beans and kombu to rolling boil, reduce heat. Cook beans until tender, about 45 minutes, remove and discard kombu. Drain beans (reserve 1 cup cooking liquid).
- Stir onion and celery into beans.
- Preheat oven to 350° F. Lightly oil a 3-quart casserole dish.
- In small bowl, stir reserved cooking liquid and all remaining ingredients into bean mixture, transfer to prepared casserole dish, cover.
- Bake 1 hour, uncover, bake an additional 15 minutes until bubbly. Serve warm.

Yield: 6 to 8 servings

---

* Lightlife Foods® makes a delicious bacon substitute, 100 percent natural, vegetarian and low in sodium with zero cholesterol.

Beets Normandy

1 bunch beets (about 4 or 5 medium)
~
3 tablespoons balsamic vinegar
2 teaspoons freshly squeezed lemon juice
2 to 3 teaspoons brown rice syrup, to taste
1½ teaspoons herbal seasoning (p. 66) or fresh dill, snipped
1 tablespoon raw carrot, grated

- Scrub beets (do not peel), remove leaves and stems leaving about 1 inch of stem intact (reserve leaves for making Sautéed Greens with Apple and Currants, p. 194), cut into chunks. Wash cutting board immediately to prevent staining from beet juice. Steam beets until tender when pierced with fork, about 20 to 25 minutes.
Note: young beets will take less time to cook.
- Transfer beets to colander, rinse briefly under cold water (skins will slip off easily with gentle rubbing), cut into ½ inch cubes, transfer to medium serving bowl.
- In a 2-cup measure, whisk vinegar and all remaining ingredients together. Pour vinaigrette over beets, tossing to coat, garnish center with grated carrot.

Yield: 4 servings

Deliciously simple. Even people not fond of beets will love this terrific rendition!

Like their cousin, the carrot, beets are high in natural sugar, iron, potassium, copper and vitamin C.

Brussels Almondine

1 pound Brussel sprouts
~
3 large cloves garlic, minced
1 tablespoon vegetarian Worcestershire sauce
1 tablespoon Dijon-style mustard
1 teaspoon prepared horseradish
2 tablespoons freshly squeezed lemon juice
1 tablespoon fresh tarragon, snipped or 1 teaspoon dried
¼ teaspoon freshly ground pepper
2 tablespoons mellow barley miso
½ cup Savory Garlic Broth (p. 8)
⅓ cup slivered almonds

- Trim ends of sprouts, remove any yellowed leaves. Using a paring knife, cut an "X" in bottom of each sprout for faster cooking. Steam sprouts until barely tender when pierced with fork, 10 to 12 minutes, drain.
- Meanwhile, in blender, combine all remaining ingredients, except almonds, process until smooth.
- Transfer sprouts to medium serving dish, pour vinaigrette over top, tossing to coat, garnish with almonds. Serve warm or room temperature.

Yield: 4 to 6 servings

I've become a devotee of this piquant dish since discovering the zesty mustard-tarragon vinaigrette. A perfect accent for the earthy flavor of the Brussel sprouts.

Brussel sprouts [a member of the crucifer family] are nearly half protein. Recently heralded for their potential ability to reduce cancer, Brussel sprouts are loaded with vitamins A and C, folic acid [an important B vitamin], phosphorus, potassium, magnesium and iron.

Lemon Dill Green Beans

16 ounces fresh green beans
~
2 tablespoons freshly squeezed lemon juice
1 teaspoon lemon zest
2 teaspoons expeller-pressed canola oil
2 teaspoons umeboshi vinegar
2 tablespoons fresh dill, snipped or 2 teaspoons dried

- Trim bean ends and cut into 2 inch pieces, steam until tender, 8 to 10 minutes.
- Whisk lemon juice and all remaining ingredients together, pour over beans, tossing to coat. Serve warm or room temperature.

Yield: 4 servings

Sautéed Greens
with Apple and Currants

Nutritious greens, so often overlooked, are versatile, easy to cook and a joy to eat.

Beet greens give this dish a pretty pink hue. Contrasting flavors of sweet [apple and currant] and bitter [beet greens] create a harmonious balance of Yin and Yang.

Beet greens are high in vitamin A, iron, calcium and folic acid [an important B vitamin] which helps rid the body of homocystine, an amino acid. High levels of homocystine have been linked to heart disease.

1½ pounds fresh beet greens
1 teaspoon garlic, minced
3 teaspoons extra-virgin olive oil
1 cup tart apple (such as Granny Smith), peeled, seeded and chopped
3 tablespoons dried currants
⅓ cup apple juice concentrate, undiluted

- Wash greens thoroughly to dislodge any dirt or sand particles, repeat, if necessary. Cut out stems and discard. Pile several leaves on top of each other, roll tightly into cigar shape, slice crosswise into ½ inch ribbons.
- In large wide-bottomed skillet, bring 2 cups water and ¼ teaspoon sea salt to rapid boil, add greens. Cover, blanch 5 minutes, stirring occasionally, drain.
- Add all remaining ingredients to skillet, sauté, stirring occasionally, until apples are tender, 4 to 6 minutes. Serve warm or room temperature.

Yield: 4 servings

Couscous Filled Orange Blossom Cups

zest from 1 navel orange
4 jumbo navel oranges
~
3 teaspoons walnut oil
2/3 cup sweet onion (such as Vidalia or Walla Walla), diced
1 1/2 cups whole wheat couscous (see Glossary)
2 cups vegetable stock (p. 8)
2 tablespoons brown rice syrup
1/2 cup golden raisins
2 whole cinnamon sticks
1/4 teaspoon sea salt
1/4 to 1/2 teaspoon Five Spice powder, to taste
2 teaspoons curry powder (p. 66)
1/3 cup fresh mint, chopped
~
1/2 cup carrot, diced
1/2 cup celery diced
1/3 cup raw pinenuts, toasted (p.10)
~
1 1/2 teaspoons crystallized ginger, finely chopped
fresh mint sprigs

- Remove zest from 1 orange using zesting tool or fine-holed grater. Cut all 4 oranges in half crosswise (reserve **2 halves** for juicing). Slice off rounded ends from remaining halves to prevent oranges from sliding off plate. Using a sharp paring knife, carefully carve orange segments from all 6 halves, cut segments into bite-size pieces. Remove as much pith (white portion) from the peel as possible, leaving shell intact.
- In medium saucepan, heat oil, over medium heat, sauté onion until soft and translucent, 4 to 6 minutes, add couscous and next 8 ingredients, bring to boil, stirring frequently to prevent sticking, reduce heat to lowest setting. Cover, simmer 5 minutes. Remove pan from heat, let stand until liquid is absorbed and raisins are plump, about 5 minutes. Uncover, discard cinnamon sticks, let couscous cool to room temperature.
- In large bowl, combine couscous mixture, carrot, celery, pinenuts, crystallized ginger, orange zest and pieces, tossing to blend.
- Spoon filling into orange shells, garnish with mint sprigs. Serve chilled or room temperature.

Yield: 6 servings

Tantalizing citrus overtones blend with sweet raisins, zesty spices and refreshing mint to lend vibrant flavor to this exotic Middle Eastern side dish.

The whole wheat variety of couscous has a light brown color, slightly nutty flavor and higher nutritive value than regular couscous.

Carrot, celery and pinenuts provide a good dose of protein, vitamins and crunch.

For a special presentation, serve for brunch or dinner with Hickory Grilled Portabellas [p. 128] and Cucumber Mint Raita [p. 187]. For dessert, savor the flavor of exotic Coconut Mango Sorbet [p. 115].

Summer Squash Medley with Limas and Millet

1½ cups millet
2 tablespoons liquid aminos
4½ cups vegetable stock (p. 8)
~
2 cups unpeeled zucchini squash, cut into bite-size pieces
2 cups unpeeled yellow crookneck squash, cut into bite-size pieces
1½ cups cooked lima beans
2 tablespoons fresh chives, snipped
2 tablespoons fresh summer savory, snipped or 2 teaspoons dried
2 tablespoons balsamic vinegar
1½ tablespoons extra-virgin olive oil
½ teaspoon freshly ground pepper

A powerhouse of nutrition, fiber and protein. Lima beans and millet are highly alkalizing, excellent for neutralizing excess acid in the body.

Serve with a salad of crisp spinach, tangy Romaine lettuce and Creamy Cucumber Dill Dressing [p. 71].

- Toast millet in large saucepan, over medium heat, stirring constantly until millet gives off a nutlike aroma, 3 to 4 minutes, add liquid aminos and stock, bring to boil, reduce heat. Cover, simmer 30 minutes. Remove pan from heat, keep warm.
- Meanwhile, scrub squash and prepare as directed, steam just until crisp-tender, about 4 to 6 minutes (do not over cook). Drain in colander, transfer to large serving bowl.
- Combine all remaining ingredients with squash, stirring to blend. Ladle mixture over millet.

Yield: 6 servings

Honey Glazed Acorn Rings

Easy to prepare, these savory-sweet rings afford a bold, colorful presentation.

Like other varieties of winter squash, acorns are low in calories and high in antioxidant carotenoids, known cancer fighters.

2 medium acorn squash (about 2½ pounds)
~
2 tablespoons extra-virgin olive oil
2 tablespoons honey
2 teaspoons ground cinnamon
½ teaspoon freshly ground nutmeg

- Preheat oven to 375° F. Lightly oil baking sheet.
- Scrub squash, cut crosswise into ½ inch rings (do not peel), remove and discard seeds. Arrange rings on prepared baking sheet.
- Prepare glaze in 1-cup measure by combining all remaining ingredients, brush glaze over top of acorn rings.
- Bake until tender when pierced with fork, 35 to 40 minutes.

Yield: 6 servings

E-Z Beanz and Greenz

3 pounds collards*
1 medium red onion, slivered
2 cups cooked cannellini (white kidney) beans
~
2 tablespoons umeboshi vinegar
2 tablespoons freshly squeezed lemon juice
1/4 cup vegetable stock (p. 8)
2 tablespoons mellow barley miso
1 tablespoon extra-virgin olive oil
2 teaspoons Dijon-style mustard
~
2 tablespoons unhulled sesame seeds

- Rinse collards thoroughly to dislodge any dirt or sand particles, repeat, if necessary. Cut center rib from between leaf. Pile several leaves on top of each other, roll tightly into cigar shape, slice crosswise into 1/2 inch ribbons.
- In large wide-bottomed skillet, bring 3 cups water and 1/4 teaspoon sea salt to rapid boil, add greens. Cover, blanch 5 minutes, stirring occasionally, add onions, blanch an additional 2 minutes. Remove pan from heat, drain. Add beans to greens, stirring to blend, transfer to medium serving dish.
- In a 2-cup measure, whisk together all dressing ingredients, pour over beans and collards, tossing to coat, sprinkle sesame seeds over top. Best served at room temperature.

Yield: 6 servings

* Mustard greens or escarole can be used in place of collards, if desired.

This traditional Southern dish is simple, nourishing, satisfying and vibrant. The dark green of the collards contrasts beautifully with the white of the beans and the red of the onion.

Cannellini beans, popular in Italian dishes, are high in iron, potassium and calcium.

Mild-tasting collards are a member of the cabbage family. One cup of collards contains more calcium than a cup of cows milk, also high in vitamin A, iron, potassium and zinc.

Umeboshi vinegar, made from umeboshi plums, gives this dressing its unusual piquant flavor. Highly alkalizing, umeboshi plums are commonly used in Japan to treat digestive upset.

Pineapple Glazed Carrots

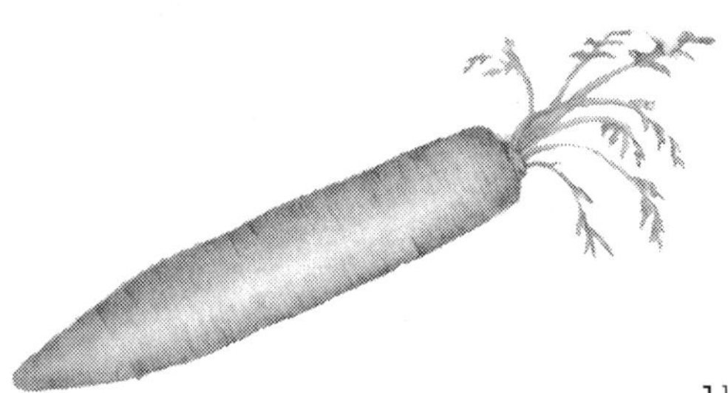

4 cups carrot, diagonally sliced
1 tablespoon kudzu dissolved in
$^3/_4$ cup pineapple juice, unsweetened
2 tablespoons honey mustard
2 tablespoons honey
$^1/_4$ teaspoon sea salt
$^1/_4$ teaspoon Five Spice powder
~
1 $^1/_2$ cups fresh pineapple, cut into bite-size chunks
$^1/_3$ cup unsweetened coconut, optional

Guaranteed, kids and adults will love these terrific-tasting carrots.

The zesty pineapple-mustard glaze lends a sunny tropical taste to this easy-to-prepare side dish. Equally delicious served with bland or tangy foods.

Carrots are a power house of vitamin A, good for supporting skin health and immune protection.

Pineapple contains bromelain, a digestive enzyme, that produces anti-inflammatory action in the body. Vitamins A and C are also present in pineapple as well as calcium and manganese.

- Prepare carrots as directed, steam until crisp-tender, about 12 to 14 minutes, drain. Set aside.
- In medium saucepan, combine all remaining ingredients, except pineapple and coconut, bring to boil, over medium heat, stirring constantly. Reduce heat, continue stirring until thickened and clear, about 2 to 3 minutes.
- Combine carrot, glaze, pineapple and coconut in medium serving bowl, tossing to coat.

Yield: 4 servings

Baked Acorn Boats
with Apple Pear Purée

2 medium acorn or butternut squash (about 2½ pounds)
juice of 1 freshly squeezed lemon
3 teaspoons extra-virgin olive oil
~
2 tart apples (such as Granny Smith), peeled, cored and coarsely chopped
2 ripe pears (such as Bartlett or Bosc), peeled, cored and coarsely chopped
¼ cup apple juice concentrate, undiluted
2 tablespoons dark amber maple syrup
1 teaspoon ground cinnamon
¼ teaspoon ground cloves
2 teaspoons fresh tarragon, snipped or 2 teaspoons dried
1 teaspoon agar flakes
~
sea salt and freshly ground pepper

- Preheat oven to 375° F. Position oven rack in center of oven.
- Cut squash in half lengthwise. Using large metal spoon, scoop out seeds and stringy flesh. Add ½ inch water to 13 by 9 inch baking dish, arrange squash, cut side up, in dish. Drizzle lemon juice over squash, baste perimeter with oil.
- Bake squash, basting every 15 minutes, until tender when pierced with fork, 45 minutes to 1 hour.
- Meanwhile, in medium saucepan, cook apple and pear in apple juice until soft, about 8 to 10 minutes. Remove pan from heat, let cool slightly, add fruit and all remaining ingredients to food processor or blender, process until smooth.
- Ladle fruit purée into squash cavities, return to oven to warm purée, 10 to 15 minutes. Season with salt and pepper to taste. Serve warm.

Yield: 4 servings

The autumn equinox heralds the harvesting of winter squash and apples.

These irresistible acorn boats are filled with a simple fruit purée, lightly sweetened with pure maple syrup. Winter squash are loaded with antioxidants, vitamins and minerals.

Cinnamon and clove help balance blood sugar by reducing highs and lows, helping to keep blood sugar normal. High blood sugar can harm arteries.

Serve with Cranberry Wheatberry Pilaf [p. 190]. Pumpkin Maple "Cheese" Cake [p. 96] rounds out this festive meal.

Oven Roasted Potatoes with Onion and Rosemary

Quick and easy. These crisp, rosemary-scented potatoes are always a hit. You might want to make a double batch—they'll disappear fast!

Potatoes are starchy carbohydrates, rich in potassium, vitamin C and folic acid; fat-free, low in sodium and calories.

A perfect accompaniment to Hacienda Breakfast Burritos [p. 58] or Garden of Eat'n Burgers [p. 177].

2 pounds small red potatoes (preferably organic), cut into bite-size pieces
1 tablespoon fresh rosemary leaves, crushed or 1 teaspoon dried
3 tablespoons extra-virgin olive oil
1 tablespoon liquid aminos
1 envelope natural onion dip*

- Preheat oven to 400° F.
- Scrub potatoes (do not peel), prepare as directed. Set aside.
- Crush rosemary leaves in mortar bowl, with pestle, to release fragrant oil. Pour olive oil and all remaining ingredients into gallon-size resealable bag, add potatoes and rosemary, re-seal bag, shake until potatoes are evenly coated. Empty contents into 13 by 9 inch baking dish.
- Bake 15 to 20 minutes. Turn, bake until outsides are crisp, another 15 to 20 minutes.

Yield: 4 servings

---

* The Spice Hunter® Five Onion and Herb Dip is excellent.

Maple Roasted Yams

You'll fall in "love at first bite" after tasting these nutty, maple-flavored gems.

Yams are rich in carotenoids, vitamin C, potassium, folic acid [an important B vitamin] and magnesium. Pecans are low in sodium, high in iron, zinc and calcium.

Serve with Figgy Cranapple Chutney [p. 88].

2 pounds yams, peeled and cut into bite-size pieces
~
2 tablespoons extra-virgin olive oil
2 teaspoons Five Spice powder
1/2 cup dark amber maple syrup
3/4 cup pecans, ground

- Preheat oven to 400° F.
- Prepare yams as directed.
- Pour oil and all remaining ingredients, except pecans, into gallon-size resealable bag, add yams, re-seal bag, shake until yams are evenly coated. Empty contents into 13 by 9 inch baking dish.
- Bake 25 minutes. Turn yams, scatter pecans over top, bake until outsides are crisp, an additional 15 to 20 minutes.

Yield: 4 to 6 servings

Bavarian Späetzle
(Miniature Dumplings)

2¼ cups Multi-Grain Baking Mix (p. 9)
¼ teaspoon sea salt
1 teaspoon herbal seasoning (p. 66)
1 tablespoon egg replacer powder
2 teaspoons aluminum-free baking powder
1 cup soy milk
~
½ cup whole grain bread crumbs
1½ tablespoons extra-virgin olive oil
¼ teaspoon Frontier® natural butter flavoring*

- In stockpot, bring 3 quarts water to rolling boil.
- Meanwhile, in medium bowl, combine baking mix and next 5 ingredients, whisking just until blended (do not over mix).
  Note: batter will be on the thin side.
- Preheat oven to 350° F. Lightly oil 3-quart baking dish.
- Position large-holed colander over stockpot. Ladle small amount of batter into colander. Using the back of a large spoon, press batter through holes into boiling water. Repeat procedure with remaining batter.
- Cook, stirring occasionally, until dumplings float to surface, about 5 minutes. Drain spaetzle thoroughly in colander, transfer to prepared baking dish.
- Combine bread crumbs, oil and butter flavoring, sprinkle mixture over späetzle.
- Bake, uncovered, until topping turns golden, about 20 to 25 minutes. Serve warm.

Yield: 4 servings

Typically, Späetzle dough is made with eggs and milk. However, this healthier version is both egg and dairy-free.

Serve with a side of Beets Normandy [p. 193] or float a few späetzle in your favorite soup.

---
* Available in natural food stores and some supermarkets.

Spicy Udon Noodles

These spicy-sweet noodles with an attitude are a perfect accompaniment to Mandarin Orange Stir Fry [p. 119]. Serve with a side of cooling Cucumber-Mint Raita [p. 187] and for dessert, a dish of exotic Coconut Mango Sorbet [p. 115].

9 ounces udon noodles
~
2 to 4 tablespoons Spicy Thai® Chili Sauce, to taste
2 tablespoons vegetable stock or Savory Garlic Broth (p. 8)
1 tablespoon low-sodium tamari sauce
3 teaspoons brown rice syrup
3 teaspoons toasted sesame oil
1/4 to 1/2 teaspoon crushed red pepper flakes, to taste

- In stockpot, bring 3 quarts water to rolling boil, add noodles, cook until tender, stirring periodically, 10 to 12 minutes, drain in colander, transfer to large serving dish. Cover to keep warm.
- Prepare sauce in 1-cup measure by combining all remaining ingredients, whisking to blend, pour sauce over noodles, tossing to coat.

Yield 6 to 8 servings

Ginger Sesame Broccoli

Slightly crunchy and intensely flavorful, this unusual treatment of broccoli really shines.

Broccoli [a cruciferous vegetable] contains the nutraceutical sulforaphane which helps cancer-fighting enzymes remove carcinogens from cells.

Delicious as a side or serve over Spicy Udon Noodles [recipe above].

1 1/2 pounds broccoli flowerettes
3 teaspoons sesame oil
2 tablespoons natural hoisin sauce
2 tablespoons freshly squeezed lemon juice
3 teaspoons fresh gingerroot, peeled and grated
2 tablespoons unhulled sesame seeds, toasted (p.10)

- In 3-quart saucepan, bring 4 cups water to rolling boil, add broccoli, blanch 3 to 4 minutes, drain thoroughly.
- Heat oil in large heavy-bottomed skillet, sauté broccoli just until crisp-tender, about 2 to 4 minutes, transfer to large serving dish. Add all remaining ingredients to broccoli, tossing to coat. Serve warm or room temperature.

Yield: 4 to 6 servings

Soups

" If we do not change our direction, we are likely to end up where we are headed."

Chinese proverb

Chestnut Apple Bisque

1½ pounds chestnuts
6 cups vegetable stock (p. 8)
2 medium carrots, chopped
½ cup onion, chopped
2 large ribs celery, chopped
1 medium parsnip, chopped
1 cup tart apple (such as Granny Smith), peeled, cored and chopped

~

¾ cup apple juice
1 tablespoon fresh tarragon, snipped
½ teaspoon sea salt
⅛ teaspoon white pepper

~

10 ounces low-fat firm silken tofu*
freshly ground nutmeg

- Using a sharp paring knife, cut an "X" partway through shell of each chestnut (flat side). In large saucepan, bring 3 quarts water to boil. Carefully drop scored chestnuts into boiling water. Reduce heat, simmer, uncovered, 20 to 25 minutes. Drain chestnuts in colander, shell when cool enough to handle.
- Prepare veggies and apple as directed. This can be done by hand or in a food processor fitted with a metal blade.
- In stockpot, over medium heat, bring ½ cup stock to simmer (reserve remainder), add carrot, onion, celery, parsnip and apple, sauté until soft, about 7 to 8 minutes. Add chestnuts, continue cooking an additional 5 minutes, stirring occasionally, add reserved stock, bring mixture to boil. Reduce heat, add apple juice and next 3 ingredients, stirring to blend, simmer 10 to 15 minutes.
- In blender or food processor, combine bisque and tofu, process in 2 or 3 batches, until smooth. Adjust seasonings to taste.
- Ladle bisque into individual bowls, grate nutmeg over top. Serve warm.

Yield: 6 servings

* Mori-Nu Lite® is excellent with only 1 percent fat.

Festive and elegant. A delightful indulgence for the holidays, guaranteed to elicit raves of praise.

While this recipe requires a fair amount of preparation time, the results are definitely worth the effort.

Chestnuts, unlike other nuts, are extremely low in fat. Boiling makes them creamy. Freshly ground nutmeg is unequalled in both taste and aroma.

Helpful Tip: for a few dollars, you can purchase a pepper-mill style grinder, specifically designed for grinding whole nutmegs, available at a kitchen specialty stores. I wholeheartedly recommend investing in one.

Asparagus Velouté

Welcome spring with this terrific soup. Sure to tantalize the taste buds. Equally delicious warm or chilled.

Traditionally, veloutés are made with cream and egg yolks to achieve their velvety texture. In this dairy-free version, asparagus and potatoes are puréed to achieve the same result.

Asparagus has a mildly pungent flavor, high in fiber, potassium, vitamins A, B-1, B-2 and C.

2 pounds asparagus
1/2 cup shallots or leeks, chopped
3 teaspoons expeller-pressed canola oil
~
1/3 cup unhulled sesame seeds, toasted (p.10)
8 cups vegetable stock (p. 8)
3 medium potatoes, peeled and chopped
2 to 3 teaspoons Gomasio (p. 67), to taste
3/4 cup carrot, diced
1/4 teaspoon white pepper
~
2 tablespoons fresh dill, snipped
~
2 tablespoons mellow barley miso
2 teaspoons Dijon-style mustard
1 cup soy milk
2 to 3 teaspoons brown rice syrup, to taste
~
fresh dill sprigs

- Rinse asparagus thoroughly under running water to dislodge dirt and sand particles from tips. Snap off tough ends and discard. Cut spears into 1 inch pieces, reserve tips.

- In stockpot, sauté shallots in oil, over medium heat, until soft, 4 to 6 minutes. Add asparagus pieces, **half** of sesame seeds and next 5 ingredients to stockpot, bring mixture to boil, reduce heat. Cover, simmer until asparagus is tender, about 8 to 12 minutes.

- In blender, process asparagus mixture, in 3 or 4 batches, until velvety-smooth. Return soup to pot, add reserved tips and dill, simmer 2 to 3 minutes. Remove pan from heat.

- In a 1-cup measure, whisk miso and next 3 ingredients together until blended, stir into soup.

- Ladle soup into individual bowls, sprinkle remaining sesame seeds over top, garnish with dill sprig. Serve warm or chilled.

Yield: 8 servings

Black Bean Soup Taos

16 ounces dried black beans
8 cups vegetable stock (p. 8)
1 6-inch strip kombu
1 large bay leaf
~
2 cups white onion, diced
6 large cloves garlic, pressed
2 large ribs celery, diced
2 large carrots, diced
2 tablespoons extra-virgin olive oil
~
2 teaspoons fennel seeds, crushed and toasted (p.10)
2 teaspoons ground cumin
2 teaspoons mild chili powder
1/8 teaspoon natural liquid hickory smoke
1 tablespoon liquid aminos
1 tablespoon vegetarian Worcestershire sauce
2 tablespoons mirin or apple juice
2 tablespoons freshly squeezed lime juice
4 tablespoons chipotle chile peppers in adobo sauce
1/4 cup fresh cilantro, snipped
1 tablespoon fresh summer savory, snipped or 1 teaspoon dried
3 large Roma tomatoes, seeded and chopped
~
2 tablespoons red hatcho miso mixed with
2 tablespoons water
1 ripe (but firm) Haas avocado, sliced

- Rinse and sort beans. In stockpot, cover beans with water, soak overnight. Drain soaking water, bring beans and next 3 ingredients to boil, reduce heat. Cover, simmer until tender, about 45 minutes. Discard kombu and bay leaf.
- Meanwhile, prepare veggies as directed. In medium heavy-bottomed skillet, heat oil, over medium heat, sauté onion, garlic, celery and carrot until soft, 6 to 8 minutes.
- Add sautéed veggies and all remaining ingredients, except miso, to beans, simmer 30 minutes. Remove pan from heat, add miso mixture to soup.
- In blender or food processor, purée **half** of soup in 3 or 4 batches, until smooth. Return puréed soup to pot, stirring to blend.
- Ladle soup into individual bowls and garnish with avocado slices (squeeze fresh lime juice over avocado to prevent browning).

Yield: 12 servings

Taos is a truly magical place nestled in the foothills of the Sangre de Cristo mountains in northern New Mexico. An eclectic blend of artists and bohemians live in harmony alongside indigenous Pueblo Indians [believed to be direct descendants of the Anasazi] there.

While dining at a local restaurant in Taos, I had the distinct pleasure of enjoying a bowl of the most awesome black bean soup I've ever tasted. As best I can recall, this recipe is a close recreation of that soup.

The fiery flavors of New Mexican cuisine shine in this savory soup redolant with smoky undertones. The slightly-sweet flavor of fennel compliments the earthy taste of the black beans.

Serve with South of the Border Skillet Cornbread [p. 42] and end with Plum Empanadas [p. 107] as the sun goes down.

Bombay Carrot Bisque

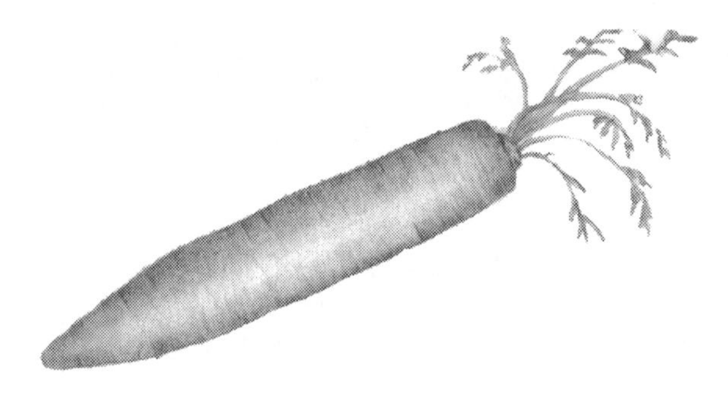

5⅓ cups vegetable stock (p. 8)
1 cup onion, finely chopped
~
6 cups carrot
1 cup apple juice
½ cup coconut milk (p. 4)
½ cup soy milk
½ teaspoon Five Spice powder
1 teaspoon ground coriander
¼ teaspoon hot pepper sauce
1 tablespoon Gomasio (p. 67)
~
3 tablespoons tahini
1 tablespoon brown rice syrup
fresh cilantro or dill sprigs

Ready to eat in 30 minutes.

A sparkling, fragrant soup loaded with great taste, high in vitamin A, helpful in supporting skin health and providing immune protection.

Serve as a first course, follow with Curry-In-A-Hurry [p. 144] and a side of Cucumber Mint Raita [p. 187].

- In stockpot, sauté onion in ⅓ cup stock (reserve remainder) until soft, 4 to 6 minutes.
- Chop carrot by hand or in a food processor fitted with a metal blade.
- Combine reserved stock, carrot and next 7 ingredients, with sautéed onion, stirring to blend.
- Whisk tahini and brown rice syrup together, add to soup, bring mixture to boil. Reduce heat, simmer until carrots are tender, 20 to 25 minutes.
- In food processor or blender, process bisque, in 2 or 3 batches, until smooth. Note: if some texture is desired, purée only ⅔ of mixture.
- Ladle bisque into individual bowls, garnish with cilantro sprig.

Yield: 6 servings

Chinatown Soup

3 teaspoons toasted sesame oil
6 large cloves garlic, minced
1 tablespoon fresh ginger root, peeled and grated
~
1/2 cup baby carrots, cut into matchstick julienne
1/2 cup bok choy, thinly sliced (include leaves and stalks)
1/2 cup red bell pepper, cut into 2 inch matchstick julienne
6 cups Savory Garlic Broth (p. 8)
4 cups water
1 6-inch strip kombu
3 tablespoons liquid aminos
~
3 ounces ramen (soba) noodles
1 cup snow pea pods, cut into matchstick julienne
3 tablespoons red hatcho miso mixed with
1/4 cup water

- In medium heavy-bottomed skillet, sauté garlic and ginger root in sesame oil, 2 to 3 minutes. Add carrot, bok choy, bell pepper and 1/2 cup broth to skillet (reserve remainder), sauté until veggies are crisp tender, 3 to 4 minutes. Remove pan from heat.
- In stockpot, combine reserved broth, kombu and liquid aminos, bring mixture to boil. Reduce heat, simmer gently until kombu is soft, 10 to 15 minutes, remove with slotted spoon, dice and return to pot.
- Break noodles in half, add to stockpot with sautéed veggies, simmer until cooked, 5 to 7 minutes.
- Add snow peas to soup, simmer 1 minute. Remove pan from heat, whisk miso into soup.
- Ladle soup into individual bowls. Serve piping hot.

Yield: 6 to 8 servings

Soup—the great healer.

Red hatcho miso, with its rich assertive flavor nourishes and heals the body, as does kombu. Perfect for those days when you're feeling under the weather.

Kombu [a mineral-rich sea vegetable] is used in China and Japan to treat thyroid disease, high blood pressure and to aid digestion. Kombu is an excellent source of potassium, iodine, calcium, magnesium, iron, niacin and vitamins A, B-2 and C.

Fresh ginger root is used to help break down high-protein foods such as meat and beans, and to lessen the damaging effect of uric acid in the body from these foods.

Helpful Tip: for easier grating, peel ginger root, freeze in airtight container with tight-fitting lid. Will keep several months. Grate, as needed.

Barley Bean Pistou

This savory winter soup is sure to give you lots of heat-generating energy to chase the cold away.

Barley is high in magnesium, calcium, iron, phosphorus and potassium. Butter beans, a member of the legume family, are an excellent source of iron, calcium, potassium and phosphorus. Both barley and beans are high in fiber and low in fat.

For an added treat, try floating a few Bavarian Späetzle [p. 201] on top.

1/3 cup pearled barley
6 cups vegetable stock (p. 8)
~
2 medium carrots, diagonally sliced
1/2 cup onion, diced
1 large rib celery, diagonally sliced
3 large Roma tomatoes, seeded and coarsely chopped
1/4 to 1/2 teaspoon Vege Sal®, to taste
1/4 teaspoon freshly ground pepper
1 teaspoon dried summer savory
2 tablespoons tomato paste
1 medium bay leaf
~
1 cup cooked butter beans
~
1/3 cup Basil-Spinach Pesto (p. 78)
2 teaspoons extra-virgin olive oil

- Rinse barley briefly under running water to remove any dust. In stockpot, combine barley and stock, bring to boil, reduce heat. Cover, simmer until tender, 45 minutes to 1 hour.
- Add carrot and next 8 ingredients to stockpot, simmer until veggies are tender, 20 to 30 minutes, add beans the last 10 minutes of cooking. Remove and discard bay leaf.
- In a 1-cup measure, whisk pesto and oil together.
- Ladle soup into individual bowls, float a dollop of pesto on top before serving.

Yield: 4 to 6 servings

Frosty Raspberry Lime
(A Chilled Soup)

1 ripe honeydew melon, seeded and chilled
1 cup fresh or frozen red raspberries, unsweetened
1 cup vanilla flavor rice milk, chilled
½ cup frozen unsweetened raspberry juice concentrate, undiluted
⅓ cup freshly squeezed lime juice
2 tablespoons liquid fruit sweetener
1 cup vanilla flavor yogurt, dairy-free
~
fresh mint sprigs

- Cut honeydew in half lengthwise. Using large metal spoon, scoop out and discard seeds. Cover and refrigerate one half for later use. Chill other half melon in freezer, for 1 hour.
- Remove melon from freezer. Scoop melon from rind (an ice cream scoop works well for this).
- In blender, combine melon, raspberries and next 5 ingredients, purée until smooth, transfer to large, nonreactive bowl. Add yogurt, whisking until fully blended. Cover with plastic wrap, chill 1 to 2 hours.
- Soup will separate after sitting, stir before serving. Ladle into individual bowls, float mint sprig on top.

Yield: 4 to 6 servings

"Summertime... and the living is easy" especially when you prepare this light, ambrosial soup that will have even the chilled-soup skeptics coming back for seconds!

For a light dinner, serve as the first course or last, as an irresistible dessert.

Honeydews are a pretty pale-green color, high in potassium, calcium, phosphorus and vitamin C.

Garden Gazpacho

3 medium Roma tomatoes, peeled, seeded and cut into chunks
1 cucumber, peeled, seeded and cut into chunks
1 medium yellow bell pepper, seeded and cut into chunks
1/2 jalapeño chile pepper, seeded and finely chopped
2 large ribs celery, cut into chunks
6 scallions (include some green)
3 cloves garlic, chopped
1/4 cup fresh cilantro, chopped
~
4 cups tomato juice*
1 cup vegetable stock (p. 8) or water
3 tablespoons red wine vinegar
1 tablespoon extra-virgin olive oil
juice of 1 freshly squeezed lime
1/2 teaspoon Vege Sal®
1/4 teaspoon white pepper
1 to 2 tablespoons brown rice syrup, to taste
1 tablespoon vegetarian Worcestershire sauce
1/4 to 1/2 teaspoon hot pepper sauce, to taste
~
fresh cilantro sprigs

- Helpful Tip: to minimize preparation time, assemble all ingredients before beginning.
- Prepare tomatoes and next 7 ingredients as directed.
  Note: if you prefer a spicier version, use the entire jalapeño, seeds and all.
- In a 6-quart mixing bowl, combine veggies and all remaining ingredients. In blender, process mixture in 3 or 4 batches until consistency is slightly chunky (do not over process), return gazpacho to bowl. Cover, chill 2 to 3 hours.
- Stir before serving. Ladle into individual bowls, float cilantro sprig on top.

Yield: 6 to 8 servings

---
* I especially like V8® Picanté.

Cool off with this zesty, chilled summer soup from Spain.

Nutraceuticals are beneficial compounds found in fruits and vegetables, essential for boosting health and preventing disease, including cancer and heart disease. This nourishing soup affords a good dose of nutraceuticals—lycopene from the tomatoes, quercetin from the onions, allicin from the garlic and capsaicin the chile peppers, as well as plenty of live-energy enzymes from the raw vegetables.

A perfect accompaniment to Quinoa and Wild Rice Avocados [p. 188]. If you prefer, serve with a medley of fresh leafy greens and Cilantro Lime Vinaigrette [p. 69] drizzled over top.

Indonesian Red Lentil Soup

1½ cups red lentils, rinsed and soaked
~
8½ cups vegetable stock (p. 8)
2 tablespoons low-sodium tamari sauce
1 cup onion, chopped
½ cup celery, diced
2 large carrots, diced
4 cloves garlic, minced
2 teaspoons fresh ginger root, peeled and grated
~
1 large bay leaf
2 whole cinnamon sticks
1 tablespoon curry powder (p. 66)
2 teaspoons cumin seeds, crushed
~
½ cup fresh or frozen peas
1 large red bell pepper, roasted (p. 3)
1 tablespoon brown rice syrup
½ cup coconut milk (p. 4)
~
curly parsley sprigs

- In stockpot, heat ½ cup stock (reserve remainder) and tamari, sauté onion and next 4 ingredients until tender, 4 to 6 minutes. Make a mirepoix (see Glossary) by blending spices into onion mixture, sauté an additional 2 to 3 minutes, stirring frequently.
- Add reserved stock and lentils to stockpot, bring to boil, reduce heat. Cover, simmer until lentils are tender, 35 to 40 minutes. Add peas to lentils the last 10 minutes.
  Note: red lentils turn brown when cooked.
- Meanwhile, roast bell pepper as directed, peel and coarsely chop. Set aside.
- Using slotted spoon, remove and discard bay leaf and cinnamon sticks. Add roasted pepper and all remaining ingredients to stockpot, stirring to blend.
- Ladle soup into individual bowls, float parsley sprig on top. Serve piping hot.

Yield: 6 to 8 servings

A wonderfully fragrant soup with tangy flavor notes of ginger, cinnamon, curry, cumin and roasted red peppers. Aromatic spices aid digestion.

Lentils [a member of the legume family] are common fare in Middle Eastern diets. Beneficial to the heart and circulation, lentils stimulate the adrenal system. High in iron, potassium and calcium, also a good source of protein.

For a complete protein, serve this exotic soup with triangles of wheat Chapati bread [p. 36].

Olde World Minestrone

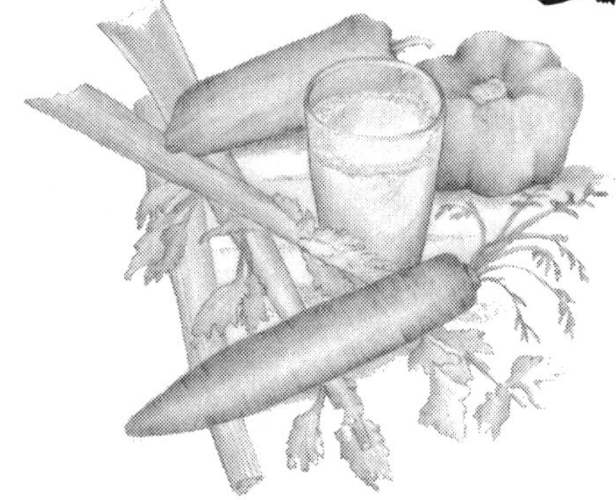

1 tablespoon extra-virgin olive oil
4 cloves garlic, minced
1 1/2 cups onion, diced
~
2 cups rhubarb chard, cut into ribbons
12 cups vegetable stock (p. 8)
2 large ribs celery, diagonally sliced
2 large unpeeled potatoes, scrubbed and cubed
3 medium carrots, diagonally sliced
1 cup fennel, coarsely chopped (white part only)
2 cups unpeeled zucchini squash, cut into bite-size pieces
~
2 cups cooked cannellini (white kidney) beans
1 cup fresh or frozen corn kernels
1/4 cup fresh basil, chopped
1/4 cup fresh oregano leaves, snipped
1/2 teaspoon Vege Sal®
2 teaspoons Italian seasoning (p. 68)
1 large bay leaf
1/2 teaspoon dried summer savory
1/2 teaspoon dried rosemary, crushed
freshly ground pepper, to taste
1 to 2 teaspoons brown rice syrup, to taste
~
1 cup uncooked spelt or whole wheat elbow macaroni
1 cup crushed tomatoes
3 cups Roma tomatoes, seeded and chopped
3 tablespoons red hatcho miso mixed with
3 tablespoons water
4 tablespoons parmesan-style cheese alternative, grated

- In medium heavy-bottomed skillet, heat oil, over medium heat, add garlic and onion, sauté until tender, 4 to 6 minutes.
- Partially fill sink with water. Rinse chard thoroughly, swirling to dislodge any dirt or sand particles, repeat if necessary. Fold each leaf in half lengthwise, holding large part of stem in one hand, tear off leaves, discard stems, coarsely chop leaves.
- In stockpot, bring stock to boil, add sautéed veggies and all remaining ingredients, except macaroni, tomatoes, miso and parmesan, return mixture to boil. Reduce heat, simmer until veggies are tender, 12 to 15 minutes.
- Add macaroni and tomatoes to mixture, simmer an additional 8 to 10 minutes. Remove pan from heat, whisk miso into soup.
- Ladle soup into individual bowls, sprinkle parmesan over top. Serve warm.

Yield: 10 to 12 servings

An Italian classic.

Whip up a pot of this much-loved regional soup for dinner. Full of old-fashioned good taste and heart-healthy nutrition. Makes a large enough quantity to enjoy throughout the week or for feeding a crowd. Feel free to vary the vegetables according to the season, keeping the macaroni and beans as your base. Adding the tomatoes at the end helps retain the bright colors of the other vegetables.

Rhubarb chard is striking with its flaming-red veins and stems, and has a flavor slightly stronger than green chard. Rich in lutein and zeaxanthin– carotenoids that appear to fend off macular degeneration in the eyes.

Serve with Amaranth Foccacia Bread [p. 35] and a salad of leafy greens splashed with Herbal Vinaigrette [p. 70].

Potato Leek Pottage

1 tablespoon extra-virgin olive oil
4 cups leeks, thinly sliced (include some green)
1 cup celery, diced
6 cups vegetable stock (p. 8)
6 cups Butter Finn or Yukon Gold potatoes, peeled and cut into 1 inch cubes
1/2 cup soy milk
1 tablespoon rice vinegar
2 tablespoons nutritional yeast flakes
1/4 teaspoon freshly ground pepper
1 teaspoon Dijon-style mustard
1 teaspoon herbal seasoning (p. 66)
1 teaspoon Gomasio (p. 67)
1 teaspoon celery seed, crushed
2 to 3 teaspoons brown rice syrup, to taste
~
3 tablespoons fresh dill, snipped
2 tablespoons mellow barley miso mixed with
2 tablespoons water
~
10 ounces low-fat firm silken tofu*
8 fresh dill sprigs for garnish

- Partially fill sink with water. Rinse leeks thoroughly, swirling to dislodge any trapped sand or tiny stones, repeat if necessary.

- In stockpot, heat oil, over medium heat, sauté leeks and celery until tender, 4 to 6 minutes, add stock, bring to boil. Add potatoes and all remaining ingredients, except dill, miso and tofu, to pot, return mixture to boil. Reduce heat, simmer until tender, 20 to 25 minutes. Remove pan from heat, add dill and miso to mixture.

- In blender or food processor, process soup with tofu, in 3 or 4 batches, until smooth. Return soup to pot.

- Ladle soup into individual bowls, float dill sprig on top. Serve warm.

Yield: 6 to 8 servings

* Mori-Nu Lite® is excellent with only 1 percent fat.

This savory soup is comfort food at its finest. Great for taking the chill out of a cold, blustery day.

Potatoes are the most universally consumed vegetable, rich in nutrients, low in sodium and calories.

Fresh dill is a must here [no substitutions please]. Silken tofu provides a creamy-rich base while adding calcium and protein.

Leeks are a nutrient-rich, high-fiber vegetable related to scallions. Leeks contain allicin compounds. Recent studies show allicin [a nutraceutical] may well lower blood cholesterol and risk of heart disease.

Serve with a Reuben James sandwich [p. 181] on the side and Almond Sun Cookies [p. 98] or Cranberry Nut Gems [p. 99] for dessert.

Savory Garlic Broth

2 to 3 bulbs garlic (about 25 cloves)
1 large bay leaf
1 tablespoon fresh thyme leaves, snipped
2 tablespoons fresh sage leaves, coarsely chopped
8 fresh parsley sprigs
pinch saffron threads
~
½ cup potato, peeled and diced
1 cup daikon, peeled and coarsely diced
1 cup carrot, peeled and diced
2 fresh serrano chile peppers,* seeded and finely chopped
8 cups water
¼ cup liquid aminos

- Rub off any loose papery skin from garlic bulbs, separate cloves from bulb (peeling is not necessary). Grind garlic to a pulp in mortar bowl with pestle. Combine garlic with next 5 ingredients to make bouquet garni (see Glossary). Set aside.
- Prepare potato, daikon, carrot and chile peppers as directed, add to stockpot with bouquet garni and all remaining ingredients. Bring mixture to a boil, reduce heat. Cover, simmer 1 hour.
- Using slotted spoon, remove and discard bouquet garni. Ladle broth into individual bowls. Serve piping hot.

Yield: 6 servings (or 8 cups)

* If serranos aren't available, substitute one jalapeño.

I call this my "decongestant" soup. Make yourself a pot when you're feeling all stuffed up.

Allicin and sulfur compounds in the garlic possess decongestant properties.

Chile peppers contain capsaicin [a nutraceutical] which gives them their heat, also a powerful decongestant.

Daikon is a long, white Japanese radish with a pungent-sweet flavor. An excellent blood cleanser, daikon helps to dissolve fat and reduce mucus.

This broth can also be used as a stock base for other recipes. Simply strain vegetables and discard bouquet garni. Will keep refrigerated 3 to 4 days, or freeze into cubes. Will keep indefinitely.

Red Pepper Velouté
with Tarragon Tomato Tapenade

The complex flavors in this velouté [velvet soup] are accented by the roasted red peppers' smoky undertones and the haunting sweet-tart flavor of the Tapenade.

1½ pounds red bell peppers, roasted (p. 3)

~

5⅓ cups vegetable stock (p. 8)
¾ cup onion, diced
3 large cloves garlic, pressed

~

3 tablespoons freshly squeezed orange juice
¼ to ½ teaspoon hot pepper sauce, to taste
⅛ teaspoon natural liquid hickory smoke, optional
2 teaspoons brown rice syrup

~

½ cup Tarragon Tomato Tapenade (p. 78)

- Roast peppers as directed, peel and coarsely chop. Set aside.
  Helpful Tip: to speed preparation time, roast peppers in advance. Store in airtight container and refrigerate until ready to use.
- In stockpot, bring ⅓ cup stock to boil (reserve remainder), reduce heat, sauté onions until tender, 4 to 6 minutes.
- Add reserved stock and all remaining ingredients, except tapenade, to pot, bring to boil. Reduce heat, simmer 10 minutes.
- In blender, process mixture, in 2 or 3 batches, until velvety smooth. Return soup to pot.
- Ladle soup into individual bowls, float dollop of tapenade on top.
  Serve warm.

Yield: 6 servings

Jamaican Salsa Soup
(A Chilled Soup)

"You are what you eat" is the core of the philosophy on which the Rastafari of Jamaica base their eating habits and exotic cuisine. They shun using additives, preservatives and all processed foods—anything which has no direct root in nature.

I created this tangy-sweet, piquant soup based on Rastafarian cuisine and philosophies. Full of live-energy enzymes. Enjoy a cool taste of the tropics in every delicious spoonful.

1 large ripe pineapple, cut into chunks (about 3½ cups)
1 ripe papaya, peeled, seeded* and cubed
1 large cucumber, peeled, seeded and coarsely chopped
4 scallions (include some green), chopped
1 mild green chile pepper, seeded and chopped
¼ cup freshly squeezed lime juice
1 cup pineapple juice, unsweetened
2 to 3 teaspoons honey, to taste

~

1 medium yellow bell pepper, finely diced
¾ cup coconut milk (p. 4)
3 tablespoons fresh cilantro, chopped

~

lime twists
fresh mint sprigs

- In blender or food processor, combine pineapple and next 7 ingredients, process, in 2 or 3 batches, until smooth.
- Transfer soup to large serving bowl, add prepared bell pepper, coconut milk and cilantro, stirring to blend. Cover, chill 2 to 3 hours.
- Stir before serving. Ladle soup into individual bowls, garnish with lime twist and mint sprigs.

Yield: 4 to 6 servings

---

* Reserve seeds and freeze for making Island Dressing (p. 72). Frozen seeds will keep several months.

Summertime Cucumber Dill
(A Chilled Soup)

4 cups cucumber, peeled, seeded and chopped
2 teaspoons walnut oil
~
2/3 cup sweet onion (such as Maui or Vidalia), coarsely chopped
1 1/2 cups vegetable stock (p. 8)
10 ounces low-fat firm silken tofu*
1/3 cup fresh dill, snipped
2 teaspoons apple cider vinegar
1 tablespoon honey mustard
3 teaspoons honey
1/4 teaspoon white pepper
1 teaspoon Gomasio (p. 67)
1 1/2 cups rice milk, chilled
~
3 tablespoons raw carrot, grated
fresh dill sprigs

- Prepare cucumber as directed. Set aside.
- In stockpot, heat oil, over medium heat, sauté onion until translucent, 4 to 6 minutes.
- In blender, combine 3 cups prepared cucumber (reserve 1 cup), sautéed onion and all remaining ingredients, except carrot and dill sprigs, process mixture, in 2 or 3 batches, until smooth. Return soup to pot, add carrot and reserved cucumber, stirring to blend, transfer to large serving bowl. Cover, chill 2 to 3 hours.
- Stir before serving. Ladle soup into individual bowls, float dill sprig on top.

Yield: 6 servings

An irresistibly delicious soup, just the thing for those "dog days of summer" when cucumbers and fresh dill are plentiful.

Cucumbers are sweet with a cooling thermal nature and contain a digestive enzyme that helps break down protein while cleansing the intestines.

Helpful Tip: can be prepared the night before to keep you out of the hot kitchen during the day.

* Mori-Nu Lite® is excellent with only 1 percent fat.

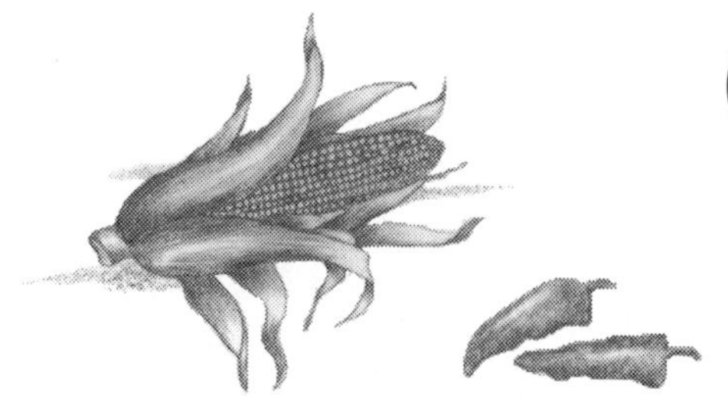

Chile Corn Chowder Cripple Creek

Tantalize your taste buds with this spirited regional meat and dairy-free corn chowder from the Great American Southwest. Typically, a chowder is a thick soup made with fish, chicken, hearty vegetables and a milk or cream base.

Pungent Cubanelle chiles are high in vitamin C and potassium. Research shows chile peppers have anticoagulant activity that tends to neutralize fatty foods' ability to form clots, causing heart attacks and strokes. Studies also show that hot, spicy foods burn calories.

Corn [or maize] is actually a native grain, usually eaten as a vegetable. American Indians used corn as the staple in their diet, cooking it with lime. Rich in vitamin A, potassium and magnesium, corn is mostly carbohydrate with about 20 percent protein content.

Chayote, native to Central America, is a pale-green, pear-shaped squash with a sweet flavor and firm texture.

2 teaspoons expeller-pressed canola oil
5⅓ cups vegetable stock (p. 8)
1½ cups sweet onion (such as Walla Wallas), diced
2 medium carrots, diced
1 mild Cubanelle chile pepper, seeded and diced (see Glossary)
2 large cloves garlic, minced
2 teaspoons ground cumin
½ teaspoon Vege Sal®
½ teaspoon chili powder
~
2 teaspoons liquid aminos
2 chayote squash, peeled, seeded, and cut into ½ inch cubes
¼ cup freshly squeezed lime juice (about 2 limes)
1 to 2 teaspoons brown rice syrup, to taste
4 cups fresh corn kernels
½ cup soy milk
~
5 ounces low-fat firm silken tofu
3 tablespoons fresh cilantro, chopped
~
1 cup Jack-style cheese alternative, grated
½ cup Southwest Chile Pesto (p. 79), optional

- In stockpot, heat oil and ⅓ cup stock (reserve remainder), over medium heat, sauté onion and next 3 ingredients until tender, 4 to 6 minutes. Make a mirepoix (see Glossary) by blending spices into onion mixture, sauté an additional 2 to 3 minutes, stirring frequently.

- Stir reserved stock, liquid aminos and next 4 ingredients into mirepoix, bring to boil. Reduce heat, simmer 10 minutes, add soy milk, simmer an additional 5 minutes. Remove pan from heat.

- In blender or food processor, combine tofu with corn mixture, process in 3 or 4 batches, until smooth. Return soup to pot, stir in cilantro.

- Ladle chowder into individual bowls, sprinkle 2 tablespoons cheese over top. Microwave on high until cheese melts, 30 to 60 seconds. Float dollop of pesto over melted cheese, if desired. Serve warm or chilled.

Yield: 8 servings

Butternut Bisque

2 medium Butter Finn or Yukon Gold potatoes
2 pounds butternut squash
~
1 tablespoon extra-virgin olive oil
1 cup onion, diced
½ cup celery, diced
½ cup carrot, diced
½ teaspoon freshly ground nutmeg
2 teaspoons ground cinnamon
¼ teaspoon ground cloves
1 teaspoon dried marjoram
½ teaspoon ground coriander
½ teaspoon Vege Sal®
~
2 ½ cups vegetable stock (p. 8)
2 tablespoons mirin
2 tablespoons brown rice syrup
~
10 ounces low-fat firm silken tofu*

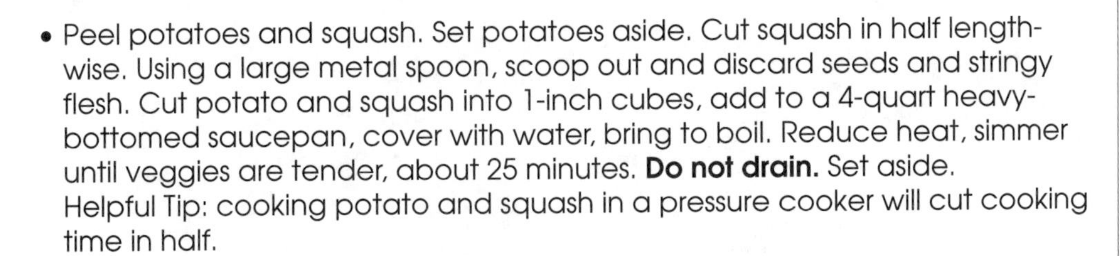

- Peel potatoes and squash. Set potatoes aside. Cut squash in half lengthwise. Using a large metal spoon, scoop out and discard seeds and stringy flesh. Cut potato and squash into 1-inch cubes, add to a 4-quart heavy-bottomed saucepan, cover with water, bring to boil. Reduce heat, simmer until veggies are tender, about 25 minutes. **Do not drain.** Set aside. Helpful Tip: cooking potato and squash in a pressure cooker will cut cooking time in half.

- In stockpot, heat oil, over medium heat, sauté onion, celery and carrot until soft, 4 to 6 minutes. Make a mirepoix (see Glossary) by blending spices into onion mixture, sauté an additional 2 to 3 minutes.

- Add potato, squash, cooking liquid and stock to stock pot, stirring to blend, simmer 10 minutes. Remove pan from heat, add mirin and brown rice syrup to mixture.

- In blender or food processor, process soup and tofu, in 2 or 3 batches, until smooth.

- Ladle bisque into individual serving bowls. Serve warm.

Yield: 6 servings

---
* Mori-Nu Lite® is excellent with only 1 percent fat.

A beautiful autumn-gold soup with a velvety texture and naturally sweet taste. Elegant enough for a special occasion, simple enough for a weeknight.

Pumpkin and butternut are two of the top ranking orange vegetables, next to yams, with a high carotenoid content. Carotenoids are known anticancer compounds.

Cinnamon and cloves help balance blood sugar. Even a little can boost the activity of the hormone insulin, speeding up its ability to dispose of blood glucose [sugar]. High blood sugar can harm arteries.

Serve with Harvest Moon Muffins [p. 46] and a winter salad of red tipped greens, radicchio and marinated beets.

Glossary

"The human body is the best picture of the human soul."

Ludwig Wittgenstein

agar (also sold as kanten) an odorless, mild-tasting, edible sea vegetable, is freeze-dried then ground into flakes or bars. Contains calcium, iron and phosphorus. Used as a gelling agent in desserts, aspics and jams, agar is easier for the body to digest than cornstarch or gelatin, which is made from beef and veal bones, cartilage, tendons and other tissue, or from pig skin. Available in natural food stores and some supermarkets.

air-cushioned baking sheets are double-insulated, double-thick with a layer of air between that prevents cookies and other baked goods from burning on the bottom before the top is done. Available in Housewares department of specialty stores and some supermarkets.

amaranth an ancient grain, was a mainstay of the Aztec's diet. The tiny seeds of this rediscovered grain are rich in lysine, an amino acid, scarce in most grains. Amaranth contains more protein than any other grain except quinoa, and is rich in calcium, phosphorus and fiber. Cooked amaranth has a sweet, nutty flavor. Available in natural food stores and some supermarkets.

amasake a sweet and creamy, pudding-like liquid made from fermented glutinous brown rice, very digestible. Used as a sweetener and leavener for baked goods and for making dairy-free puddings and pie fillings. Almond amasake is high in calcium. Available in natural food stores and some supermarkets.

Anasazi beans plump cranberry-colored beans with cream-colored splotches and a sweet flavor. These beans are easier to digest than many of the common varieties. Available in natural food stores and some supermarkets.

arame a thin mild-flavored sea vegetable, rich in protein, iodine, calcium and iron. Arame can be mixed with soups, salads or rice. Cooking arame before using is not necessary, will fall apart when soaked. Available in natural food stores and some supermarkets.

arborio rice a short-grained rice from Italy, usually slow-simmered with stock. Arborio is used to make the classic Italian dish, risotto, whose high starch content gives the dish its characteristic creamy texture. Available in Mediterranean markets and some supermarkets.

arrowroot powder a delicate cooking starch extracted from the tubers of several tropical plants, is used to thicken soups, sauces and gravies. Arrowroot can be substituted, measure for measure, in place of corn or potato starch. Arrowroot is 100 percent vegetarian and thickens at lower temperatures. Dissolve in cold water and add at the *end* of cooking, as it tends to break down if cooked too long. Store in a cool, dry place. Available in natural food stores and supermarkets.

balsamic vinegar an aromatic, dark-amber vinegar with robust complex flavor. Made from white Trebbiano grapes by aging them for years in wooden barrels. Complements most greens, excellent mixed with extra-virgin olive oil for a vinaigrette. Available in most supermarkets.

barley the oldest grain known to man, commonly used in making soups. Barley is a good heat-generating food; its high-gluten content gives it a pasta-like consistency. Whole barley, with only the outer husk removed, is rich in fiber and high in protein, niacin, folic acid, B vitamins and the minerals magnesium, calcium, iron, phosphorus and potassium. *Pearled barley* is put through a refining process to remove the bran covering (outer husk), making it easier to cook but less nutritious than whole barley. Whole barley is available in natural food stores.

barley malt syrup a processed, sprouted whole-barley grain syrup with a light molasses-like flavor similar to brown rice syrup. Retaining about 40 percent of its carbohydrates, barley malt syrup contains some vitamins and minerals and is half as sweet as honey, but very sticky. Oiling a spoon before measuring is recommended. It is also a healthier replacement for sugar or molasses and probably the least expensive of the natural sweeteners. Store in a cool dry place in a glass container. Available in natural food stores and some supermarkets.

black-eyed peas small, tan Asian legumes with a black circular "eye," introduced to American via the African slave trade. Available fresh, dried or canned, in natural food stores and supermarkets.

bouquet garni a seasoning pouch of fresh and/or dried herbs wrapped in cheesecloth and tied with kitchen string, added to soups, sauces and stews during cooking for heightening the flavor. Discard before serving.

brown rice syrup at least half the composition of this grain-based sweetener is the nutrients found in whole grains and barley. It contains maltose and a good percentage of complex sugars, which take much longer to digest than the simple variety. This smooths out the blood-sugar peaks and valleys associated with the consumption of highly refined sweeteners. Brown rice syrup is not highly processed and is made by adding dried sprouted barley or barley enzymes to cooked brown rice and fermenting the mixture until the rice starch breaks down to complex sugars. Similar in consistency to honey. Available in natural food stores and some supermarkets.

bulgur a quick-cooking grain made from wheatberries that are steamed, dried, cracked and crushed between stone rollers. This process makes bulgur a *precooked* grain that is usually soaked in boiling water, rather than cooked. Let bulgur sit in boiling water 15 minutes, drain and fluff with a fork. Commonly used in Middle Eastern cooking.

capers small green buds from a prickly shrub native to the Mediterranean. Capers come pickled in a vinegar-base brine or preserved in coarse sea salt. They add a wonderful zestiness to salads, soups, pastas and stews. Stores specializing in Mediterranean ingredients will have the best selection of the different-size capers. Also available in most supermarkets.

carob centuries-old carob trees originally grew in the Mediterranean, now cultivated in southern California for food. Carob is a healthy caffeine and stimulant-free substitute for candy or chocolate. The pulp or flesh of the carob pod is made into chips, flour or syrup. It is an excellent energy food containing about 47 percent natural sugars and 7 percent protein. Rich in calcium and phosphorus with some iron, copper and magnesium. Carob flour or powder should be stored in a cool place. Available in natural food stores and Mediterranean markets.

chard (*also sold as Swiss chard*) grown in several varieties, the most popular being *rhubarb chard* with bright red stems and veins. *Green chard* with white stems and veins has a somewhat milder flavor than the rhubarb variety. Chard is one of the most nutritious of the dark, leafy greens, high in vitamin A with a fair amount of calcium.

chickpeas (also sold as garbanzo beans) are small, round, legumes, tan in color and rich in protein. Commonly used in Middle Eastern cooking. Available dried or canned in supermarkets.

chile peppers there are a myriad of peppers in this category. Chilies vary in flavor and hotness. Their heat content is rated in Scoville units on a scale of 1 to 10. Unless specifically called-for, seeding the chiles is optional. However, be aware that the seeds add extra heat. (I always test a minute piece of fresh chile to determine its possibilities before deciding how much to add). Wearing rubber gloves is recommend when handling chiles as the volatile oils irritate sensitive skin as well as any cuts or abrasions you may have. If you remove the seeds, cut pod in half and scrape out the seeds under cold running water. Wash hands in warm, soapy water immediately after preparing chiles. Keep hands away from eyes and face for several hours.

Helpful Tip: when buying fresh chiles, select only those with firm, smooth skins and glossy appearance. To store, wrap in paper towels (moisture from plastic causes them to decay). Will keep refrigerated up to 2 weeks or 6 months, if frozen.

The following chilies are used in *The Light Body:*

~ ***anaheim*** closely related to and interchangeable with the New Mexico chile *(commonly known as mild green chiles)*. Anaheims are long, smooth and bluntly pointed with medium-thick flesh, 5 to 7 inches long, 1 to 2 inches wide, ripening to glossy green, orange-red or bright scarlet with a clear-cutting, sweet, earthy flavor. Used in many Southwestern dishes.

Scoville rating: between a 2 and 4

~ ***cayenne*** long, thin-fleshed with sharply pointed pods, either straight or curled at the tip, 6 to 10 inches long, 1 inch wide, ripening to brick red. Cayennes have an acidic, tart flavor and are used fresh in salsas, also commonly ground into a spice known as cayenne pepper or processed into hot pepper sauces such as Tabasco.

Scoville rating: an incendiary 8

~ ***chipotle*** dried, smoked jalapeños with a smoky-sweet flavor, usually packed in a mild red adobo sauce. Chipotles are perfect for salsas and chili.

Scoville rating: 5

~ ***cubanelles*** are anaheim chiles left on the plant until they ripen to red.

Scoville rating: between a 2 and 4

~ ***jalapeño*** plump, blunt and bullet-shaped with thick-skinned flesh, 1 to 2 inches long, 1/2 to 1 inch wide, shiny medium-green, red or purple when ripe. Jalapeños are commonly used in salsas, stews and sauces.

Scoville rating: a fiery 6

~ ***poblano*** thick-fleshed, shaped like a bell pepper with collapsed sides tapering to a point, 3 to 5 inches long, 2 to 3 inches wide near the stem, dark green, becoming dark red when fully matured. Poblanos have a smoke-roasted, raisin-like flavor, excellent for roasting, delicious in soups and sauces.

Scoville rating: a comfortable 3

~ ***serrano*** torpedo shaped, thick-fleshed, 1 to 3 inches long, 1/4 to 1/2 inch wide, dark green, becoming red when fully matured, but sometimes brown, orange or yellow. Serranos have a pleasantly acrid flavor with clean biting heat, delicious roasted in salsas and sauces.

Scoville rating: a blazing 6 or low 7

citrus oil an intensely flavored oil derived from lemon, lime and orange peel. Available in specialty stores or by mail order.

collards have wide, flat dark-green leaves with white ribs. A member of the cabbage family, collards are high in calcium, phosphorus and vitamins A and C.

cornmeal made from yellow, white or blue corn. Nutritionally, yellow cornmeal is fairly high in vitamin A, while white and blue cornmeal have none. Whole grain also has three times as much calcium and twice as much fiber, iron, potassium, phosphorus, riboflavin and niacin as de-germed cornmeal. Whole grain stone ground cornmeal has the best flavor and nutrition with two distinguishing characteristics—light and dark specks from the germ and the bran. If the cornmeal is uniformly gold, it has probably been de-germed and will have substantially fewer nutrients and lack the sweetness of whole grain cornmeal. When purchasing whole grain cornmeal, buy from a store that does a brisk business, such as a health or natural food store. Whole grain cornmeal is highly susceptible to rancidity and should be stored in an airtight container in your refrigerator or freezer.

couscous tiny seedlike grains of pasta made from durum wheat. The *whole wheat* variety is somewhat darker in color than traditional couscous and more nutritious. Can be used in a variety of warm or cold grain dishes and desserts. Available in natural food stores and some supermarkets.

daikon a crisp, white Oriental radish with a pungent taste, commonly used in macrobiotic cooking, ranging in size from 6 to 15 inches long and 2 to 3 inches in diameter. Can be eaten raw in dips and salads, or cooked in soups, stews and stir-fries. Cooking sweetens its flavor. Daikon is an excellent blood purifier, helpful in digesting greasy foods by countering or breaking up fat in the body. Available in Asian markets and produce sections of well-stocked supermarkets.

date sugar a granulated, unrefined, natural sweetener made from dried dates, about two-thirds as sweet as table sugar. Date sugar contains iron, potassium and other minerals and vitamins. Use in baked goods in place of brown sugar. Store in an airtight container in a cool, dry place. Available in natural food stores.

dried currants a tiny variety of grapes, often used in baking. Not to be confused with fresh red or black currants which are used in jellies, pies and wine. Available in natural food stores and bulk section of some supermarkets.

egg replacer powder an egg substitute made primarily from potato starch, tapioca flour and leavening agents that bind cooked and baked foods together. Fat and cholesterol-free with no animal products, lactose, sodium, preservatives, sugar or artificial flavorings. Available in natural food stores and baking products section of some supermarkets.

expeller-pressed oils unrefined oils extracted without the use of solvents. They have more flavor, aroma and nutrition than refined oils. However, expeller-pressed oils have a shorter shelf life and should be kept refrigerated.

extra-virgin olive oil is the highest quality olive oil from the first pressing of the olives, without the addition of water, heat or solvents. Color can range from yellow to green depending on the region the olives were grown in and when they were harvested. One of the healthiest oils for cooking, olive oil is mainly a mono-unsaturated fat, making it more stable to heat degradation than polyunsaturated oils, also helps lower LDL cholesterol, which is implicated in coronary artery disease.

fennel a crisp, fragrant, pale-green vegetable with a mild licorice flavor and feathery fronds reminiscent of dill. Fennels' edible bulb and stalk can be used like celery in stir-fries or eaten raw in salads. Available in most supermarkets.

five spice powder (also sold as Chinese Five Spice). Most commercial blends usually include star anise, ginger, cinnamon, fennel and black pepper, commonly used in Asian and Middle Eastern cooking. Available in Asian markets and supermarkets.

flax seed tiny glossy-brown or golden seeds with emulsifying properties, high in Omega 3 fatty acids. Available in natural food stores.

ginger root the fresh root of a tropical plant native to Asia, with a pungent, aromatic flavor. Available in Asian markets and most supermarkets.

herbs de Provence an aromatic blend of dried herbs associated with the South of France. Most commercial mixes usually include basil, lavender, marjoram, rosemary, sage, summer savory and thyme. There are probably as many recipes for this mix as there are chefs. The herbs used may vary, but they are always dried, so the pungency of each herb is prominent. Available in kitchen specialty stores and some supermarkets.

hoisin sauce a thick, reddish-brown sauce with a spicy-sweet taste, used in Chinese cooking. Commercially prepared hoisin sauce is a mixture of soybeans, garlic, chile peppers and other spices. Available in Asian markets, natural food stores and some supermarkets.

Kalamata olives large, purplish-black, imported unpitted from Greece with a glossy veneer and salty, sweet, meaty flavor. Usually packaged in a wine-vinegar marinade or olive oil.

kale has dark blue-green leaves that are deeply ruffled to the stem. The leaves should have a supple, moist feel. When cooked, kale has a mild cabbage-like flavor, which is good in soups, pastas and even on pizza. High in vitamins A and C, calcium, iron, magnesium and potassium.

kamut an ancient grain dating back to the time of the pyramids, is closely related to common wheat. Kamut grows three times larger than wheat and has a hump in the middle. Although kamut contains gluten, it appears to be less allergenic than wheat and contains 20 to 40 percent more protein. It is higher in 8 minerals, especially magnesium and zinc, than modern bread wheat. Kamut has a slightly buttery-sweet flavor, pleasant aroma and satisfying, chewy texture. The whole grain is commonly ground into unrefined flour, which is light and powdery, resulting in light-textured pastas and baked goods. It is also delicious in soups, salads and stews. Stored in an airtight container in a cool, dry place, kamut will keep for months. Available in natural food stores and some supermarkets.

kasha (cracked, roasted buckwheat) isn't really a grass but a thistle plant that produces fragrant flowers, followed by the buckwheat groats. Toasting turns tan-colored raw groats a reddish-brown and gives them an assertive, earthy flavor. Because kasha's consistency, flavor and nutrient content are so much like those of grains, it is essentially treated like one. Rich in fiber, potassium, calcium, iron and B vitamins, kasha is a quick-cooking grain. Available in natural food stores and some supermarkets.

Kashi™ a mixture of whole, unprocessed oats, long-grain brown rice, rye, hard red winter wheat, triticale, buckwheat, barley and sesame seeds. Kashi contains no additives, salt or sugar, and has a satisfyingly chewy texture and nutty flavor. Cooks in 30 minutes. Available in natural food stores and some supermarkets.

kombu a member of the kelp family. This wide, flat, olive-green sea vegetable comes packaged in 6- to 8-inch strips. Extremely rich in potassium, iodine, calcium, magnesium, iron, niacin, vitamins A, B2, C and alginic acid, which helps cleanse the body of toxic metallic elements. Used in China and Japan to treat thyroid disease and high blood pressure, kombu is the natural form of MSG. Cooked with dried legumes, kombu improves flavor and digestibility while adding nutrients. Excellent in soups and stocks. Available in natural food stores and some supermarkets.

kudzu a thickening and gelling agent extracted from a plant that grows in the Southeastern United States. Indigenous to the Orient, kudzu is similar to arrowroot but with twice the gelling strength and no starchy taste. Has a soothing effect on the nerves and digestive system, also good for digestive disorders. Crush lumps before measuring. Available in natural food stores and some supermarkets.

lecithin a yellow substance derived from the soybean. Available in liquid or granular form. Used as an emulsifying agent in place of eggs. Available in natural food stores.

liquid aminos a vegetable protein made from soybeans, similar in taste to tamari but unfermented, containing no alcohol, additives or wheat. Liquid aminos have a lower sodium content than soy or tamari and are a good source of amino acids. Use in vegetable stock for a beef-like flavor. Liquid aminos can replace soy or tamari measure for measure. Store at room temperature. Available in natural food stores and some supermarkets.

liquid fruit sweetener a concentrated, natural sweetener with the consistency of honey, made from a variety of fruits. Available in natural food stores and some supermarkets.

liquid hickory smoke a flavoring made by burning hickory without the use of chemicals or preservatives. A small amount gives sauces and marinades a smoky flavor. Available in most supermarkets.

mace a spice which is the outer covering of nutmeg, used to flavor desserts and baked goods. Lighter in color and milder in flavor than nutmeg.

millet (also sold as sorghum) a tiny, yellow grain whose origins go back thousands of years to China. Non-glutenous and the only grain that is alkalizing in nature, millet assists in heating the body in cold or rainy climates. High in protein, fiber, iron, magnesium and potassium. Use in breakfast cereals, soups and pilafs. Available in natural food stores and some supermarkets.

mirepoix a savory sauté commonly used in French cuisine as a base for flavorful soups, made from diced vegetables (usually onion, celery and carrot) and aromatic spices cooked together before liquid is added.

mirin a Japanese cooking wine made from sweet rice. The low alcohol content evaporates quickly when heated. Mirin has a subtle quality that mixes well with a variety of dressings, marinades, sauces, glazes, sautéed vegetables and dips. Use in place of sherry or white wine. Available in natural food stores and some supermarkets.

miso a paste made from fermented, crushed soybeans, sea salt and sometimes grains such as barley, rice or wheat. Miso plays a dual role as both a seasoning and thickening agent. Long-aged darker varieties tend to be stronger flavored and lend themselves well to heartier dishes while light mellow misos work well in more delicate recipes. When mixed with a small amount of water or other liquid, miso becomes smooth and creamy making it the perfect substitute for dairy products and eggs in many dishes. *When using miso in a recipe, cut back or eliminate any salt called for.* Misos' versatility lends richness and depth of flavor to gravies, sauces, soups, dressings, beans, spreads and dips, and contains valuable enzymes which aid digestion. Isoflavones (nutraceuticals) in miso have been shown to help prevent certain forms of cancer, also a powerful systemic detoxifier. Available in Asian markets, natural food stores and some supermarkets.

nonreactive bowls or pans made of glass, porcelain, pottery, enamel or stainless steel. Used in recipes containing acidic ingredients such as tomatoes and citrus juices which tend to discolor some materials such as aluminum.

nutritional yeast an inactive yeast and dietary food supplement with a distinct, pleasant aroma and delicious cheesy taste. Nutritional yeast is different from baking yeast and has no fermenting power, rich in highly-assimilated protein, B vitamins, phosphorus and other minerals. Store in a cool, dry place or refrigerate. Will keep indefinitely if stored properly. Available in flakes or powder at natural food stores.

onions (and their cousins - chives, leeks, scallions and shallots) encompass a wide range of colors, shapes, sizes and flavors. Depending on the season and variety, onions may be mild or spicy-hot, sweet or quite pungent. Some onions taste best raw and lose their flavor when cooked, while others are too pungent to eat raw, but become mellow and sweet when cooked. All varieties belong to the genus *allium* and contain certain phytochemicals that in laboratory tests appear to block the earliest changes in cells that enable tumors to grow. Alliums contain antioxidant quercitin and sulfur compounds. A number of promising studies show that people who eat a lot of onions are less likely to develop cancer. Stored in a cool, dry, well-ventilated place, most varieties should keep up to a month.

~ ***Maui, Vidalia and Walla Walla*** onions, named for the regions they are grown in, are sweet not hot, prized for their fruity, distinct flavor. Their main season is April through June, though Walla Wallas are available through mid-August. Delicious raw in salads or topping a garden burger.

~ ***red*** onions are best when eaten raw, cooked they turn watery and lose their beautiful color.

~ ***white*** onions are typically the most pungent with a sharp flavor and strong bite. Because they contain more water than yellow onions, white onions have a shorter shelf life. Used predominantly in Mexican dishes. Available year-round.

~ ***chives*** have edible, purplish flowers and hollow, grasslike leaves. Used raw as a seasoning and garnish, chives are wonderful in a variety of salads. Buy only what you can readily use, since they are a *fresh* onion and won't keep long.

~ ***leeks*** have a sweet, delicate flavor. Small leeks are delicious grilled whole, while larger leeks shine in soups and stews. Clean leeks thoroughly, as they tend to be gritty. Leeks are at their peak in fall, winter and spring, although most supermarkets carry them year-round. Buy only what you can readily use, since they are a *fresh* onion and won't keep long.

~ ***scallions*** have a fresh, onion flavor that is slightly assertive. They are wonderful raw and are often used as a garnish. At their peak in May and June, scallions are available in supermarkets year-round. Buy only what you can readily use, as they are a *fresh* onion and won't keep long.

~ ***shallots*** are crisp with a refined, delicate flavor, more intense than onions but less hot. Shallots can be eaten raw, excellent in vinaigrettes. Available in supermarkets year-round.

orzo (also sold as Rosa Marina) are tiny rice-shaped pasta. Available in Italian groceries, natural food stores and some supermarkets.

pepitas (also known as pumpkin seeds) a popular ingredient in Mexican dishes, the seeds are dark green with a delicate flavor. Raw, unsalted pepitas are available at Mexican markets and natural food stores.

pine nuts (also known as pignolias or pinons) are actually edible seeds from a Mediterranean pine tree. Their piney flavor is enhanced by toasting. Pine nuts are a key ingredient in pesto and are used extensively in cuisines of Africa, Eastern Europe and Spain. Available in the ethnic or imported section of some supermarkets as well as Italian and natural food stores.

polenta coarsely ground Italian cornmeal simmered in stock or water, like porridge, then served soft or cooled and cut into wedges, usually topped with tomato sauce. Available in most supermarkets.

portabella a popular cultivated, domestic mushroom. Portabellas are giants of the mushroom family, ranging in size from 3 to 6 inches across, with pale brown mottled caps, thick stems and a dense, meaty flavor and texture. Excellent grilled. Available year-round in the produce section of many well-stocked supermarkets.

prune purée a fat substitute for butter, shortening or oil in baked goods, also adds sweetness. Easy to make in a food processor (see recipe, p. 4).

"quick" bread does not contain a leavening agent (yeast-free). Instead, rising occurs from gases that form bubbles or air pockets in the batter.

quinoa an ancient grain originally grown by the Incas and now grown in Colorado, contains more protein than other grains. It contains all eight amino acids which the body can't produce on its own, in the correct proportions, and is also high in iron and calcium. Rinse in a fine mesh sieve before cooking to remove the natural saponin coating. Though perhaps more expensive than other grains, quinoa *expands almost 5 times* during cooking. Versatile with a light texture, quinoa lends itself to a variety of dishes from breakfast cereal to pilafs and even desserts. Available in natural food stores and some supermarkets.

rice milk a slightly sweet, dairy-free beverage, made from brown rice with the appearance and consistency of 2 percent milk. Available in natural food stores and some supermarkets.

rice vinegar slightly sweet and naturally brewed from fermented brown rice, rice vinegar has half the acid level of apple cider vinegar resulting in a more delicate flavor. B*rown rice vinegar* has a high amino acid content due to the fact that it's made from whole brown rice. Widely available in Asian markets, natural food stores and most supermarkets.

Roma tomatoes (also sold as Italian or plum tomatoes) small, pear-shaped and fleshy with few seeds, excellent for making sauce or tomato paste. Widely available in supermarkets.

saffron an aromatic spice with threadlike stamen from the autumn crocus. Popular in Spanish, Indian and North African cooking, saffron imparts a distinct, delicate flavor and soft yellow color to dishes. Although relatively expensive, a little goes a long way. Available in kitchen specialty stores, natural food stores and most supermarkets.

sea salt a crystalline seasoning evaporated from sea water. Unlike table salt, it is usually free of additives and contains some natural trace minerals. Available in natural food stores and supermarkets.

silken tofu white, easily digestible curd made from cooked soybeans with a soft, custard-like consistency. Available in soft, firm and extra-firm textures. Silken-style tofu comes packaged in 10 1/2 ounce aseptic packages and plastic tubs (the aseptic packages do not require refrigeration until opened), high in protein and nutrients, terrific in dressings, sauces, soups, smoothies and baked goods. Available in natural food stores and some supermarkets.

soba noodles made from buckwheat, they resemble fettucine noodles in appearance. Popular in Asian cooking, soba noodles are available in Asian markets, natural food stores and some supermarkets.

soy milk made from ground and boiled soybeans, rich in genistein (an isoflavone) which appears to protect against breast cancer, heart disease, osteoporosis and menopausal symptoms. Use in cooking and baking in place of cows milk. Available in natural food stores and some supermarkets.

spirulina (rhymes with ballerina) a traditional *food* of some Mexican and African peoples. A primordial life form, spirulina is planktonic blue-green algae found in warm-water, alkaline, volcanic lakes. Spirulina is among the richest food sources of protein (about 65 percent), beta-carotene, an essential fatty acid and powerful antioxidant, gamma-linolenic acid (GLA), vitamin E, B12, iron and chlorophyll and a host of other food factors. (Note: spirulina is **not** chlorella or the blue-green algae harvested from Klamath Lake, Oregon). Spirulina is different from most other algae in that it is easily digested. Scientific literature is full of information concerning the benefits and safety of humans eating spirulina. It has been found to help lower serum cholesterol (LDLs). Available in natural and health food stores in powder form, usually sold in bulk.

tahini (tah-HEE-nee) a thick, smooth paste made from ground sesame seeds. Popular in Middle Eastern cooking, tahini is high in calcium and protein with a wonderful texture and peanutlike flavor that makes it ideal, in small amounts, for use in spreads, sauces and dressings. It is not hydrogenated. Stir tahini before using as the oil separates from the ground seeds; refrigeration helps prevent some separation and extends the life of the product. Available in natural food stores and some supermarkets.

tamari sauce (tuh-MAH-ree) a naturally-brewed soy sauce, does not contain sugar or wheat. Low-sodium formula available in natural food stores and some supermarkets.

tamarind concentrate a paste made from the dried pods of the tamarind, or Indian date, which is sour-tasting and very sticky. Though much stronger than lemon, lemon is often used as a substitute. Available in Indian markets and the ethnic section of some supermarkets.

tempeh a traditional Indonesian food made from fermented soybeans that have been split and hulled. Grains such as millet and quinoa are often added to produce different flavors. Tempeh is highly nutritious and rich-tasting with a hearty texture and neutral flavor that readily absorbs seasonings during cooking or marinating. Available in several flavors in the frozen food section of Asian markets, natural food stores and some supermarkets.

toasted sesame oil expressed from sesame seeds with a strong sesame flavor. Unlike plain sesame oil, toasted sesame oil is used mainly as a flavor enhancer rather than as a cooking oil. Available in Asian markets, natural food stores and some supermarkets.

tomatillos (tohm-ah-TEE-oh) also sold as Mexican green tomatoes. Tomatillos are a small fruit, related to tomatoes and gooseberries, with a papery husk and lemony flavor with apple and herb overtones. Available in Mexican markets and produce sections of well-stocked supermarkets.

TVP (texturized vegetable protein) made from flour that remains after oil is expressed from the soybean. The flour is then mixed with water and extruded into granules of various sizes resembling ground meat in texture and chewiness. Available in natural food stores and some well-stocked supermarkets.

udon noodles long, flat noodles made from whole wheat flour, used primarily in Japanese cooking. Available in Asian markets, natural food stores and some supermarkets.

umeboshi vinegar made from sour, immature ume plums fermented in salt. The vinegar has a fruity-citrus flavor, cherry aroma and reddish color. Umeboshi vinegar is very strong and a little goes a long way. Because it contains salt, it is not technically a vinegar. Considered a seasoning agent by the Japanese, it is often used for its medicinal properties. *If using umeboshi vinegar in a recipe, omit any additional salt called for.*

unbleached flour with germ a white-wheat flour in which the endosperm (see wheat germ) is still intact making it more nutritious than regular unbleached flour. Lends itself especially well to baked goods. Available in natural food stores and cooperatives.

wheat germ the vitamin, mineral, protein and oil-rich embryo of the wheat berry, high in fiber. It is a concentrated source of vitamins with a slightly nutty taste. Store in an airtight container in refrigerator or freezer to prevent rancidity. Available plain or toasted in health food stores and most supermarkets.

wild rice a Native American staple. Wild rice is actually a grain, not a rice, with twice as much protein as regular rice, and more niacin, riboflavin, iron and phosphorus than brown rice. Though more expensive than other types of rice, it expands three to four times to make a sizable amount. Available in natural food stores and supermarkets.

zest the outermost, colored rind of citrus fruits. Zest is easily removed with a relatively inexpensive zester tool, (available in kitchen specialty stores) or by lightly rubbing the peel up and down across a fine stainless steel or ceramic grater. Adds a tartness to dressings, sauces, baked goods and desserts. Be sure to scrub fruit well before zesting. If available, buy organic.

Index

"After a time comes the turning point. The powerful light that has been banished returns. There is movement, but it is not brought about by force... The movement is natural, arising spontaneously. For this reason, the transformation of the old becomes easy. The old is discarded and the new is introduced. Both measures accord with time; therefore no harm results."

I Ching

A

agar G–iii
air-cushioned baking sheets G–iii
almond butter
  "Almond Sun Cookies" 98
amaranth G–iii
  "Amaranth Focaccia" 35
  "Cranberry Wheatberry Pilaf" 190
  how to cook 7
amasake G–iii
anaheim G–iv
Anasazi beans G–iii
antipasto
  "Caponata" 23
"Appetizers" 11–23
apple cider
  "Cranberry 'Mulled' Cider" 29
apples
  "Apple Spice Cake" 91
  "Baked Acorn Boats" 199
  "Chestnut Apple Bisque" 205
  "Cinnamon Apple Butter" 65
  "Figgy Cranapple Chutney" 88
  "Harvest Moon Muffins" 46
  "Sauteed Greens" 194
apricots
  "Apricot Glazed Carrot Cake" 92
  "Coconut Apricot Balls" 102
  "Mandarin Orange Stir Fry" 119
  "Orange Apricot Bars" 103
  "Orange Wheatberry Salad" 172
  "Rise 'n Shine Granola" 61
  "Thanksgiving Hubbard" 140
arame G–iii
arborio rice G–iii
arrowroot powder G–iii
artichokes
  "Artichoke Paté" 16
  "Artichoke Stuffed Portabellas" 129
  "Pasta Monterey" 157
asparagus
  "Asparagus Risotto" 124
  "Asparagus Velouté" 206
  "Far East Noodle Salad" 149
  "Orange Wheatberry Salad" 172
avocados
  "Black Bean Soup Taos" 207
  "Garden Patch Bagels" 180
  "Hacienda Breakfast Burritos" 58
  "Holé Guacamole" 18
  "Quinoa and Wild Rice Avocados" 188

B

balsamic vinegar G–iii
bananas
  "Banana Coconut 'Cream' Pie" 106
  "Banana Date Bread" 37
  "Banana Nut Waffles" 55
  "Cranberry Pumpkin Bread" 39
  "French Toast Mimosa" 56
  "Fruits of the Sun Fiesta" 60
  "Ginger Scented Banana Muffin" 45
  "Hawaiian Ti Bread" 38
  "Honey Drop Cookies" 100
  how to keep 4
  "Island Dressing" 72
  "Kona Banana Bake" 109
  "Pooh Bear Smoothie" 30
barley G–iii
  "Barley Bean Pistou" 210
  "Dilly Barley Salad" 171
  how to cook 7
barley malt syrup G–iii
basil
  "Basil Spinach Pesto" 78
beans
  Aduki*
    how to cook 6
  Anasazi
    "Anasazi Bean Burgers" 178
    how to cook 6
    "Scorned Woman Chili" 139
  black
    "Black Bean Enchiladas Grande" 123
    "Black Bean Hummus" 13
    "Black Bean Primavera" 126
    "Black Bean Soup Taos" 207
    how to cook 6
    "Pueblo Tortilla Casserole" 133
    "Scorned Woman Chili" 139
    "Squaw Salad" 167
    "Stuffed Peppers Ranchero" 138
    "Toasted Cumin Black Bean Sauce" 85
  butter
    "Barley Bean Pistou" 210
  cannellini (white kidney)
    "E-Z Beanz and Greenz" 197
    "Olde World Minestrone" 214
  garbanzo
    "Black Bean Hummus" 13
    "Curry In A Hurry" 144
    "Garden of Eat'n Burgers" 177
    "Gnocchi and Garbanzos" 152
    "Holé Guacamole" 18
    how to cook 6
    "Moroccan Tagine" 125
  Great Northern
    how to cook 6
    "Mom's Baked Beans" 192
    "Sweet 'n Sour Salad" 166

green
"Curry In A Hurry" 144
"Lemon Dill Green Beans" 194
"Moroccan Tagine" 125
how to cook 6
kidney
"E-Z Beanz and Greenz" 197
how to cook 6
"Scorned Woman Chili" 139
lima
how to cook 6
"Summer Squash Medley" 196
navy
how to cook 6
pinto
how to cook 6
turtle
how to cook 6
beet greens
"Sauteed Greens" 194
beets
"Beets Normandy" 193
"Heart-Beet Dressing" 70
"Roasted Veggie Medley" 136
"Sweet 'n Sour Salad" 166
"Beverages" 25–31
black-eyed peas G–iii
how to cook 6
blueberries
"Blueberry Griddle Cakes" 57
"Blueberry Muffins" 47
"Blueberry Peach Crisp" 110
"Blueberry-Heaven Smoothie" 27
"Lemon Saffron Granita" 114
bouquet garni G–iii
bread
"Amaranth Focaccia" 35
"Banana Date Bread" 37
"Chapatis" 36
"Cranberry Pumpkin Bread" 39
"French Toast Mimosa" 56
"Hawaiian Ti Bread" 38
"Savory Sunflower Bread" 44
"Seven Grain Bread" 43
"South of the Border Skillet Cornbread" 42
"Breads, Muffins and Rolls" 33–49
"Breakfast and Brunch" 51–61
broccoli
"Black Bean Primavera" 126
"Broccoli Salad" 165
"Ginger Sesame Broccoli" 202
"Kealakekua Stir Fry" 120
"Pesto Pasta Salad" 150
brown rice syrup G–iii
brunch
"Breakfast and Brunch" 51–61
brussel sprouts
"Brussels Almondine" 193
buckwheat
how to cook 7
bulgur G–iii
how to cook 7
burgers
"Anasazi Bean Burgers" 178
"Garden of Eat'n Burgers" 177
burritos
"Hacienda Breakfast Burritos" 58
buttermilk substitute
how to make 3

C

cabbage
"Mediterranean Cabbage Rolls" 121
cakes
"Apple Spice Cake" 91
"Apricot Glazed Carrot Cake" 92
"Celebration Cake" 93
"Chocolate Surprise Cake" 94
"Hawaiian Gingerbread" 95
"Plum Kuchen" 53
"Pumpkin Maple 'Cheese' Cake" 96
capers G–iii
carob G–iv
carrots
"Apricot Glazed Carrot Cake" 92
"Black Bean Enchiladas Grande" 123
"Bombay Carrot Bisque" 208
"Chile Dilly Carrot Paté" 14
"Confetti Roll-Ups" 158
"Curry In A Hurry" 144
"Dilly Barley Salad" 171
"Garden of Eat'n Burgers" 177
"Mandarin Orange Stir Fry" 119
"Olde World Minestrone" 214
"Pineapple Glazed Carrots" 198
"Quinoa Tabouleh" 168
"Roasted Veggie Medley" 136
"Scorned Woman Chili" 139
"Sedona Sauce" 87
"Shepherdess Pie" 143
cauliflower
"Black Bean Primavera" 126
"Cauliflower Leek Quiche" 59
"Curry In A Hurry" 144
"Shepherdess Pie" 143
cayenne G–iv
champagne
"'Champagne' Spritzer" 29
chapatis
"Chapatis" 36
chard G–iv
"Olde World Minestrone" 214
"Pasta Monterey" 157
chayote
"Chayote Kamut Medley" 127
chestnuts
"Chestnut Apple Bisque" 205
chickpeas G–iv
how to cook 6

chile peppers G–iv
"Anasazi Bean Burgers" 178
"Black Bean Enchiladas Grande" 123
"Black Bean Soup Taos" 207
"Border Salsa" 76
"Chile Corn Chowder Cripple Creek" 220
"Chile Dilly Carrot Paté" 14
"Garden Gazpacho" 212
"Hacienda Breakfast Burritos" 58
"Harissa" 68
"Howling Coyote Hot Sauce" 80
"Jamaican Salsa Soup" 218
"Orzo Salad" 151
"Penne Four Pepper Pasta" 156
"Potatoes El Greco" 135
"Salsa Verde" 77
"Savory Garlic Broth" 216
"Scorned Woman Chili" 139
"Southwest Chile Pesto" 79
"Squaw Salad" 167
chili
"Scorned Woman Chili" 139
chipotle G–iv
chives G–vii
chocolate
"Chocolate Surprise Cake" 94
chutney
"Figgy Cranapple Chutney" 88
cider
"Cranberry Mulled Cider" 29
citrus oil G–iv
coconut
"Coconut Mango Sorbet" 115
coconut milk
how to make 4
collards G–iv
"E-Z Beanz and Greenz" 197
condiment
"Basil Spinach Pesto" 78
"Border Salsa" 76
"Cinnamon Apple Butter" 65
"Figgy Cranapple Chutney" 88
"Harissa" 68
"Mint Chutney" 65
"Salsa Verde" 77
"Southwest Chile Pesto" 79
"Tarragon Tomato Tapenade" 78
"Zesty Ketchup" 75
cookies
"Almond Sun Cookies" 98
"Chewy Molasses Energy Cookies" 101
"Coconut Apricot Balls" 102
"Cranberry Nut Gems" 99
"Honey Drop Cookies" 100
"Orange Apricot Bars" 103
corn
"Cajun Creole" 142
"Chile Corn Chowder Cripple Creek" 220
"Golden Corn Waffles" 54
"Olde World Minestrone" 214
"Scorned Woman Chili" 139
"Squaw Salad" 167
"Stuffed Peppers Ranchero" 138
"Three Sisters Stew" 146
cornbread
"South of the Border Skillet Cornbread" 42
cornmeal G–iv
"Cornmeal Dumplings" 191
how to cook 7
couscous G–v
"Couscous Filled Orange Blossom Cups" 195
how to cook 7
"Lemon Couscous Salad" 170
"Mediterranean Cabbage Rolls" 121
"Moroccan Tagine" 125
cranberries
"Cranberry Nut Gems" 99
"Cranberry Pumpkin Bread" 39
"Cranberry Wheatberry Pilaf" 190
"Figgy Cranapple Chutney" 88
cranberry juice
"Cranberry Mulled Cider" 29
cubanelles G–iv
cucumbers
"Creamy Cucumber Dill Dressing" 71
"Cucumber Mint Raita" 187
"Garden Gazpacho" 212
"Jamaican Salsa Soup" 218
"Summertime Cucumber Dill" 219
curry
"Curry In A Hurry" 144

D

daikon G–v
"Savory Garlic Broth" 216
"Zesty Daikon Dip" 16
date sugar G–v
dates
"Almond Date Crust" 104
"Banana Date Bread" 37
"Chewy Molasses Energy Cookies" 101
"Mediterranean Cabbage Rolls" 121
"Pineapple Date Bran Muffins" 48
"Rise 'n Shine Granola" 61
"Desserts" 89–116
dill
"Chile Dilly Carrot Paté" 14
"Creamy Cucumber Dill Dressing" 71
"Dilly Barley Salad" 171
"Onion Dill Dip" 18
dips
"Onion Dill Dip" 18
"Zesty Daikon Dip" 16

dressing
"Asian Marinade" 74
"Cilantro Lime Vinaigrette" 69
"Citrus Poppy Seed Dressing" 69
"Creamy Cucumber Dill Dressing" 71
"Dijon Eggless 'Mayo'" 74
"Heart Beet Dressing" 70
"Herbal Vinaigrette" 70
"Island Dressing" 72
"Mango Fandango Dressing" 72
"Pineapple Dressing" 165
"Raspberry Walnut Vinaigrette" 164
"Thousand Island Dressing" 71
"Zorba the Greek Dressing" 73
"Dressings, Sauces, Etc." 63–88
dried currants G–v
dumplings
"Bavarian Spaetzle" 201
"Cornmeal Dumplings" 191

E

egg replacer powder G–v
eggplant
"Baba Ganouj Pockets" 179
"Caponata" 23
eggs
how to cook without 5
enchiladas
"Black Bean Enchiladas Grande" 123
"Entrées" 117–138
expeller-pressed oils G–v
extra-virgin olive oil G–v

F

fennel G–v
"Asparagus Risotto" 124
"Lemon Pineapple Kabobs" 131
"Moroccan Tagine" 125
"Olde World Minestrone" 214
"Penne Four Pepper Pasta" 156
figs
"Figgy Cranapple Chutney" 88
Five spice powder G–v
flax seed G–v
focaccia
"Amaranth Focaccia" 35
frozen desserts
"Coconut Mango Sorbet" 115
"Lemon Saffron Granita" 114

G

garlic
"Garlic Polenta" 137
"Herbed Pomadoro Sauce" 86
"Ratatouille Ragout" 134
"Savory Garlic Broth" 216
garlic broth
how to make 8
ginger root G–v
gingerbread
"Hawaiian Gingerbread" 95
gnocchi
"Gnocchi and Garbanzos" 152
grains
how to cook 7
granola
"Rise 'n Shine Granola" 61
grape juice
"'Champagne' Spritzer" 29
"Purple Passion Lemonade" 28
grape leaves
"Dolmades" 20
grapes
"Canadice Grape Pie" 105

H

herbs de Provence G–v
hoisin sauce G–v
honey
"Honey Drop Cookies" 100
hummus
"Black Bean Hummus" 13
"Hummus Canapes" 17

I

iced tea
"Iced Relaxation Tea" 30

J

jalapeño G–iv

K

Kalamata olives G–v
kale G–v
"Amazing Grains" 154
kamut G–v
"Chayote Kamut Medley" 127
how to cook 7
kasha G–v
Kashi™ G–vi
kombu G–vi
kudzu G–vi

L

lasagna
"Confetti Roll-Ups" 158
lecithin G–vi
leeks G–vii
"Cauliflower Leek Quiche" 59
"Potato Leek Pottage" 215

lemons
"Figgy Cranapple Chutney" 88
"Lemon Couscous Salad" 170
"Lemon Dill Green Beans" 194
"Lemon Pineapple Kabobs Maui" 131
"Lemon Saffron Granita" 114
"Lemon Tempeh Picatta" 122
"Purple Passion Lemonade" 28
lentils
how to cook 6
"Indonesian Red Lentil Soup" 213
liquid aminos G–vi
liquid fruit sweetener G–vi
liquid hickory smoke G–vi

M

mace G–vi
mangoes
"Coconut Mango Sorbet" 115
"Fruits of the Sun Fiesta" 60
how to prepare 5
"Mango Fandango Dressing" 72
"Nectar of the Gods" 28
Maui onions G–vii
melon
"Frosty Raspberry Lime" 211
millet G–vi
"Acropolis Pilaf" 191
how to cook 7
"Summer Squash Medley" 196
mint
"Mint Chutney" 65
mirepoix G–vi
mirin G–vi
miso G–vi
mousse
"Razzle Berry Mousse" 116
muffins
"Blueberry Muffins" 47
"Breads, Muffins and Rolls" 33
"Ginger Scented Banana Muffins" 45
"Harvest Moon Muffins" 46
"PB & J Muffins" 49
"Pineapple Date Bran Muffins" 48
multi-grain pancake mix
how to make 9
mung beans
how to cook 6
mushroom stock
how to make 8
mushrooms
"Amazing Grains" 154
"Artichoke Stuffed Portabellas" 129
"Asparagus Risotto" 124
"Braised Mushroom Caps" 19
"Chayote Kamut Medley" 127
"Hickory Grilled Portabellas" 128
"Mesquite Summer Grill" 183
"Pasta Monterey" 157
"Swedish 'Nut' Balls" 21
"Wild Mushroom Stroganoff" 159

N

nonreactive bowls or pans G–vi
noodles
"Spicy Udon Noodles" 202
nutritional yeast G–vi
nuts
how to toast 10

O

oats
how to cook 7
onions G–vi
"Onion Dill Dip" 18
orange juice
"Citrus Poppy Seed Dressing" 69
"Nectar of the Gods" 28
"Orange Wheatberry Salad" 172
oranges
"Coconut Apricot Balls" 102
"Couscous Filled Orange Blossom Cups" 195
"Figgy Cranapple Chutney" 88
"Orange Apricot Bars" 103
"Orange Quinoa Pudding" 113
"Sunny Citrus Sauce" 82
orzo G–vii

P

pancakes
"Blueberry Griddle Cakes" 57
papaya
"Coral Reef" 31
"Fruits of the Sun Fiesta" 60
"Jamaican Salsa Soup" 218
"Kealakekua Stir Fry" 120
"Pasta" 147–159
paté
"Artichoke Paté" 16
"Chile Dilly Carrot Paté 14
peaches
"Blueberry Peach Crisp" 110
"Peach Melba Croustade" 111
"Peachy Keen Frappe" 27
peanut butter
"PB & J Muffins" 49

pears
"Baked Acorn Boats" 199
peas
"Cajun Creole" 142
"Curry In A Hurry" 144
"Indonesian Red Lentil Soup" 213
"Mandarin Orange Stir Fry" 119
"Moroccan Tagine" 125
"Saffron Scented Rice" 187
"Shepherdess Pie" 143
"Sweet 'n Sour Salad" 166
"Three Sisters Stew" 146
pecans
"Pecan Lime 'Chick' Fingers" 132
pepitas G–vii
peppers
bell
"Black Bean Enchiladas Grande" 123
"Black Bean Primavera" 126
"Broccoli Salad" 165
"Cajun Creole" 142
"Chayote Kamut Medley" 127
"Confetti Roll-Ups" 158
"Curry In A Hurry" 144
"Far East Noodle Salad" 149
"Garden Gazpacho" 212
"Garden of Eat'n Burgers" 177
"Hasta la Pasta" 169
"Howling Coyote Hot Sauce" 80
"Indonesian Red Lentil Soup" 213
"Jamaican Salsa Soup" 218
"Kealakekua Stir Fry" 120
"Mandarin Orange Stir Fry" 119
"Mellow Yellow Sauce" 81
"Mesquite Summer Grill" 183
"Moroccan Tagine" 125
"Penne Four Pepper Pasta" 156
"Pesto Pasta Salad" 150
"Pueblo Tortilla Casserole" 133
"Quinoa Tabouleh" 168
"Ratatouille Ragout" 134
"Red Pepper Veloute" 217
"Scorned Woman Chili" 139
"Sedona Sauce" 87
"Squaw Salad" 167
"Stuffed Peppers Ranchero" 138
"Sweet 'n Sour Salad" 166
"Wild Mushroom Stroganoff" 159
how to roast 3
pesto
"Basil Spinach Pesto" 78
"Pesto Pasta Salad" 150
"Southwest Chile Pesto" 79
pie crust
"Almond Date Crust" 104
"Whole Wheat Crust" 104
pies
"Banana Coconut 'Cream' Pie" 106
"Canadice Grape Pie" 105
"Pie Crusts" 104
"Plum Empanadas" 107
"Shepherdess Pie" 143
"Strawberry Glazed Tart" 108
pine nuts G–vii
pineapple
"Broccoli Salad" 165
"Celebration Cake" 93
"Fruits of the Sun Fiesta" 60
"Hawaiian Gingerbread" 95
"Hawaiian Ti Bread" 38
"Jamaican Salsa Soup" 218
"Kealakekua Stir Fry" 120
"Lemon Pineapple Kabobs" 131
"Orzo Salad" 151
"Pineapple Date Bran Muffins" 48
"Pineapple Glazed Carrots" 198
pineapple juice
"Nectar of the Gods" 28
plums
"Far East Noodle Salad" 149
"Gingery Plum Sauce" 82
"Plum Empanadas" 107
"Plum Kuchen" 53
poblano G–iv
pockets
"Baba Ganouj Pockets" 179
"Pockets, Sandwiches and Wraps" 173–183
polenta G–vii
portabella mushrooms G–vii
potatoes
"Asparagus Velouté" 206
"Butternut Bisque" 221
"Curry In A Hurry" 144
"Garden of Eat'n Burgers" 177
"German Potato Salad" 163
"Olde World Minestrone" 214
"Oven Roasted Potatoes" 200
"Potato Leek Pottage" 215
"Potatoes El Greco" 135
"Roasted Veggie Medley" 136
"Shepherdess Pie" 143
"Preparation and Technique" 1–10
prune purée G–vii
how to make 4
pudding
"Orange Quinoa Pudding" 113
"Razzle Berry Mousse" 116
"Tropical Dream Tapioca" 112
pumpkin
"Cranberry Pumpkin Bread" 39
"Harvest Moon Muffins" 46
"Moroccan Tagine" 125
"Pumpkin Maple 'Cheese' Cake" 96

Q

quiche
  "Cauliflower Leek Quiche" 59
"quick" bread G–vii
quinoa G–vii
  "Anasazi Bean Burgers" 178
  how to cook 7
  "Orange Quinoa Pudding" 113
  "Quinoa and Wild Rice Avocados" 188
  "Quinoa Tabouleh" 168
  "Stuffed Tomatoes Provencale" 145

R

raisins
  "Apple Spice Cake" 91
  "Chewy Molasses Energy Cookies" 101
  "Couscous Filled Orange Blossom Cups" 195
  "Rise 'n Shine Granola" 61
raspberries
  "Berry Green Salad" 164
  "Frosty Raspberry Lime" 211
  "Peach Melba Croustade" 111
  "Razzle Berry Mousse" 116
red onions G–vii
rice
  "Asparagus Risotto" 124
  "Black Bean Enchiladas Grande" 123
  "Cajun Creole" 142
  "Cauliflower Leek Quiche" 59
  "Dolmades" 20
  "Garden of Eat'n Burgers" 177
  how to cook 7
  "Quinoa and Wild Rice Avocados" 188
  "Saffron Scented Rice" 187
  "Swedish 'Nut' Balls" 21
  "Thai Rice Bake" 189
  "Zesty Glazed Neat Loaf" 130
rice milk G–vii
  "Holiday Nog" 31
  "Pooh Bear Smoothie" 30
rice vinegar G–vii
risotto
  "Asparagus Risotto" 124
rolls
  "Breads, Muffins and Rolls" 33
  "E-Z Tarragon Rolls" 41
  "Honey Wheat Rolls" 40
Roma tomatoes G–vii

S

saffron G–vii
  "Saffron Scented Rice" 187
salad, bean
  "Squaw Salad" 167
salad, grain
  "Dilly Barley Salad" 171
  "Lemon Couscous Salad" 170
  "Orange Wheatberry Salad" 172
salad, green
  "Berry Green Salad" 164
  "Broccoli Salad" 165
salad, pasta
  "Far East Noodle Salad" 149
  "Hasta la Pasta" 169
  "Orzo Salad" 151
  "Pesto Pasta Salad" 150
  "Puttanesca Insalate" 152
salad, potato
  "German Potato Salad" 163
salad, vegetable
  "Pinwheel Salad" 165
  "Sweet 'n Sour Salad" 166
"Salads" 161–172
salsa
  "Border Salsa" 76
  "Salsa Verde" 77
sandwiches
  "Garden Patch Bagels" 180
  "Mesquite Summer Grill" 183
  "Reuben James" 181
  "Sloppy Josettes" 182
  "Tofuna Waffle Club" 176
sauce
  "Alfrézo Sauce" 83
  "Gingery Plum Sauce" 82
  "Herbed Pomadoro Sauce" 86
  "Holiday Gravy" 84
  "Horsey Sauce" 85
  "Howling Coyote Hot Sauce" 80
  "Mellow Yellow Sauce" 81
  "Sedona Sauce" 87
  "Sunny Citrus Sauce" 82
  "Sweet 'n Sour Sauce" 81
  "Toasted Cumin Black Bean Sauce" 85
  "Tomato 'Cream' Sauce" 83
scallions G–vii
sea salt G–vii
seasoning
  "Curry Powder" 66
  "Garam Masala" 67
  "Gomasio" 67
  "Herbal Seasoning" 66
  "Italian Seasoning" 68
seeds
  how to toast 10
serrano G–iv
shallots G–vii
"Sides" 185–202
silken tofu G–vii
snow peas
  "Chinatown Soup" 209
  "Far East Noodle Salad" 149
soba noodles G–viii
sorbet
  "Coconut Mango Sorbet" 115
"Soups" 203–221
soy milk G–viii
  "Pooh Bear Smoothie" 30

soybeans
how to cook 6
spinach
"Basil Spinach Pesto" 78
"Berry Green Salad" 164
"Confetti Roll-Ups" 158
"Spinach Balls" 22
spirulina G–viii
split peas
how to cook 6
squash
"Baked Acorn Boats" 199
"Butternut Bisque" 221
"Cajun Creole" 142
"Chayote Kamut Medley" 127
"Chile Corn Chowder Cripple Creek" 220
"Hasta la Pasta" 169
"Honey Glazed Acorn Rings" 196
"Mesquite Summer Grill" 183
"Pinwheel Salad" 165
"Shepherdess Pie" 143
"Summer Squash Medley" 196
"Thanksgiving Hubbard" 140
"Three Sisters Stew" 146
stew
"Cajun Creole" 142
"Moroccan Tagine" 125
"Ratatouille Ragout" 134
"Scorned Woman Chili" 139
"Three Sisters Stew" 146
stir fry
"Kealakekua Stir Fry" 120
"Mandarin Orange Stir Fry" 119
stock
freezing 9
how to make 8
"Savory Garlic Broth" 216
strawberries
"Coral Reef" 31
"French Toast Mimosa" 56
"Strawberry Glazed Tart" 108
stuffing
"Thanksgiving Hubbard" 140
sun-dried tomatoes
"Artichoke Stuffed Portabellas" 129
how to make 3
"Hummus Canapes" 17
"Pasta Monterey" 157
syrup
"Apricot Orange Syrup" 55
"Cinnamon Blueberry Syrup" 57

T

tabouleh
"Quinoa Tabouleh" 168
tahini G–viii
tamari sauce G–viii
tamarind concentrate G–viii
tarragon
"E-Z Tarragon Rolls" 41
"Tarragon Tomato Tapenade" 78
tea
"Iced Relaxation Tea" 30
tempeh G–viii
"Lemon Tempeh Picatta" 122
"Mock Chicken Wraps" 175
"Reuben James" 181
toasted sesame oil G–viii
tofu
"Alfrézo Sauce" 83
"Banana Coconut 'Cream' Pie" 106
"Butternut Bisque" 221
"Cajun Creole" 142
"Chestnut Apple Bisque" 205
"Chile Corn Chowder Cripple Creek" 220
"Chocolate Surprise Cake" 94
"Confetti Roll-Ups" 158
"Cornmeal Dumplings" 191
"Cranberry Nut Gems" 99
"Creamy Cucumber Dill Dressing" 71
"Dijon Eggless 'Mayo'" 74
"Fruits of the Sun Fiesta" 60
"Golden Corn Waffles" 54
"Hacienda Breakfast Burritos" 58
"Holiday Nog" 31
"Island Dressing" 72
"Mandarin Orange Stir Fry" 119
"Mellow Yellow Sauce" 81
"Onion Dill Dip" 18
"Pecan Lime 'Chick' Fingers" 132
"Potato Leek Pottage" 215
"Pumpkin Maple 'Cheese' Cake" 96
"Razzle Berry Mousse" 116
"Summertime Cucumber Dill" 219
"Thousand Island Dressing" 71
"Tofuna Waffle Club" 176
"Zesty Daikon Dip" 16
tomatillos G–viii
"Salsa Verde" 77
tomatoes
"Acropolis Pilaf" 191
"Barley Bean Pistou" 210
"Black Bean Soup Taos" 207
"Border Salsa" 76
"Cajun Creole" 142
"Caponata" 23
"Curry In A Hurry" 144
"Garden Gazpacho" 212
"Garden Patch Bagels" 180
"Hacienda Breakfast Burritos" 58
"Hasta la Pasta" 169
"Herbed Pomadoro Sauce" 86
"Howling Coyote Hot Sauce" 80
"Lemon Pineapple Kabobs" 131
"Mesquite Summer Grill" 183
"Mock Chicken Wraps" 175
"Moroccan Tagine" 125
"Olde World Minestrone" 214

"Pinwheel Salad" 165
"Pueblo Tortilla Casserole" 133
"Puttanesca Insalate" 152
"Quinoa and Wild Rice Avocados" 188
"Quinoa Tabouleh" 168
"Ratatouille Ragout" 134
"Reuben James" 181
"Scorned Woman Chili" 139
"Shepherdess Pie" 143
"Sloppy Josettes" 182
"Stuffed Peppers Ranchero" 138
"Stuffed Tomatoes Provencale" 145
"Tarragon Tomato Tapenade" 78
"Tofuna Waffle Club" 176
"Tomato 'Cream' Sauce" 83
"Tomato Zucchini Bolognese" 153
"Zesty Ketchup" 75
"Zorba the Greek Dressing" 73
tortillas
"Baked Tortilla Chips" 13
"Black Bean Enchiladas Grande" 123
"Hacienda Breakfast Burritos" 58
"Mock Chicken Wraps" 175
"Pueblo Tortilla Casserole" 133
TVP (texturized vegetable protein) G–viii
"Sloppy Josettes" 182
"Lemon Couscous Salad" 130

U

udon noodles G–viii
umeboshi vinegar G–viii
unbleached flour with germ G–viii

vegetable stock
how to make 8
vegetables
"Basic Vegetable Stock" 8
Vidalia onions G–vii

W

waffles
"Banana Nut Waffles" 55
"Golden Corn Waffles" 54
Walla Walla onions G–vii
walnuts
Swedish 'Nut' Balls 21
wheat germ G–viii
wheatberries
"Cranberry Wheatberry Pilaf" 190
how to cook 7
"Orange Wheatberry Salad" 172
white onions G–vii
wild rice G–viii
wraps
"Hacienda Breakfast Burritos" 58
"Mock Chicken Wraps" 175

yams
"Hawaiian Ti Bread" 38
"Kealakekua Stir Fry" 120
"Lemon Pineapple Kabobs" 131
"Maple Roasted Yams" 200

Z

zest G–viii
zucchini
"Black Bean Primavera" 126
"Cheezy Zucchini Squares" 15
"Chocolate Surprise Cake" 94
"Honey Drop Cookies" 100
"Olde World Minestrone" 214
"Ratatouille Ragout" 134
"Scorned Woman Chili" 139
"Summer Squash Medley" 196
"Tomato Zucchini Bolognese" 153